Jonah – The Epistle of Wild Grace

Stephen John March

ISBN 978-1-291-94596-6

First published in the United Kingdom
in 2014 by LULU

www.lulu.com

This book is also available in hardback ISBN 978-1-291-66834-6
and in e-book format ISBN 978-1-291-94609-3

This book is also available in French "Jonas - L'Épître de la grâce déchaînée".

Other writing
(with David E. Bjork) As Pilgrims Progress - Learning how Christians can walk hand in hand when they don't see eye to eye, Aventine Press, 2006, 240p, ISBN 1-59330-367-X

Blogs

sjmarch.wordpress.com (English)
plusdunefoi.wordpress.com (French)

Personal website

www.marchsite.com

About the cover image

The cover image with a Celtic picture of a wild goose is purposely chosen.

In the Celtic Christian tradition the Holy Spirit was represented, not as the dove of biblical imagery, but rather as the wild goose (*An Geadh-Glas*).

Their rationale in choosing this image for the Holy Spirit was as follows:

- Wild geese aren't controllable. They cannot be tamed or bent to the will of man.
- If you have ever heard a wild goose you will know that they make a lot of noise! No gentle dove-like cooing – a calming and gentle sound - but rather a loud, disturbing and raucous honk! A sound which is challenging, not consoling; strong, not weak, even disquieting.
- Historically, geese often functioned as guard-dogs. They are not a little scary[1].

In this book we will see how all of this is highly appropriate imagery for the Holy Spirit's action in and around the person of Jonah.

When God's Spirit comes like a gentle dove that is one thing; when He comes like a wild, noisy goose that it is entirely another.

The colour is also chosen purposefully. In the writing of icons, blue is the colour of heavenly grace. As the book of Jonah is pervaded by the amazing grace of God, this is appropriate.

---

[1] See the article 'Celtic Christianity' at
http://www.thisischurch.com/christian_teaching/celticchristianity.htm accessed on 18/06/14.

Dedication

This book is dedicated to my mom, Jean March, a woman who has lived the Good News of Jesus Christ with passion and authenticity.

Table of Contents:

Table of Figures:

List of Tables:

Acknowledgements:

This book has been some 12 years in the making. The Rev. Clive Burnard and the Rev. Duncan Ridgeon first started the ball rolling by inviting me to speak at a Men's Breakfast event in Iford Baptist Church, England in 2001. For some unknown reason I chose Jonah as my topic and spent several weeks preparing.

When it came time to share my message with the men gathered there that Saturday morning, such was the anointing of God on this time that even I was unable to miss that somehow God had put Jonah on my heart in a special way.

I continued to study Jonah and, after a few years, I had learned so much and been so blessed that I decided to try and write a book. I wanted to be able to share with others all the blessing my studies had brought to me. This process has taken 12 years! I kept discovering more and more in this wonderful book!

At this point I want to give my thanks to the people who have given me encouragement along the way. I actually tried to give up this project several times but I never quite managed it! So, to all those 'encouragers', here is the result of my failure to give up; and it's partly your fault!

My darling wife receives especial thanks, she has had to put up with way too many theological conversations about Jonah and for that she deserves eternal merit! She has also a very fine ear for the English language and her advice and help 'polishing' the final text have been invaluable.

I also offer my thanks to my friend Andy McIntyre, a Scottish poet in the Celtic tradition. I suggested to Andy that Jonah might make an ideal subject for Celtic poetry; partly due to the intense involvement of the Creator in His creation that pervades the book, and partly because Jonah – the man himself – has a real feel of a Celtic saint about him. Andy agreed and subsequently wrote a series of four poems drawn from the Jonah story – poems that he has kindly allowed me to reproduce in this book. I'm confident that Andy's poems will be a joy and delight to readers and will help them gain a new perspective on Jonah's story.

What kind of a book is this?

This book has been written as a meditational commentary on the book of Jonah.

A standard commentary will help you understand the meaning of a biblical text; giving you the cultural and literary insights necessary to deepen your appreciation and understanding of the text. This commentary does that too. In particular I hope that the cultural insights I have included regarding aspects of the Assyrian / Babylonian and Jewish cultures will really enrich your understanding and appreciation of the story. You will discover how God was amazingly at work behind the scenes, placing certain elements in Assyrian culture that will help the Ninevites to recognize that Jonah and his message are of divine origin. This in-depth divine preparation is something God does in Jonah himself. All Jonah's adventures, as he seeks to escape God's call, only serve to better prepare him for his mission to Nineveh!

A meditational commentary then goes beyond where standard commentary's leave off. Beyond helping you develop an appreciation of the richness of the cultural background of the text, a meditational commentary has for its goal the desire to lead you into a personal meditation on the **application** of the text's message. What does this message mean for **you**, for **your church fellowship** and for **your engagement with God** in His project for the redemption of the universe? This is achieved through the provision of questions at the end of each study which lead you into a time of personal meditation (followed ideally by a time of group sharing and discussion). Through this process you will learn how to **apply the message of Jonah** into the nitty-gritty of your **Real Life Situation**.

The book has been structured around 40 individual meditations that can be undertaken daily, or at a rhythm which suits. The forty day period also makes the book suited to use during Lent or Advent. It is my hope that individuals, and especially groups, will use this book as an aid to going deeper in their engagement with the Bible.

As one of my Bible college professors used to say, "Every Christian **IS** an applied theologian – it's just that some do a better job of it than others!" What he meant by this was that simply being a Christian necessarily involves applying the Bible to every area of our life. The Bible is the "manual" for the Christian life – a manual God has given to us in order that we might understand the nature of our earthly existence and live it well. Any engagement with Jesus Christ which is worthy of the name requires that we take seriously what God has revealed to us in His Word and put it into practice in our lives.

I also remember from my college days someone stating that the only scriptures you **REALLY** know are the ones you **OBEY**. This statement stopped me in my tracks then, and still gives me pause to think today.

You see, for Christians, Bible study is not an end in itself - simply an intellectual exercise in order to be better **INFORMED**. Rather, the goal of interacting with the Bible is that we might be **TRANSFORMED** by the encounter. Transformed by our encounter with God through the reading and studying of His word - an encounter that is only possible through the Holy Spirit's action in us.

> *And we all, who with unveiled faces contemplate the Lord's glory,*
> *are being transformed into his image with ever-increasing glory,*
> *which comes from the Lord, who is the Spirit.*[2]

This transformation, whilst significant in itself – in making us more like the people God calls us to be – has an even greater level of importance. Our ability to interact with God, to know Him and to experience His presence and His love in our lives is determined by our level of transformation. So as we study the Bible, we engage in a process that should transform our attitudes, alter our behaviour and modify our character. This deep and profound transformation will then permit us to experience God Himself in a new way. If that doesn't motivate us to come enthusiastically to the Bible, then I don't know what will!

Given the nature of this activity, we can imagine that it will be neither quick nor easy. However, it is one of the most crucial activities of our whole life.

Our performance in fulfilling this assignment will be one of the key measures of the success of our human existence.

It is therefore a serious task that we undertake in studying God's word. It is a task in which we often need the help and inspiration of others. I hope that this book will inspire you, as my own studies have inspired me. I also hope and pray that as you study Jonah the Holy Spirit will work in you to transform you - which is the whole point of it all.

---

[2] 2 Corinthians 3 :18, NIV

How do I use this book?

The 40 individual studies can be done daily, or at a rhythm that suits the individual or the group. As our goal is personal transformation, speed is not of the essence. It is better to take things slowly, to spend time meditating and thinking through the issues raised, rather than rushing on in order to finish quickly.

The following program is recommended:

Individually – Each Day (or an agreed number of times per week)
Take some time to read, to meditate upon and to pray through the study. I believe that there is a spiritual momentum which builds up when we interact regularly with the Word of God, particularly as we engage with the same portion of scripture over a significant period of time.

Begin each study with a period of **prayer**. This will help you 'centre' yourself and to open yourself to the Holy Spirit. It will also help you remember what you are actually doing here – coming to meet with God Himself, through His Word. So take time to pray asking God to meet with you.

To help you in your **meditation** of what you will discover in the fascinating story of Jonah, there are questions at the end of each section. These questions will help you to focus on the issues raised and will help you in your calling as an 'applied theologian'; **to apply the truths contained in Jonah into your life**. It will also help if you **write down your responses** to these questions. Your written answers will also be useful for the following step.

In a Small Group – Once a Week (or at an agreed rhythm)
I encourage you to benefit from the spiritual dynamic created by studying God's word with a friend or with a small group. Do the studies individually and then, once a week (or at an agreed rhythm), meet up in a group to share your thoughts and questions, explore the issues raised, discuss your answers to the study questions and respond in prayer together to what the Holy Spirit has revealed to you.

Working through this material with others will definitely lead to you getting more out of your study. Sharing and discussing together the questions that Jonah raises will bring a wider perspective to the issues raised and will also enable you to benefit from the life experiences of others in your group. It is also vitally important to not just consider the individual life application of these truths, but also to focus on the application of these truths to your local church/group/fellowship/community.

5

These group meetings will also enable you to pray for each other. Each time God speaks we need to give thanks to Him and also to ask Him to help us put into practice what we have heard. Transformation is never easy; being surrounded by the prayers of others will be a real help.

Jonah is **THE** most amazing book! As I have interacted with this book I have been by turns blessed, astonished, amazed, shaken, troubled, encouraged, mystified and even amused. But at the end I am left with a deeper love for God, a greater humility before His awesome greatness and a greater hope and expectation that His grace is as unlimited as it is unpredictable.

May God's grace and peace be with you.

Stephen John March

Introducing Jonah

[**Note to the Reader**: The following sections give detailed background information about the nature of the book of Jonah, they discuss some of the complexities of its inclusion in the Bible and outline the historical context in which the story takes place. All of which is fascinating stuff, but not strictly necessary before beginning the studies. So please feel free to skip these sections and go straight to the first study. You can always come back and read them later!]

The book of Jonah is by any estimation an extraordinary story about an unusual man. It is also a masterpiece of minimalist writing. In only a few hundred Hebrew words, 689 to be exact, (or a tiny 0.25% of the Old Testament[3]), the author weaves a complex tapestry of plot twists and turns. The scene changes rapidly within the course of the story. The story moves from mainland Israel, to the port of Joppa and then onto the open sea. Jonah's journey takes him from the hold of a cargo ship, to the innards of a sea monster, to the depths of the ocean, to the very gates of *Sheol*. Finally vomited onto a beach, Jonah then crosses the desert until he reaches the great city of Nineveh. He is only there a brief time before he relocates to a ramshackle shelter outside of the city in the surrounding desert.

In addition to this rapid change of location, the reader is also introduced to an amazing variety of different characters - Jonah, the Sailors, the Captain, the Sea Monster, the Ninevites, the King of Nineveh and, primarily, to God.

The literary genre also changes regularly, from narrative to reported speech, from poetry to the inmost personal prayer of a soul in turmoil, from divine communication to prophetic preaching. In this little book we encounter inspired psalmody of deep spiritual beauty but also the deepest psychological trauma of a man whose understanding of his God and his world is being ripped to shreds before his very eyes. This experience is so intense that Jonah seems more than once to be almost suicidal.

The story itself is by turns funny, amazing, frightening, encouraging, and often perplexing! But we are not left as mere observers. The author draws us into the story, forcing us to evaluate the words and actions of the characters, to try to work out their thoughts and feelings. We are forced to try to find answers to many questions, such as, 'Is Jonah the hero or the villain?' and 'Why does God seemingly have more compassion on pagan sailors and cruel Ninevites than one of His own prophets?' Indeed, this aspect of the book of Jonah is crucial and is

---

[3] Sasson J.M. *Jonah – The Anchor Bible Vol. 24b*, New York: Doubleday, 1990, pxi.

emphasised by the fact that the book itself is formed around 14 questions and ends provocatively with an unanswered one![4]

Yet this tiny and often confusing book has for 3,000 years inspired people of faith - Jews, Christians and Muslims. Indeed, the story of Jonah has so deeply entered the human consciousness that it continues to resonate even today.

Figure 1 - Replica Whale Tooth[5]

On 30th November 2008 American and Iraqi soldiers visited the Mosque *Nabi Yunus*, outside of Mosul, one of the possible locations of Jonah's tomb. Their visit was a good-will gesture, as the mosque had lost one of its prize possessions – a

[4] Limburg J. *Jonah*, Louisville: Westminster/John Knox Press, 1993, p25. How can you sleep? (1:6); Who is responsible (1:8); What do you do? (1:8); Where do you come from? (1:8); What is your country? (1:8); From what people are you? (1:8); What have you done? (1v10); What should we do to you? (1:11) [Note that the sailors ask 7 questions of Jonah]; Will I ever see you Holy Temple again? (2:4); Who knows? (3:9); O Lord, is this not what I said? (4:2); Have you any right to be angry? (4:4); Do you have any right to be angry? (4:9); Should I not be concerned about this great city? (4:11)
[5] Image by Staff Sgt. JoAnn Makinano used with permission, source http://www.dvidshub.net/image/133813/tomb-jonah-complete-again#.UTC-faK8GSo

whale tooth. The soldiers presented them with a replica in a display case in order to 'restore harmony' to the mosque. This is just one recent example which shows that Jonah and his story continue to have significance, even today.

Why is Jonah in the Bible?

This is a serious question and raises a serious problem. Jonah is not classified within the Jewish scriptures as an historical book, but as a prophetic book. Yet the book contains only one sentence of prophecy – only five words in Hebrew – and this is a prophecy which doesn't come to pass!

To make things more confusing, the prophetic books of the Old Testament are addressed primarily to the nation of Israel. When other nations are addressed, it is only in the context of their relationship with Israel. Yet this is absolutely not the case with Jonah! Jonah is solely addressed to the people of Nineveh, a Gentile nation.

Also, in the other prophetic books of the Old Testament, the prophet's own life and circumstances are largely incidental to the main plot. The main focus is the message received from God, the delivery of that message and the nation of Israel's response to that message. All of which is clearly **NOT** the case in the book of Jonah; for here it is Jonah himself and his troubled relationship with God that form the focus of the book.

So why then, given all these idiosyncrasies, is Jonah included in the Hebrew canon? There are several possible responses;

1   Perhaps Jonah's direct conversations with God in chapter four helped to authenticate the divine inspiration of the work.

2   Another possibility is the fact that there is a prophet called Jonah mentioned in 2 Kings 14.

> *In the fifteenth year of Amaziah son of Joash king of Judah, Jeroboam son of Jehoash king of Israel became king in Samaria, and he reigned for forty-one years. He did evil in the eyes of the Lord and did not turn away from any of the sins of Jeroboam son of Nebat, which he had caused Israel to commit. He was the one who restored the boundaries of Israel from Lebo Hamath to the Dead Sea, in accordance with the word of the Lord, the God of Israel, spoken through his servant Jonah son of Amittai, the prophet from Gath Hepher.[6]*

The prophet Jonah mentioned here was a contemporary of the prophets Hosea and Amos. His prophetic calling was to announce to the Northern Kingdom of Israel that the time of their divine punishment was coming to an end; from now on God was going to bless them. This would mean the re-establishment of their

---

[6] 2 Kings 14:23-25, NIV

borders, that they would be delivered from the foreign oppression that they had been suffering and that they would regain political control of their region.

We are told that this Jonah's prophecies were fulfilled and so he was accepted by the Israelites as a true prophet of the Lord.

If the book of Jonah was written by the same person – a nationally recognised prophet of the Lord - then his prophetic credentials were already assured by his previous ministry and that may be why the Jewish religious authorities accepted this strange book into the canon. Perhaps in support of this view, we note that the Jonah of 2 Kings 14 was a writer. The literal translation of 2 Kings 14:25b reads,

'...*as-word-of*| *Yahweh* |*God-of*| *Israel* | *that* | *he-spoke* | *by-hand-of*| *servant-of-him* | *Jonah* | *son-of*| *Amittai* | *the-prophet* | *who* |*from-Gath-of*| *the-Hepher*[7]

God spoke 'by the hand of' Jonah, which means that the Jonah of 2 Kings 14 was a writing prophet. His messages were delivered in written form as opposed to a preaching prophet who delivers his messages in verbal discourse. This lends support to the possibility of the book of Jonah being written by the prophet himself.

3   One other possible reason for Jonah's inclusion in the Jewish canon is that it presents a strong argument in favour of a particular way of understanding how Israel's future blessing would affect the surrounding nations. At the time when Jonah was written there were two competing views fighting for dominance.

Some prophets saw the future glorification of Israel as being at the expense of the surrounding nations[8], whilst others saw the Gentile nations as being included in the blessing of Israel[9]. The book of Jonah can be clearly seen as a strong argument in support of the view that sees the Gentiles included in the blessing of Israel.

Understood in this way, the book of Jonah warns Israel against the danger of seeing her status as God's chosen people as a reason to look down upon the other nations. The book makes clear the concern of God for the pagan nations and shows Him to be active amongst them. Furthermore, the story shows the role that Israel herself was meant to play - demonstrating and communicating

---

[7] Kohlenberger III J.R. *The Interlinear NIV Hebrew-English Old Testament*, Grand Rapids : Zondervan, 1987, p471
[8] Haggai 2:22f, Zechariah 9.
[9] Isaiah 49:6, Zechariah 8:20-23.

God's love to the surrounding nations. Israel was called to be God's special agent for mission; a role that Israel, like Jonah, was reluctant to undertake.

In conclusion, we must recognise the fact that the spiritual value of the book of Jonah is something that has been appreciated by Jews, Christians and Muslims. All these faiths have considered it to be of great value and they have all included Jonah's story in their holy writings.

Jonah and the story of his mission, is also of immense significance in the history of God's activity in the world. For, as Von Orelli noted, it is,

...an epoch-making event,
the first mission of a prophet of the true God to a centre of the heathen world[10]

Some theologians regard the book of Jonah as a work of imaginative fiction, a parable with no basis in history. Certainly it is an unusual book and contains some bizarre elements. Others, however (me included), continue to regard the story as an account of a real historical event. We note that those closest in time to the writing of Jonah understood it in this way. Flavius Josephus, in his 'Antiquities of the Jews' written in 93 A.D. presents Jonah as a historical figure[11].

Recent archaeological discoveries have also given support to a historical understanding of Jonah. For example, the incredible size of Nineveh, (often pointed to as a reason for understanding the book as a work of fiction) has actually proved to be an accurate reflection of the true size of the Nineveh and its surrounding administrative area (Rehoboth Ir, Calah and Resen)[12].

The presence of certain supernatural elements have also led some to discount the historicity of Jonah - the sending and the stilling of the storm, the fact of Jonah being swallowed alive by a sea monster and surviving three days inside it, the miraculous conversion of the Ninevites. However, these are, to my way of thinking, no reason to question the historicity of the story. We either believe in a God who acts in supernatural ways, or not; a God who reveals himself through concrete actions in the lives of real people, or not.

If we take out all the supernatural events recounted in Scripture, we quickly discover that there isn't much scripture actually left, and what is left isn't very useful! The Bible is the story of God's involvement in His world, and if He doesn't actually do anything then there's not much of a story!

---

[10] Von Orelli C. *On the Minor Prophets*, Edinburgh : T & T Clark, 1893, p171.
[11] Josephus F. (tr. Whiston W.) *The Works of Josephus*, Peabody: Hendrickson Publishers, 1987, pp259-261.
[12] See Genesis 10v11f

Perhaps the more helpful approach is to treat Jonah as a historical account of a real person's actual experiences. However, even if you believe Jonah to be a work of imaginative fiction, the important spiritual lessons that the book teaches are not diminished. Readers are free to come to their own conclusions on this matter, we will consider the evidence during our studies.

We also need to remember that the inclusion of a book in the canon of scripture was primarily determined by the appreciation of the book's usefulness by the people of God, both for liturgical use and in terms of promoting personal piety. The books which found a place in the canon (Jewish and Christian), did so only because successive generations found these books useful; they found these writings encouraged them and helped them in their walk with God. They were convinced that God was able to speak through these texts and on that basis their divine origin was affirmed. I am convinced that each person who sets himself/herself to seriously study the book of Jonah will have the same experience.

Background to Jonah

If the Jonah of 2 Kings 14 is identified as the author of the book we are studying, then the dating of Jonah is tied to Jeroboam II's reign (approx. 771-753 B.C.) If we also consider the book to be a record of an actual historical event, then the date is further limited by the destruction of Nineveh in 612 B.C.; since obviously Jonah must have visited Nineveh prior to this time. Apart from this we have no other clues to help us date the events in the book, neither is there any indication of when (or by whom) it was written.

The people to whom Jonah is sent are the Assyrians in their great city of Nineveh. The Assyrians were one of the leading world powers of the time and the city of Nineveh had already been an important centre for millennia. Its earliest remains date from around 4,500 B.C.

The Assyrian empire was founded on a military tactic of 'shock and awe'. They treated those they conquered with a degree of cruelty that was legendary, even in an age when violence was common. Their stock-in-trade was gratuitous atrocity. It seems to have been a trait of which they were particularly proud, since frescoes have been discovered in one of the Assyrian emperor's palaces which graphically portray soldiers barbarously mutilating vanquished enemies (see fig. 2).

Military action, threatened or enacted, was indispensable to the growth of the Assyrian empire. Intimidation, facilitated by Assyria's well-earned reputation as a brutal and merciless military opponent, was often successful in convincing states to assume vassal status[13]

An inscription from the time of Ashur-nasir-apli II (883-859 B.C.) found in the temple at Ninurta at Kalach gives a real sense of Assyrian pride, their delight in cruelty and their sense of total superiority,

I approached the city of Suru ... Awe of the radiance of Ashur my lord overwhelmed them. The nobles (and) elders of the city came out to me to save their lives ... I erected a pile in front of his gate, I flayed as many nobles as had rebelled against me (and) draped their skins over the pile, some I spread out within the pile, some I erected on stakes upon the pile, (and) some I placed on stakes around about the pile. I flayed many right through my land (and) draped their skins over the walls. I slashed the flesh of the eunuchs (and) of the royal eunuchs who were guilty. I

---

[13] Timmer D. The Intertextual Israelite Jonah Face à l'Empire: The Post-Colonial Significance of the Book's Context and Purported Neo-Assyrian Context, Journal of Hebrew Scriptures, Vol. 9, Art. 9, 2009, p6

brought Ahi-yababa [the ruler of Suru] to Nineveh, flayed him, (and) draped his skin over the wall of Nineveh.[14]

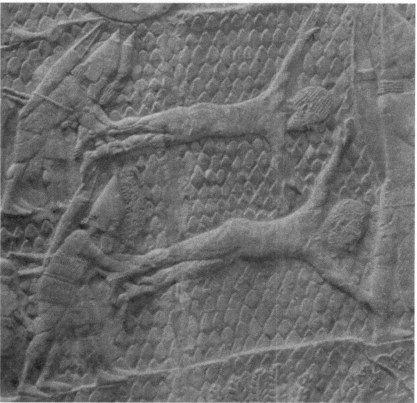

Figure 2 - The Flaying of Prisoners at Lachish[15]

Nineveh was itself a synonym for bloodthirstiness and cruelty. Prophesying a century or so after Jonah (approx. 663-612 B.C.) the prophet Nahum would exalt in the destruction prophesied for it with the following words;

> *Woe to the city full of blood,*
> *Full of lies,*
> *Full of plunder,*
> *Never without victims!...*

---

[14] Grayson, A.K. Assyrian royal inscriptions. Part 2. From Tiglath-pileser I to Ashur-nasir-apli II. (Records of the Ancient Near East, Vol. II.,)Wiesbaden: Otto Harrassowitz, 1976, cited in Timmer D. ibid., p6/7
[15] Stone panel from the South-West Palace of Sennacherib, Nineveh. Displayed in the British Museum (Room 36, no. 10), Photograph by Mike Peel (www.mikepeel.net). [CC-BY-SA-2.5 (http://creativecommons.org/licenses/by-sa/2.5)], via Wikimedia Commons.

Everyone who hears about you claps his hands at your fall,
For who has not felt your endless cruelty? [16]

By this time the Assyrians had conquered the Northern Kingdom of Israel (722-721 B.C.), so the shocking ferocity and gruesome brutality of the Assyrians was something the prophet knew of first-hand.

We need to keep in mind this understanding of the character of the people of Nineveh, it will help us as we try to understand Jonah's thoughts and actions as our story progresses.

---

[16] Nahum 3:1, 19b NIV

Ionah : the first part - Morfil Gwr (Whale man)

Angry winds tore at the sails of the distressed little ship
Waves crashed and harried intent on destruction
Below he hid, shaking with fear and loathing
Begging to be cast into the storming, broiling waters
To escape the eyes and the voice in his head.

Remembering how he stood at the edge of the dock
Watching tides swirl in and out with hypnotic intent
Fear in his mind forcing him to flight
Away he ran trying to feel unnoticed and small
Still he found no peace for his plight.

Down he sank into the maelstrom deep, lives saved
By his supposed good deed, mind going blank
Down he went, down he sank
To the depths he fell cold and black
'Welcome death!' he cried, his body slack.

Out of the deep with jaws open wide he came
Great fish of the deep, sifting the sea, Morfil by name
And swallowed the man, his grief, anger and all
Shaking with anger, tears streaking his face
Admitting defeat asked to be restored to his place.

With a great gush of vomit spewed onto the beach
Found him gasping as air filled his lungs
Grudgingly yet he ventured into the city
Looking at all his eyes full of pity
And they flocked to hear the words that he spoke.

Out to the wastes with anger in his heart
Leaving the people and city behind
Angry with them and the creator
Hiding away like some spoiled child
Under the searing heat of the mid-day sun.

Yet then the creator saw and loved the man still
Despite his tantrums and anger within
Sent help to feed and shade his head
And still the man asked and wished he was dead
'Why Me?' was the song that he continued to sing.

A.P. McIntyre 2012.

1 - Jonah and his Mission (Jonah 1:1-2)

The word of the Lord came to Jonah son of Amittai:
'Go to the great city of Nineveh and preach against it,
because its wickedness has come up before me.'

Jonah 1:1-2, NIV

Now we come to our first day's study. Hopefully, in the light of the background information we have just covered, these verses will have a new resonance.

The name Jonah means "dove" in Hebrew. It is clear that we are meant to make the connection with the dove in the story of Noah's ark[17], where the dove, released by Noah, returned with a freshly picked olive leaf; thus announcing the end of the flood.

This dove was therefore the sign of the end of chaos
and the re-creation of the world.
It was the sign too of Noah's salvation. [18]

From this point on, doves were associated in Hebrew culture with bearing good news. Doves are also used in scripture as a symbol of Israel[19]. The word dove was also used as a term of endearment between lovers[20]. In another word picture, the dove was also the sin offering to be made by the poorest members of society[21], in which case a 'jonah' is a sacrifice for sin[22]. This will be significant as our story progresses, because we will see Jonah offering himself as a sacrifice in order to save the Gentile sailors.

So whilst the book of Jonah is, on the surface, a story about a specific prophet and the story of his mission to the city of Nineveh, there is also a secondary level of meaning in which Jonah symbolises the nation of Israel. In particular in her failure to undertake the missionary task to the nations to which she was called.

We note from these opening verses that Jonah's family name was *"Amittai"* which means *"truth"*. What a great name Jonah has for someone whose ministry is mission! Jonah, the dove, was to be the bearer of good news, to come to the Ninevites with the 'Amittai' (truth) of God!

---

[17] Gen. 8:8-12

[18] Burrows D.P. *Jonah, the Reluctant Missionary*, Leominster: Gracewing, 2008, p5

[19] See Hosea 7:11-13, 11:8-11, Psalm 68:13, 74:19 etc.

[20] Song of Songs 2:14, 5:2, 6:9

[21] Leviticus 5:7-10

[22] Burrows D.P. *ibid.*

Jonah is also a 'type' of Christ, that is to say, someone in the Old Testament who prefigures Jesus. Like Jesus, Jonah will offer himself as a sacrifice to save others[23]. Jonah will also spend three days and nights in the belly of a big fish before being released onto dry land; an event that Jesus himself will use as an image of his death and resurrection[24].

In all these ways, Jonah has the great privilege of pointing us towards Jesus the Messiah.

Also, like Jesus, Jonah came from Galilee. He was born in Gath-Hepher, a town only about four miles from Nazareth where Jesus would live. This is quite remarkable because this region had a very bad reputation in Israel. The inhabitants of Galilee were unfavourably viewed as 'irreligious' by the pious Jews of Judah and Jerusalem because they lived in close proximity with Gentiles. As an illustration of this we note the words of the Pharisees to Nicodemus, when he sought to defend Jesus before them;

Are you from Galilee?
Look into it, and you will find that a prophet does not come out of Galilee.[25]

In fact the Pharisees were wrong! Jonah came from Galilee! But Jonah and Jesus are 'the exceptions that prove the rule', being the only two prophets ever recorded in scripture as coming from this area. No doubt for Jesus growing up in Nazareth, Jonah was a religious hero – his story well-known and well-loved.

A rabbinic tradition included in the *'Pirke de Rabbi Eliezer'*, a ninth - century work but which is attributed to Rabbi Eliezer son of Hyrcanus, a figure from the first century A.D., identifies Jonah as the son of the widow of *Zarephath* (1 Kings 17:7-24). This would mean that Jonah could have been a Gentile who converted to Judaism. Given that Jonah's story is about a mission to save gentiles, this would give a further nuance to the story[26].

---

[23] Jonah 1:12
[24] Matthew 12:40f
[25] John 7:52, NIV
[26] Friedlander G. *Pirke de-Rabbi Eliezer*, London: Kegan Paul, Trench, Trubner & Co Ltd, 1916, p240

Questions for Reflection and Discussion

1   In Jonah's place, how would you have reacted to God's call? Think particularly of the character of the Assyrians and their cruelty. Perhaps it might help you to think about the most bloodthirsty and inhumane cruelty that you have recently been made aware of by the T.V. news. Think of what your reaction would be should God call you to go and take a message to these people.

2   Jonah was a successful prophet with a nationally recognised ministry; he sent messages to the king himself. Can you imagine what his life might have been like in Israel? What will it cost him to be obedient to God's command?

2 - God's Call (Jonah 1:1-3)

The word of the Lord came to Jonah son of Amittai: 'Go to the great city of Nineveh and preach against it, because its wickedness has come up before me.' But Jonah ran away from the Lord and headed for Tarshish. He went down to Joppa, where he found a ship bound for that port. After paying the fare, he went aboard and sailed for Tarshish to flee from the Lord.

Jonah 1:1-3, NIV

Even if we identify Jonah as the prophet of 2 Kings 14, we know almost nothing about him prior to his call. Only one single verse speaks of him and his activity. This is significant. Jacques Ellul has made the remark;

He begins to be important only when the word of the Lord is on him[27].

Another important point to be aware of is that the events recounted in the Bible are not there primarily to tell us about individuals or nations - although incidentally they do give us such information. Rather, the events reported in scripture are there primarily to tell us about God. These stories were included in the holy writings of the Jewish nation because they were believed to reveal something of the nature of God and of His activity in the world.

From a reader's perspective this means that the stories can leave us frustrated. We would often love to have more information about the fascinating people and the amazing places that scripture mentions. To our great disappointment, both characters and locations are often sketched out very much 'in the rough'.

Sometimes we are not even sure if key protagonists are presented to us as heroes to be emulated or villains whose stories are to be a warning to us. This ambiguity is deliberate; it forces us to reflect, to enter more deeply into the text and to meditate on it. This enables us in turn to really profit from what God reveals to us in His word.

This unresolved ambiguity with regard to the people in the Bible is also important as it shows us that scripture is true to life. Life is complex. Often the same person will display both great qualities and serious failings. In fact, scripture is often brutally honest about the flaws and failings of even its greatest characters. We are shown their great holiness as well as their worst sins. For example we see the holiness, courage and faith of David, but we also get to see his weak fatherhood, his lecherous adultery and his murderous attempt to cover up his sin.

---

[27] Ellul J. (tr. Bromily G.W.) *The Judgement of Jonah*, Grand Rapids: W.B. Eerdmans, 1971, p22

24

The book of Jonah follows the same approach. We have no information about Jonah's life and activity before God's word comes to him, and we have no information in scripture to tell us what happens to him after he finally obeys God's command. Neither is it obvious what we are to make of him as a man.

We are therefore not reading a biography of Jonah; a book written with the purpose of helping us to understand a man and his life. Instead we are reading the story of one episode, a defining episode, in a man's complicated relationship with God. Jonah loves God, that is clear, yet he also struggles to understand God - both in His nature and His actions.

Through Jonah's very human story we are encouraged to evaluate our own ways of thinking about the nature and the activity of God. Like Jonah, we often misunderstand. Like Jonah we often struggle to come to terms with why God acts in certain ways. It is exactly in order to provoke this kind of reflection that the book of Jonah was written.

Given that Jonah has so many misconceptions about God and that he struggles to understand God's actions, we might ask the reasonable question, why did God choose Jonah for this mission? Furthermore, as will become clear in our later considerations, Jonah is by character, attitude and temperament unsuited for the task to which God assigns him.

If we step back and consider the many examples within the Bible, we discover a confusing picture regarding the suitability of God's chosen agents. Sometimes God seems to select people for tasks which are very much in harmony with their personality, natural gifts and experience. David, for example, was a courageous, charismatic, attractive and gifted individual. All of which contributed to the success of his leadership of the nation of Israel.

Yet, in contrast, the selection of Peter as leader of the disciples seems a strange decision. Some of Peter's natural characteristics, his impetuousness, his egocentricity and his weakness, made him a somewhat less than ideal candidate for recruitment to the leadership of the Church; these characteristics would certainly be a block to his recruitment to a leadership position in many churches today!

Why does God seem to be so inconsistent in his recruitment and selection processes? As we look more deeply into the Bible we can see clues that help us understand some of the reasons for God's choice of 'unsuitable' candidates, we can also take heart in the fact that perfection is not an essential attribute for involvement in the activity of God!!

The first reason for God's surprising choice of operatives is seen in the story of Gideon[28]. In this story God tells Gideon to reduce the size of his army before engaging the enemy. We might see this as foolishness, but God makes clear His purpose – it is in order that it would be clear to all that the military victory Gideon was about to obtain was the result of God's involvement and not due to the strength of the Israelite army.

> The Lord said to Gideon, 'You have too many men. I cannot deliver Midian into their hands, or Israel would boast against me, "My own strength has saved me."[29]

Therefore, in order to demonstrate His hand in what was about to happen, God reduces the army of Gideon to only 300 soldiers.

This same kind of motivation is cited by St. Paul as the reason why God uses people of remarkable ordinariness as messengers of the gospel;

> We have this treasure in jars of clay
> to show that this all-surpassing power is from God not us.[30]

The second reason for God's surprising choice of candidates is demonstrated in the life of St. Peter. Throughout the New Testament, we see clear signs of a development and a growing maturity of character. The later St. Peter is less impetuous, wiser and gentler, in comparison to the young St Peter. This transformation of character is the key activity of God in our lives. God puts us into situations and gives us certain experiences in order to change us.

So we see that God uses challenges that are beyond our natural capability in order to force us to confront our weaknesses and to accept our need of the Holy Spirit; the power of God in our lives.

We can see many other examples of this transformation process e.g. Moses and Joseph. Moses' forty years in the desert with Jethro and Joseph's fifteen years in slavery in Egypt were periods of trial and tribulation which transformed them. The divine objective was to prepare them for a future task to which they were presently unsuited.

It is the same for us today. We are being transformed in order to be able to do something that we are currently incapable of. Transformation is the indispensable pre-qualification for the future task. To work with God on our own

---

[28] Judges chapters 3-8
[29] Judges 7v2, NIV
[30] 2 Corinthians 4v7, NIV

Transformation is the prequalification for partnership with God in his activity in the world.

Questions for Reflection and Discussion

1   If your life story were to be written as an account of God's activity in the World, what would it be like? What lives have been touched by God through you – by your actions, your words, your prayers?

2   What examples can you think of in your own life and experience of God choosing people to accomplish tasks that they were either suited to, or unsuited to? For the latter cases did it lead to transformation or not? Did it prepare the individual for some future task?

Consider the following texts and ask yourself, "What do these scriptures teach us about the agent, the goal and the mechanism of our transformation?"

> *Do not conform to the pattern of this world,*
> *but be transformed by the renewing of your mind.*
> *Then you will be able to test and approve what God's will is –*
> *his good, pleasing and perfect will.*
>
> Romans 12:2, NIV

> *You show that you are a letter from Christ, the result of our ministry,*
> *written not with ink but with the Spirit of the living God,*
> *not on tablets of stone but on tablets of human hearts...*
> *And we all, who with unveiled faces contemplate the Lord's glory,*
> *are being transformed into his image with ever-increasing glory,*
> *which comes from the Lord, who is the Spirit.*
>
> 2 Corinthians 3:3, 18, NIV

> *But the fruit of the Spirit is love, joy, peace, forbearance, kindness, goodness,*
> *faithfulness, gentleness and self-control. Against such things there is no law.*
>
> Galatians 5:22f, NIV

3 - Jonah's Response (Jonah 1:1-3)

The word of the Lord came to Jonah son of Amittai:
'Go to the great city of Nineveh and preach against it,
because its wickedness has come up before me.'
But Jonah ran away from the Lord and headed for Tarshish.
He went down to Joppa, where he found a ship bound for that port.
After paying the fare, he went aboard and sailed for Tarshish to flee from the Lord.

Jonah 1:1-3, NIV

God comes to Jonah with an assignment. From the moment God speaks, Jonah's life takes on a radical new direction. It does not matter that Jonah's first response is disobedience. God is much stronger than our refusal. Even more surprising, God is capable of weaving our disobedience into His plans and purposes in order to make them even more glorious. God sets Jonah apart by His call. After that **everything** Jonah does is significant.

God's assignment for Jonah is to send him to the 'great' city of Nineveh to deliver a message of impending judgement. Here we see for the first time one of the important stylistic features of the book. The Hebrew word translated as the adjective 'great' here appears 14 times in the book[31] (note also that there are also 14 questions that form the skeleton for the book[32]). In 8 of the uses of this adjective it has the meaning of 'great' or 'important'[33]; in the other 6 instances it has the meaning 'key / chief / major'[34].

Another stylistic touch is the repetition of the word translated here as 'wickedness'. This word appears 9 times[35] and is variously translated as 'evil'[36], 'trouble / disaster / misery / difficulty / harm'[37]. Indeed the very ambiguity of the term is significant. Does God mean that He sees Nineveh's 'trouble', or that He sees her 'wickedness'?

At this particular time, Nineveh was undergoing one of the most troubled periods of her history. Famine, plague and political upheaval were an almost constant presence. It is therefore distinctly possible to understand the word as 'trouble'. Certainly for the first hearers of this story the ambiguity of this term is significant and it hangs in the air, unresolved, as the story progresses.

---

[31] Stuart D. Hosea – Jonah – Word Biblical Commentary – Volume 31, Nashville: Thomas Nelson, 1987, p437
[32] See section 'Introducing Jonah' page 7
[33] 1:4 (twice), 10, 12, 16, 2:1, 4:1, 6
[34] 1:2, 3:2, 3, 5, 7, 4:11
[35] Stuart D. *ibid.*
[36] 3:8, 10
[37] 1:2, 7, 8, 3:10, 4:1, 2, 6

This said, most commentators are of the opinion that the word should be translated 'wickedness' in this verse. As we have seen, the Assyrians were the great world power of the time and were a notoriously cruel people. They took delight not only in conquering their enemies but also in torturing and mutilating them prior to killing them. Along with their cruelty in war, they are also accused in scripture of prostitution, witchcraft, and commercial exploitation[38]. Not surprising then, that God should come against such a people and their great city of Nineveh in judgement. It may well have been something that devout Jews, such as Jonah, had even been praying for!

So the news that God intends to send divine judgment upon Nineveh and the detested Assyrians would no doubt have been good news for Jonah and all pious God-fearing Jews of this time. As McBirnie reminds us,

The Jew of Jonah's day did not desire that the peoples of the earth should be saved. Rather, he looked for a grand vengeance that should pay back the tyrannies that the brutal heathen had exercised upon Israel.[39]

As we consider Jonah and his prophetic mission, one point to remember is that the Bible does not present prophets as a kind of fortune teller; those who simply predict the future. Rather they are people who have been granted an intimate knowledge of God.

With this exclusive knowledge, the prophet is charged with a responsibility and a mission. It is imperative upon him or her to spread the message to the community.[40]

If we remember the strong possibility that Jonah is an experienced prophet with a good track-record in ministry, we might assume he would respond obediently to God and hurry to fulfil his assignment. After all, it is the business of a prophet to receive messages from God and to deliver them!

However, this is a mission Jonah wholeheartedly refuses! Instead of heading off towards Nineveh, Jonah immediately flees in the opposite direction. Why would an experienced and attested prophet baulk at receiving another assignment from God? Jonah's reaction also seems excessive. Why jump on a boat and flee? Why not just simply stay where he is and get on with his life? Why not just ignore God's call?

In terms of where Jonah is headed, Tarshish, (most likely located in Southern Spain) is in the opposite direction to Nineveh, so perhaps there is a certain logic

---

[38] Nahum 3
[39] McBirnie W.S. *Seven Sins of Jonah*, Wheaton: Tyndale House, 1981, p10
[40] Schwarz J. *Yunus the Prophet - The Qur'anic Story of Jonah*, Muslim-Jewish Journal, 2008, p1

in his chosen destination. In order to get there, however, Jonah has to undertake a long ocean voyage and, in Jewish culture, the sea was considered as a godless and demonic place. Rabbi Eliezer, quotes a Jewish tradition in which Jonah states,

The whole earth is full of his glory (Isa. 6:3);
behold, I shall escape to the sea, to a place where His glory is not proclaimed.[41]

Therefore the sea is not so much a place where God's presence is absent, but a place where there is no-one to prophesy to[42].

Another Jewish perspective on Jonah's flight holds that it was an attempt by Jonah to flee God's voice, to escape to a place that God's voice could not reach. Seen in this way, Jonah's flight was,

...not so much a physical running away as an attempt to shut out the messages
from his own mind.[43]

As such, his attempt is doomed for, once someone has become a prophet of Yahweh,

...he cannot on his own return to the tranquillity of the uninitiated ...
prophecy is a perpetual condition.[44]

Poor Jonah seems to have been so determined to avoid doing what God asked him to do that he was prepared to pay a small fortune to escape it. The Hebrew says that Jonah paid its (i.e. the ship's) fare. This unusual phrase is interpreted in some rabbinic traditions as meaning Jonah paid for the whole ship, that is to say he hired it completely - he chartered the entire ship as a getaway vehicle!

Also it was normal to pay one's fare when disembarking from the ship at the end of a voyage, here Jonah is stated as paying up-front[45]. All of which gives us a deeper sense of the intensity of Jonah's desire to escape his mission.

But why was Jonah so determined not to do what God asked him to do?

There are several possibilities.

---

[41] Ben Hyrcanus E. *ibid.*, p66
[42] Ginzberg L. *The Legends of the Jews*, Vol. IV, Philadelphia : The Jewish Publication Society of America, 1913, p248
[43] Blumenthal F. *Jonah the Relcutant Prophet – Prophecy and Allegory*, Jewish Bible Quarterly, Vol. 35, No. 2, 2007, p104
[44] *ibid.*, p105
[45] Ben Hyrcanus E. *ibid.*, p67

Fear - God's call, to go to a city of a people notorious for their violence and cruelty in order to tell them that God was going to destroy them, is certainly not the most attractive assignment in the world! Other prophets have had similar reactions to 'difficult' callings. Elijah was afraid of the mission God gave him[46], and the prophet Uriah was actually murdered because of his message[47]. Even some of the greatest characters in the Bible, men such as Moses, Jeremiah and Gideon, felt fear and were only too aware of their own weakness in the face of what God was asking them to do[48].

Distance - Nineveh was a very long way away - some 800 km (500 miles) from Gath-Hepher. However, in his attempted flight from God, Jonah is willing to travel from Joppa to Tarshish, some 3,700 Km (2,400 miles) ! So travelling the 800 Km to Nineveh doesn't seem to have been the key problem.

The Content of the Message – We see examples from the ministries of Jeremiah, Amos and Isaiah of the fact that the message God gives is not always one His prophet agrees with.

My own conviction is that this last possibility is the most likely to have been Jonah's real problem – Jonah had theological objections to his assignment!

So what was it about the message that was so objectionable to the messenger?

The first indication of the message Jonah is to carry is very brief. We have only the shortest of statements which speaks of impending judgement in the face of great wickedness. But later statements by Jonah (in chapter four) make it clear that this first revelation was only the beginning of an extended process of clarification between him and God[49].

The writer doesn't give us this extra information right away; he is cleverly preserving the dramatic tension of the story. However, it seems clear that a long, drawn-out conversation went on between Jonah and God, in which Jonah obtained clarification from God about just exactly what he was being asked to do. Once he comprehends the detail of his assignment and just what God intends to do in Nineveh, Jonah is so shocked and outraged that he is ready to jump onto a boat and sail to the end of the world.

---

[46] 2 Kings 19:1-3
[47] Jeremiah 26:20-24
[48] Exodus 4:10, Jeremiah 1:6, Judges 6:15
[49] Jonah 4:2

He prayed to the Lord, 'Isn't this what I said, Lord, when I was still at home? That is what I tried to forestall by fleeing to Tarshish. I knew that you are a gracious and compassionate God, slow to anger and abounding in love, a God who relents from sending calamity.[50]

So what was it that so shocked Jonah? Amazingly, it is the fact that God's motivation for this mission is not judgement but mercy. The message of imminent judgement is actually a divine invitation to the Ninevites to repent and experience the mercy of Jonah's God for themselves.

Sin cannot be repented of unless it is revealed. Revelation of our sin, with its inevitable and disastrous consequences, also opens up to us the possibility of repentance, confession and ultimately forgiveness. In fact, the greatest curse anyone can receive from God is to be left alone in their sin. Being allowed 'to get away with it' is the worst curse that human beings can experience. Without an awareness of sin there is no possibility of repentance.

Sometimes God chooses to allow us to experience the results of sinful choices in our lives[51]. He temporarily abandons us to our sins. But this is only in order that we can see what results sin has in our lives, our families and our communities. Then we can be fruitfully called to repentance and restitution.

As Jonah spoke with God and received clarification about his mission, he came to realise that God's motivation for the mission was not destruction but salvation. I believe that **this** was Jonah's real problem. He was so appalled by this that he was ready to leave his homeland, his family, his friends and to embark on a voluntary, lonely exile to the limits of the known world; so horrified was he that the Ninevites might be allowed to experience God's grace.

But why was Jonah so appalled by this possibility of mercy for the Ninevites? It is possible that it was simply because of the merciless brutality of the oppressive Assyrian empire. Perhaps Jonah considered people like them had no right to benefit from God's grace, they deserved only punishment.

Or maybe things are more complex than this....

Jonah knew that the Assyrians posed a continual threat to Israel. If they were to experience God's salvation then that threat would remain. Their destruction, however, would eliminate forever the threat that they posed to Jonah's homeland (and the surrounding nations).

---

[50] Jonah 4:2, NIV
[51] Deuteronomy 31:16f, 1 Corinthians 5:5, 1 Timothy 1:20

A Jewish legend holds that Jonah feared that the Assyrians would respond to God's call to repent, (something the Jews constantly failed to do!), and so would ultimately supplant the Jews as God's chosen people[52]. If so, the people of Israel, would have no glorious future in God but would simply withdraw into obscurity[53].

Seen from this perspective it become possible to understand Jonah's rebellion and flight as the actions of a national hero, someone who is willing to endure personally the anger of God and exile in order to protect his people. Such an optic would transform Jonah from a curmudgeonly misanthropist into a tragic hero.

Fears about the future threat Assyria might pose to Israel would be proved correct by later events when, between 732 and 721 B.C., a resurgent Assyria utterly destroyed Northern Israel[54].

Another possible factor in Jonah's motivation is revealed when we remember that in order for a prophet to be accepted as 'true', his words have to bear fruit. What he reveals as God's intended actions need to be validated by subsequent events; otherwise he is a 'false' prophet. A Jewish legend holds that Jonah had experienced exactly this situation. The legend says that God had sent him to prophesy destruction upon the people of Jerusalem - a destruction that God did not carry out. Thus, Jonah was considered to be a false prophet by his contemporaries.

Whatever the truth of this non-biblical legend, it is a possibility that Jonah's refusal to go to Nineveh is perhaps driven by a desire not to repeat this shaming experience[55]. Given that we now know that the ultimate purpose of Jonah's mission to the Ninevites is that they might repent and so avoid destruction; it is clear that Jonah's prophecy of destruction must prove false if Nineveh is to be saved. He must announce a divine judgement that ultimately will not take place. Jonah has to become a 'false' prophet if Nineveh is to be saved.

It is therefore Jonah's disgrace that is to be the key that unlocks the Ninevites salvation[56]. This is not a price Jonah wishes to pay.

---

[52] Ginzberg L. *ibid.*, p247

[53] de Monléon Dom J. *Commentaire sur le Prophète Jonas*, Clermont Ferrand : Editions de la Source, 1970, p47

[54] Ferguson P. *Who was the king of Nineveh?*, Tyndale Bulletin, vol.47 no.2, Nov. 1996, p302 and Blumenthal F. *Jonah the reluctant prophet – Prophecy and Allegory*, Jewish Bible Quarterly, vol.35 no.2, 2007, p105

[55] Ginzberg L. *ibid.*

[56] Bolin T.M. *Eternal delight and deliciousness : The book of Jonah after ten years*, The Journal of Hebrew Scriptures, vol.9 no.4, 2009, p6

Questions for Reflection and Discussion

1.   How do you respond to the idea that God's mission to the barbaric Assyrians was about mercy and not judgement? In your opinion, what was the most likely motivation for Jonah's flight?

2.   We saw above that prophets often had difficulty accepting the assignments God gave them. Have you had experience in your own life of God coming to you, or to your fellowship, with a difficult assignment? How did you respond?

4 - The Horror of Grace (Jonah 1:1-3)

*The word of the Lord came to Jonah son of Amittai: 'Go to the great city of
Nineveh and preach against it, because its wickedness has come up before me.'
But Jonah ran away from the Lord and headed for Tarshish. He went down to
Joppa, where he found a ship bound for that port. After paying the fare, he went
aboard and sailed for Tarshish to flee from the Lord.*

Jonah 1:1-3, NIV

In 2004 we saw an amazing modern parallel of the world situation which is
presented to us in the book of Jonah. The U.S.A. and her allies went to war
against the Iraqi regime of Saddam Hussein. The justification for this attack was
that Saddam Hussein was an evil, war-mongering, ruthless dictator, who formed
part of an 'axis of evil'. The U.S.A. saw themselves as carrying out God's
judgement against this oppressive regime. Even more interestingly, the ancient
city of Nineveh was actually located in modern Iraq, near to the modern city of
Mosul.

Perhaps this parallel can help us to understand something of Jonah's problem
about going to Nineveh. Imagine how a contemporary, nationally famous,
American religious leader would have felt being sent to modern Iraq in order to
invite Saddam Hussein and his regime to receive God's mercy and forgiveness.
Does that give you an insight into Jonah's struggle?

In trying to understand Jonah in his disobedience there is a tendency to see him
in a very negative light. He is often presented simply as a bigot, someone who
simply just didn't want pagans to be saved. However, I think this evaluation of
Jonah over-simplifies the reality. As we considered in the previous study, Jonah's
motivation was far more complex and probably had more to do with how he
expected Nineveh's repentance to impinge on his own nation of Israel. For
example,

*If the people of Nineveh repent quickly it will shame the Jews
in the eyes of the nations and of God* [57]

An eager responsiveness by the Ninevites to the message of God will reflect
badly on the Israelites, who had a long history of refusing to listen to the
messages God sent them. The Jews will therefore be shamed by the Ninevites'
willingness to respond to God.

---

[57] Schwarz J. *Yunus the Prophet - The Qur'anic Story of Jonah*, Muslim-Jewish Journal, 2008 accessed
online at http://www.themuslimjewishjournal.com/articles/yunus-the-prophet-the-quranic-story-of-
jonah.shtml on 15/01/13

Or maybe Jonah was simply seeking to protect his nation from the possibility of a future Assyrian attack. The Assyrians had been for many years the greatest military threat to Northern Israel, often imposing vassal status upon Northern Kingdom. Jonah knew first-hand the reality of living in the presence of oppressive powers. His attitude could therefore be interpreted as demonstrating acute political *nous*. He knows that,

> *For Yahweh to extend the hand of divine mercy rather than act in judgement is therefore, too much. It enables such powers to continue to oppress.* [58]

Jonah's problem is therefore not so much with God's mercy but with God's indiscriminate exercise of that mercy[59], particularly in the light of the likely negative consequences of that mercy for Israel.

Seen from this viewpoint, Jonah is a tragic hero willing to sacrifice himself, his ministry, his reputation and his family ties in order to save his nation[60]. This has been put most strongly by Sawyer, who states that in undertaking God's mission of mercy to the Ninevites,

> *Jonah was being asked to sign his own peoples' death warrant* [61]

If these theories about Jonah's motivation are true, then Jonah might well have seen himself and his actions as standing in the heroic tradition of Moses and David – who both offered their lives to God in order to save their nation[62].

Whatever the reality of Jonah's struggle with his mission, the ultimate result is that, at the end of a drawn out period of struggling with God and his conscience, Jonah decides to flee.

But to where does Jonah flee? Not just anywhere – he specifically chooses Tarshish. This location is given particular emphasis by the structure of the Hebrew text. The text of verse 3 has a particular shape. It follows a specific Hebrew literary form which follows an ABCDCBA chiasmus structure[63]. This is represented graphically as follows;

---

[58] Dray S. Facing the powers – A Biblical Framework for those Facing Political Oppression, Carn Brae Media, 2013, p71.

[59] Fretheim T.E. *ibid.* p119.

[60] Bolin T.M. *Eternal delight and deliciousness : The book of Jonah after ten years*, The Journal of Hebrew Scriptures, vol.9 no.4, 2009, p6.

[61] Sawyer, J.F.A Prophecy and the Prophets of the Old Testament, Oxford: OUP, 1987, p114

[62] See Exodus 32:32 and 2 Samuel 24:17

[63] Fretheim T.E. *ibid.*, p79.

A. To flee to *Tarshish* **from the presence of the Lord.**

B. He *went down* to Joppa.

C. He found a ship.

D. Going to *Tarshish*

C. He paid his fare.

B. He *went down* into the ship.

A. To go with them to *Tarshish* **from the presence of the Lord**.

We see a three-fold repetition of the word 'Tarshish' at the beginning, middle and end of the phrase. The use of such a literary structure serves the function of emphasis. By this repetition of *Tarshish*, Jonah's destination is given prominence.

Tarshish was probably a port at the western limit of the Mediterranean trading area. Plinius and Strabo writing in the first century A.D. located it at the end of the Guadalquivir valley in Southern Spain[64]. The name 'Tarshish' is derived from the verb 'to smelt' , and it seems to have been a centre for metal production.

By contrast, Nineveh was just about at the eastern limit of the Mediterranean trading area. Jonah was therefore trying to put himself as far away from Nineveh as was physically possible at the time. He wanted to put himself at the opposite end of the world to where God wanted to send him, and so he set off on a voyage of around 3,700 km (2,400 miles) in exactly the opposite direction! We can therefore see the significance of Tarshish. It is literally a world away from where God wants Jonah to go.

Questions for Reflection and Discussion

1   Jonah was uncomfortable with what God was trying to say to him and how God was seeking to direct his life, so he tried to take himself *out of the arena of God's proclamation*. In what circumstances and by what means do contemporary Christians try to do this? How do we seek to escape God's uncomfortable presence?

2   What conclusions do you draw from the modern parallels of the world situation in Jonah?

---

[64] Blaiklock E.M. 'Tarshish' in *The Illustrated Bible Dictionary – vol.3*, Leicester: IVP, 1980, p1518.

5 - Joppa - The Port of Grace (Jonah 1:1-3)

The word of the Lord came to Jonah son of Amittai: 'Go to the great city of Nineveh and preach against it, because its wickedness has come up before me.' But Jonah ran away from the Lord and headed for Tarshish. He went down to Joppa, where he found a ship bound for that port. After paying the fare, he went aboard and sailed for Tarshish to flee from the Lord.

Jonah 1:1-3, NIV

There is a wonderful resonance in the fact that Jonah's journey begins in the port of Joppa. In 700 years' time a Jewish man we now call St. Peter will also be staying in Joppa. From this very same spot, he too will begin an unexpected 'voyage' taking the message of God's grace to Gentiles[65].

One afternoon, whilst Peter is having a siesta, God sends him the most disturbing vision. He sees a blanket descend from heaven full of animals that are religiously 'unclean' for Jews – animals that God has instructed Jews not to eat.

God then speaks to Peter and tells him to 'kill and eat'. Peter refuses. He is scandalised that God could ask him - a devout, practising Jew, to break the Kosher regulations laid down by God Himself for His people. God replies to Peter's refusal by saying,

Do not call anything impure that God has made clean

This event is repeated three times. Peter finally awakes, no doubt sweating, certainly in a state of anguish and totally confused by this vision.

Then he hears a knock at the door of the house. Just at that moment God speaks to Peter again and tells him to go with these men. He goes downstairs and what does he find? Two servants of a Roman Centurion named Cornelius, accompanied by a Roman soldier. They have been sent by the Centurion (a Gentile, or 'non-Jew') to bring the Peter, the Jew, to him!

Clearly, Peter had already made some progress in modifying the ceremonial constraints of Judaism. The house in which he was staying was the home of a tanner - an activity which required continual contact with dead animals, and so was considered by devout Jews as an 'unclean' profession. However, to go into the home of a Gentile, to accept his hospitality, was a still an enormous cultural taboo for Peter.

---

[65] Acts 10:1-10

Yet not only does Peter accept their invitation to go to the home of Cornelius the following day, but he invites these men, including the accompanying Roman soldier, into the home where he is staying and lets them stay the night!

The next day sees Peter in the home of Cornelius. Peter hears their story and then begins to preach the gospel to them. While he is still preaching, the Holy Spirit falls on these Gentiles in such a way that Peter is convinced that God is at work amongst them. He draws the inevitable conclusion - if God accepts Gentiles, if He gives them His Spirit, then the Christian Church (up to that point essentially Jewish) must accept them too!

Jonah has the honour in scripture of being, in Dean Stanley's phrase, *'the first apostle to the Gentiles'*[66]. And, 700 years later, in exactly the same town, Peter will become the second. With a divine relish, God even works in the detail that Peter is literally 'the son of Jonah',

Jesus replied, 'Blessed are you, Simon son of Jonah...'[67]

Peter, the son of a man called Jonah, is also the 'spiritual' son of Jonah the prophet. Like Jonah, Peter learns the same message; that God's grace extends to Gentiles, even when they form a ruthless military empire! Like Jonah, Peter will take God's message to Gentiles and see them enter into a new relationship with God.

Such a mental shift was not easy for Peter, and it was even harder for Jonah.

If Peter, in the same Joppa, needed a heavenly vision before he set foot in the first heathen house, a still stronger Divine interposition was necessary in the Old Covenant to overcome the resistance of the spirit of national self-righteousness which deemed the impure heathen fit objects of Divine wrath, but denied to them God's mercy.[68]

That Joppa was the scene for these two events is amazing! It is one of the glorious wonders of scripture that such resonances occur again and again. It reminds us that there is a supernatural intelligence at work in the formation of Scripture. The Holy Spirit has, over millennia, been constantly at work, inspiring many different authors, in many different places, yet revealing one coherent message.

---

[66] Quoted in Kennedy J. *On the book of Jonah*, London: Alexander and Shepheard, 1895, p13
[67] Matthew 16:17, NIV
[68] Von Orelli C. *ibid.*, p172

This link between the stories of Jonah and of Peter reminds us that God's character has not changed: 700 years separate the two, yet God is still trying to help his people understand that His grace has no limits. It reaches out to all, even to those who, in our estimation, do not deserve it. How wonderful that both journeys start in the same place – Joppa - a place whose name means 'beautiful'.

Questions for Reflection and Discussion

1   We could call Joppa the *'Port of Grace'* for both Jonah and St Peter. Their whole way of understanding the world changed there. What *Port of Grace* experiences can you think of, moments when God's revelation has changed a person's complete way of thinking?

2   Is it significant for you that these two 'journeys towards the Gentiles' started from the same place?

6 - God's Call and Jonah's Response – Conclusions (Jonah 1:1-3)

The word of the Lord came to Jonah son of Amittai: 'Go to the great city of Nineveh and preach against it, because its wickedness has come up before me.' But Jonah ran away from the Lord and headed for Tarshish. He went down to Joppa, where he found a ship bound for that port. After paying the fare, he went aboard and sailed for Tarshish to flee from the Lord.

Jonah 1:1-3, NIV

Jonah's story is quite scary. It forces us to face some frightening facts;

1   A Successful Past Does Not Prove Spiritual Maturity:

Jonah had been significantly used by God[69], yet his story reveals to us someone who is still churlish, angry and curmudgeonly. The Bible tells us plainly that God's choices are not always ours, that God chooses to use the weak and the foolish in order to confound the wise, but somehow it still surprises us when we see it!

But God chose the foolish things of the world to shame the wise;
God chose the weak things of the world to shame the strong.
God chose the lowly things of this world and the despised things
– and the things that are not – to nullify the things that are...[70]

When we see God using someone who has major flaws in their character or in their morality we get so confused. Why does God use people like that? The answer is, "Just because he chooses to"!

This doesn't mean that God accepts their faults and failings, or that God approves of them. There is no justification in the Bible for such a viewpoint. God is always against everything that diminishes human life and therefore **ALL** forms of sin. We know that bad choices will always have negative consequences in life on earth, as well as in eternity. However, these failings do not mean that God will not use a person.

We need to remember that no-one **deserves** that God should use them. No-one can ever by their perfection merit such an honour. It is therefore **never** to a person's credit that God works through them. It is always an act of grace on God's part.

If God extends that grace to those in whom we see gross failings, we should rather rejoice than complain. It means that God can use us too!

---

[69] 2 Kings 14:25
[70] 1 Corinthians 1:27-28, NIV

2   A Successful Past Does Not Prove You Share God's Heart:
God had used Jonah in a mighty way in the past, yet Jonah is still a long way from sharing God's heart. Although Jonah never utters a statement that is theologically incorrect (in fact Jonah's theology shines through as being of the highest order), he doesn't share God's heart for lost sinners. Jonah has a view of mission that is completely upside-down. For Jonah, mission is about limiting God's grace to those who deserve it[71]. It is a matter of restricting the gospel to those who are living well, who are making a concerted effort to do what's right.

It was this same mentality that caused the religious elite to condemn Jesus. He too proclaimed God's grace to 'undeserving sinners'. When the self-appointed 'guardians of grace' challenged Jesus, his answer was;

It is not the healthy who need a doctor, but the sick [72]

Jonah had the same mind-set as these 'guardians of grace' Pharisees. He too thought sinners deserved only judgement. God comes to him with a training program in order to show him that God's grace is wild. The grace of God cannot be contained, restrained, limited. It bursts out of any limits that we try to place on it. It reaches into the most unexpected of places and transforms the most unlikely of people. That is the glory and wonder of grace.

3   A Successful Past Does Not Guard Against Future Failure:
In spite of his previously successful ministry[73], we see Jonah flagrantly disobey God. To Jonah's credit he is honest about this. He owns up to the fact that he has deliberately put himself in opposition to God's will for his life. He is so open about this that he doesn't even hide it from the people around him[74].

There is a saying in sporting circles that you are only as good as your last performance. Which is to say that you get no credit for what might have been achieved in the past, it is what you are capable of **NOW** that counts. In the spiritual life is the same. We cannot live on past successes. Our relationship with God is dynamic, not static. We are either growing closer to God, moving on, developing; or we are moving further away, growing colder in our love, stepping back in our level of commitment.

---

[71] For a development of this see, Fretheim T.E. *ibid.*, p24.
[72] Matthew 9:12 NIV.
[73] 2 Kings 14:25
[74] Jonah 1:10

To be fair towards Jonah, his refusal to obey God's call is pretty much the natural human response. We see this clearly in the pages of the Bible, as well as in our own experience. When God comes to us with an assignment, our first response is nearly always refusal. This refusal is often based on very reasonable grounds – the assignment seems too difficult, beyond our capabilities, we don't have sufficient experience etc. We make excuses to God, or we try to convince God that there is somebody more suited to the task; we say, *'There he is, send him!'* rather than, *'Here am I, send me'* [75]

In Merville's classic book, 'Moby Dick', Father Mapple preaches a sermon based on Jonah 1:17. In speaking of Jonah's disobedience he reminds the congregation that,

> *...all the things that God would have us do are hard for us to do*
> *– remember that –*
> *and hence, he oftner commands us than endeavours to persuade.*
> *And if we obey God, we must disobey ourselves;*
> *and it is this disobeying ourselves, wherein the hardness of obeying God consists* [76]

The whole point of God involving us in His purposes is that God wants to use the assignment to transform us, to draw us closer to Him and to prepare us for future service. This necessarily entails a displacement of our desires, our understandings; even our sense of what is just or appropriate.

It is a fundamental truth to grasp that God can do anything He wants without us! He is God after all! So if God involves us in His activity, He does so in order to accomplish something in us – to transform us, to take us deeper in our relationship with Him, to help us to share something of His heart for humanity.
The more incongruous the assignment in relation to our character, our past experience and our abilities, then the more likely it will be that people will perceive it is God who is at work and not us. He will have revealed Himself through our activity.

Questions for Reflection and Discussion

1   If backsliding and spiritual failure remain a possibility for even the greatest of Bible characters, what does that teach us about our own spiritual life, and the life of our faith community?
2   Have you ever run away from an assignment God gave you? If so what was the 'Tarshish' that you ran to?

---

[75] Isaiah 6:8 NIV
[76] Melville H. *Moby Dick*, Evanston: Northwestern University Press, 1991 (1851), p42f

3   What can we practically do to avoid such spiritual failure? In the first instance try to think of your own ideas, then evaluate them in the light of the following biblical texts.

Therefore put on the full armour of God, so that when the day of evil comes, you may be able to stand your ground, and after you have done everything, to stand. Stand firm then, with the belt of truth buckled round your waist, with the breastplate of righteousness in place, and with your feet fitted with the readiness that comes from the gospel of peace. In addition to all this, take up the shield of faith, with which you can extinguish all the flaming arrows of the evil one. Take the helmet of salvation and the sword of the Spirit, which is the word of God. And pray in the Spirit on all occasions with all kinds of prayers and requests. With this in mind, be alert and always keep on praying for all the Lord's people.

Ephesians 6:13-18, NIV

And let us consider how we may spur one another on towards love and good deeds, not giving up meeting together, as some are in the habit of doing, but encouraging one another – and all the more as you see the Day approaching.

Hebrews 10:24-25, NIV

If I speak in the tongues of men or of angels, but do not have love, I am only a resounding gong or a clanging cymbal. If I have the gift of prophecy and can fathom all mysteries and all knowledge, and if I have a faith that can move mountains, but do not have love, I am nothing. If I give all I possess to the poor and give over my body to hardship that I may boast, but do not have love, I gain nothing.
Love is patient, love is kind. It does not envy, it does not boast, it is not proud. It does not dishonour others, it is not self-seeking, it is not easily angered, it keeps no record of wrongs. Love does not delight in evil but rejoices with the truth. It always protects, always trusts, always hopes, always perseveres.
Love never fails. But where there are prophecies, they will cease; where there are tongues, they will be stilled; where there is knowledge, it will pass away. For we know in part and we prophesy in part, but when completeness comes, what is in part disappears. When I was a child, I talked like a child, I thought like a child, I reasoned like a child. When I became a man, I put the ways of childhood behind me. For now we see only a reflection as in a mirror; then we shall see face to face. Now I know in part; then I shall know fully, even as I am fully known.

And now these three remain: faith, hope and love. But the greatest of these is love.

1 Corinthians 13:1-13, NIV

7 - God Sends a Storm (Jonah 1:4-5)

Then the Lord sent a great wind on the sea,
and such a violent storm arose that the ship threatened to break up.
All the sailors were afraid and each cried out to his own god.
And they threw the cargo into the sea to lighten the ship.

Jonah 1:4-5 NIV

God responds to Jonah's disobedience by using an element of His creation to do something in Jonah's life. This is the first of several such interventions. In the short book of Jonah we see a storm, a sea monster, a gourd, a worm and a hot desert wind all being used to bring Jonah into alignment with the mind and heart of God.

The great question is 'Why?' Why does God bother to pursue Jonah? God gave him a command, an assignment, Jonah refused, why doesn't the story stop there? It isn't like God needs Jonah - that without Jonah, God is incapable of doing what He wants to do. So why does God pursue Jonah, rearrange the created order around Jonah in order to intercept him, to bring him to a stand-still, to force him to reconsider his actions and his motivations?

The first answer, the foundational truth, is simply love; God loves Jonah and so God wants the best for him. As one of God's covenant people, God is committed to bringing Jonah back into a healthy relationship with Himself.

The second reason is that God has simply chosen to do something through Jonah. When God makes a choice it is definitive. God's call is irrevocable. God has chosen Jonah as His agent. God knows beforehand what struggles this will entail for Jonah, He also knows what fruit this experience will bear in Jonah's life and how his story will bear fruit in the lives of others. God does not make mistakes! He makes choices and then brings those choices to their desired end.

Let's look at the first element of the creation that God uses to bring Jonah around – the storm.

In our 21st century Western context, we have grown up surrounded by a culture that believes the universe operates **on its own**. This mechanistic viewpoint sees the universe as simply following certain intrinsic principles and unchanging laws.

People holding this mechanistic view believe that they can explain (or eventually will be able to explain, as human knowledge develops) every phenomena they witness, without any need of an outside agency such as supernatural forces, or God.

45

However, this way of seeing the world is completely foreign to the Bible. For Jonah and his contemporaries the supernatural was an intrinsic part of everyday life. For them nothing happened without the direct activity of an outside agency - be it the gods, spirits etc.

Whilst our base-line assumption tends to be that **nothing** is supernatural; their base-line assumption was that **everything** was supernatural.

For the Christian also, God is at the centre of everything and is the origin of everything.

"For in him we live and move and have our being"[77]

Jesus himself is understood as having a mystical role at the centre of the created order, not simply in the past as the agent of its creation, but as dynamically holding it in existence moment by moment.

"The Son is the image of the invisible God, the firstborn over all creation.
For in him all things were created: things in heaven and on earth, visible and
invisible, whether thrones or powers or rulers or authorities;
all things have been created through him and for him.
He is before all things, and in him all things hold together." [78]

"The Son is the radiance of God's glory and the exact representation of his being,
sustaining all things by his powerful word."[79]

So from a Christian optic, the universe is not a blindly-operating mechanism but the continuing expression of the creative Word of God. Each moment of existence is a grace, an expression of the goodness, glory and love of God. Each moment of life is in itself a reason for giving thanks and glory to God.

So if we accept that God is at the origin of everything that happens in the universe, even 'naturally-occurring events', the question we must ask of each event is 'What is this event's purpose? What does God intend by this event?' In regard to our text, what was the point God wished to make in sending a storm upon Jonah?

As we consider what the Bible teaches about the universe and God's activity within it, we find that while the Christian faith maintains that God is the origin of everything, it does not however support an outlook on life where every difficulty

---

[77] Acts 17:28a, NIV
[78] Colossians 1:16-17, NIV
[79] Hebrews 1:3a, NIV

is seen as a divine punishment and every good thing is interpreted as an evidence of divine blessing. The reality is far more complex than that.

In the first covenant that God made with Israel there were blessings for obedience and curses for disobedience[80]. From a simply logical perspective, it would seem natural that following God's rules for human society should lead to good results. God's laws for Israel promoted justice, provided structures for resolving conflict and difficulties, and kept in balance the social relationships which are a normal part of human beings trying to live together. So, to a certain degree, the blessings can be considered the natural outworking of a healthy model of society. Yet we read in Deuteronomy 28 that the blessings God promises will accompany obedience go far beyond what could be expected as merely the natural result of a good social model. They include fertility (both of humans and of livestock) as well as the promise of military and economic success.

On the other hand, God promises that certain curses will fall upon the nation if they are disobedient to the terms of the covenant. Again, these curses go beyond what might naturally be expected to be the result of a poor social model and include infertility, economic failure, disease, social confusion and military attack.

This double mechanism – blessings for obedience and curses for disobedience – is God's strategy to help His people choose the right path, to do what is best. **Both** aspects are an expression of God's love for Israel. Certainly blessing is the most natural expression of God's nature of love. The difficulties that God brings upon His people, in response to their sin, is described by Isaiah as God's 'strange work'; something contrary to His nature.

> *The Lord will rise up as he did at Mount Perazim,*
> *he will rouse himself as in the Valley of Gibeon –*
> *to do his work, his strange work,*
> *and perform his task, his alien task.*[81]

Like every good parent, God's love does not allow Him to let us take the wrong road in our lives. He knows that rejection of His will and His ways will only lead to our harm, and so He does all He can to bring us to our senses and to repentance and restitution in our relationship with Him.

---

[80] See Deuteronomy 28
[81] Isaiah 28:21, NIV

But it is wrong to imagine that happy, healthy, wealthy people are blessed by God and must therefore be good Christians with whom God is pleased - and vice versa. Jesus' disciples made this error and He had to correct them for it.

As he went along, he saw a man blind from birth. His disciples asked him, 'Rabbi, who sinned, this man or his parents, that he was born blind?'
'Neither this man nor his parents sinned,' said Jesus, 'but this happened so that the works of God might be displayed in him'.[82]

Jesus warns His disciples against this over-simplistic outlook. The reality is far more complex. Often good people have a hard time, whilst many wicked people have an easy life – how can this be understood? Many psalms express the struggle to come to terms with this -

This is what the wicked are like –
always free of care, they go on amassing wealth.
Surely in vain I have kept my heart pure
and have washed my hands in innocence.
All day long I have been afflicted,
and every morning brings new punishments.[83]

So whilst the Bible indicates that there is some causal link between obedience to God's will and blessing, and between disobedience and cursing, it is not a simple relationship. There are other elements at work which we must take into account;

-   That God uses difficulty in our lives to enable us to grow in our faith.
-   That the created universe is damaged by man's sin and the fall. Sickness and death therefore touch all of us indiscriminately. The natural world is wild and dangerous sometimes.
-   That Satan is at work, as well as God. He actively opposes God's activity and all those who are involved in it.

All of which means that to understand a specific event we need spiritual discernment – the gift which enables us to perceive the spiritual realities behind the physical reality that we experience. It is only by exercising this gift of the Spirit that we can find out if what we are experiencing has a spiritual component (from God or from Satan) or if it is simply a natural event, arising from the inherently damaged nature of the universe.

We mustn't forget the fact that God's wisdom is beyond our understanding. God's actions in this world will always remain, at least to some degree,

---

[82] John 9:1-3, NIV
[83] Psalm 73:12-14, NIV

incomprehensible to us. If we consider the life of Saint Paul, we are told that he had some kind of a physical problem which he called his 'thorn in the flesh'.

...because of these surpassingly great revelations. Therefore, in order to keep me from becoming conceited, I was given a thorn in my flesh, a messenger of Satan, to torment me. Three times I pleaded with the Lord to take it away from me. But he said to me, 'My grace is sufficient for you, for my power is made perfect in weakness.'[84]

This unspecified problem caused Saint Paul suffering. He prayed three times asking God to release him from this (remember that St Paul had a ministry of healing[85]) and yet God refused his request. What God did do, was to show him that his suffering was not an accident, that it had a purpose. It was meant to be of spiritual benefit in his life; to prevent him from becoming proud. Knowing this enabled Saint Paul to come to terms with his situation and accept God's will.

It is often said that God is more interested in our holiness than our happiness. Empirically we know that is often in the times of suffering that people most turn towards God, that they make the greatest spiritual progress.

In conclusion there are a few truths that we need to take hold of;

- Normally we can expect God's blessing upon a life or a community that is turned towards God and following His guidance.
- If we rebel against God and His guidance for our lives, we can expect negative consequences, as God expresses His love for us in trying to bring us to our senses.
- In the fallen universe, there are forces of evil at work that oppose God and His people.
- Creation is not in its original perfect state. Therefore there are negative elements – sicknesses and dangers – which are an integral aspect of what it means to live in this world.
- God and His ways are above and beyond our comprehension. There will inevitably be times when the 'why' of a situation cannot be known – at least this side of eternity. But we can draw strength from the fact that God has expressed his love for us in an irrefutable fashion through Jesus on the cross.

So we can conclude from our reading of Jonah that the storm was indeed sent by God; that it was an expression of God's love for Jonah; that its intended purpose is to draw Jonah back to the path of obedience. Later on we will see how God

---

[84] 2 Corinthians 12:7-9a, NIV
[85] See Acts 14

uses the storm to accomplish even more in Jonah's life; it actually prepares him for his mission.

Questions for Reflection and Discussion

1   In what ways do you discern the presence of God in and through His creation? In your own life has God used elements of His creation in order to reveal Himself and His will to you?

2   What are the benefits and the dangers of believing that God is present in a proactive way in His creation?

8 – The Structure of the Storm (Jonah 1:11-15)

Then the Lord sent a great wind on the sea, and such a violent storm arose that the ship threatened to break up. All the sailors were afraid and each cried out to his own god.
And they threw the cargo into the sea to lighten the ship.
But Jonah had gone below deck, where he lay down and fell into a deep sleep. The captain went to him and said, 'How can you sleep? Get up and call on your god! Maybe he will take notice of us so that we will not perish.'
Then the sailors said to each other, 'Come, let us cast lots to find out who is responsible for this calamity.' They cast lots and the lot fell on Jonah. So they asked him, 'Tell us, who is responsible for making all this trouble for us? What kind of work do you do? Where do you come from?
What is your country? From what people are you?'
He answered, 'I am a Hebrew and I worship the Lord, the God of heaven, who made the sea and the dry land.'
This terrified them and they asked, 'What have you done?'
(They knew he was running away from the Lord, because he had already told them so.)
The sea was getting rougher and rougher. So they asked him,
'What should we do to you to make the sea calm down for us?'
'Pick me up and throw me into the sea,' he replied, 'and it will become calm. I know that it is my fault that this great storm has come upon you.'
Instead, the men did their best to row back to land. But they could not, for the sea grew even wilder than before. Then they cried out to the Lord, 'Please, Lord, do not let us die for taking this man's life. Do not hold us accountable for killing an innocent man, for you, Lord, have done as you pleased.' Then they took Jonah and threw him overboard, and the raging sea grew calm.

Jonah 1:11-15, NIV

The author here describes to us the breaking of the storm and the frantic conversations and desperate actions which follow as the sailors try desperately to avoid death by drowning. This is such an exciting piece of narrative that we can miss the fact that it is actually very carefully constructed. In fact there seems to be a particular literary structure to this story of the storm. This structure is one that is very common in Hebrew literature and is variously called an ABCCBA, a chiastic, or a concentric structure[86]. Represented graphically it looks like this:

---

[86] This analysis of the structure of the passage follows that detailed in Limburg, *ibid.*, p47

```
A         The Lord hurls the storm (v.4)
    B         The sailors pray and act (v.5ab)
        C         Jonah acts (lies down and sleeps) (v.5c)
            D         The captain / sailors question Jonah (v.6-8)
                E         Jonah speaks (v.9)
            D'         The sailors question Jonah (v.10-11)
        C'         Jonah speaks - hurl me - (v.12)
    B'         The sailors act and pray (v.13-14)
A'         The sailors hurl Jonah and the storm ends (v.15)
```

The underlining, italics and emphasis reveal the presence of mirrored elements in the passage. The reason for using such a structure is always in order to focus attention on the central element (E), in this instance it is Jonah's confession of faith. At this key point Jonah states his cultural identity, *I am a Hebrew*, and his religious persuasion, *I worship the Lord, the God of heaven, who made the sea and the land*. To quote James Limburg,

> *Jonah's words in 1:9, a confession of faith, have been carefully placed at the midpoint of this concentric structure. There are 94 words in the Hebrew text from the scene's beginning in 1:4 to the beginning of the speech in 1:9 ("I am a Hebrew") and 94 words in 1:10-15 ... Both the concentric structure and the exact balance of number of words serve to place the focus for this section on the confession in 1:9*[87]

We also notice that in the Hebrew text the same verb is used three times, *to hurl*. First, God is said *to hurl* the storm. Second, Jonah tells the sailors *to hurl* him over the side of the boat. Third, the sailors finally carry out Jonah's instructions and *hurl* him into the raging sea.

Such stylistic features help to remind us that the Bible is art as well as theology. In scripture divine revelation is clothed in human artistry. Whilst translations can preserve the sense and the meaning of the original language, we sometimes miss the artistry and the literary beauty of their form in our translations.

The structure of this passage with its emphasis at the central point, serves to remind us that Jonah has been set apart by the call of God as a **prophet**, and focuses our attention on Jonah's **confession of faith**.

Remember that Jonah has been called to proclaim the truth about God to the Gentile people of Nineveh. He has chosen to disobey God and has refused to fulfil his calling. But God doesn't leave things there. Even in his disobedience, God places Jonah in a situation in which he is forced to carry out his prophetic

---

[87] Limburg, *ibid.*, p48

function. Even in the midst of his rebellion against God and in the heat of his outrage and refusal to preach to the Gentiles, Jonah finds himself proclaiming the truth about God to Gentiles!

This is an incident in scripture which makes it clear to us that *God's gifts and His call are irrevocable*[88]. Once God has decided to use a person in a certain way, He will use them in that way - either in disobedience or in obedience. He can use them with their active co-operation, which will work to their spiritual blessing and eternal reward, or, as here with Jonah, He can use them in spite of their active rebellion, to their eternal shame.

As we will see later, every single time Jonah opens his mouth to speak to Gentiles, those Gentiles turn to God in repentance and faith, such is the nature of God's anointing upon his life.

It is interesting to note in passing the parallels between this experience of Jonah and the storm which fell upon Jesus and his disciples in Matthew 8.

Biblical Refs.	Nature of the Storm	The Solution	The Situation	The Fear	The Result
Jonah 1:4-15	A divinely appointed storm	Only Jonah has the solution to the situation	Jonah is asleep	The sailors are terrified	Jonah is thrown overboard and God stills the storm
Matt 8:23-27 Mark 4:36-41 Luke 8:22-25	A demonic storm	Only Jesus has the solution to the situation	Jesus is asleep	The disciples are terrified	Jesus stills the storm with a word

Table 1 - Parallels between storm experiences of Jonah and the disciples

---

[88] Romans 11:29 NIV

The gospel accounts of the storm event show Jesus as master of the elements. Their purpose is to make His divine nature evident; it is this event that leads the disciples to first worship Him[89].

In the Jonah story we see that the point of the storm is to call wayward Jonah back to obedience. Through it Yahweh also reveals Himself and His power to the pagan sailors, they come to know *the Lord, the God of heaven, who made the sea and the dry land* – and respond by worshipping Him.

Some Bible commentators have pictured the conflict between Jonah and his God as a 'spat' or a 'lover's tiff'. God certainly loves Jonah and Jonah seems to love God too, however at this point Jonah is struggling to come to terms with a God whose character is different from that which he had always understood. Unfortunately the poor pagan sailors are caught up in the middle of it and it is a terrifying experience for them. This will ultimately prove to be a blessing as they will not only emerge unharmed, but with a new knowledge of God.

This is no accident;
it is what is supposed to happen when Gentiles get in the way of the altercation
between the Lord and His beloved[90]

Questions for Reflection and Discussion

1   What is the significance of the literary dimension of scripture? Why is it important for us to recognise that the Bible is comprised of elements written in different literary genre (e.g. poetry, legal documents, historical narrative etc.)?

2   What are the implications of the fact that God's gifts and His call are irrevocable?

3   Who knows more about God – Jonah or the sailors? Who is closer to God – Jonah or the sailors?

---

[89] Stuart D. *ibid.*, p467
[90] Cary P. *Jonah – SCM Theological Commentary*, London: SCM Press, 2008, p47

9 – In the Eye of the Storm (Jonah 1:5-6)

> *All the sailors were afraid and each cried out to his own god.*
> *And they threw the cargo into the sea to lighten the ship.*
> *But Jonah had gone below deck, where he lay down and fell into a deep sleep.*
> *The captain went to him and said, 'How can you sleep? Get up and call on your*
> *god! Maybe he will take notice of us so that we will not perish.'*
>
> Jonah 1:5-6, NIV

The storm hits the ship and chaos follows. The sailors, even with all their experience of life at sea, are terrified. There are some indications that this must have been an exceptional storm which came upon them without warning. This is shown by the fact that the sailors haven't had time to put into port, to find safe harbour. Indeed, the sailors seem to have sensed straight away that there was something supernatural in this storm; a storm that looks like being the end of them all.

The first reaction of the sailors is to pray. It is a bald fact that in moments of crisis there are surprisingly few atheists! These sailors, totally helpless in the face of a storm the like of which they have never experienced before, begin to cry out to their gods.

In the ancient world the gods of the pagans were of three types – personal, family and national. So each sailor would be crying out to his own god, his family's chosen god and also the god of his nation[91].

A Jewish tradition, recounted in the writings of the great Talmudic scholar, Rabbi Eliezer ben Hyrcanus (40-120 A.D.), interprets the phrase 'every man' to have particular significance - to indicate that there were representatives on board the ship from every single one of the 70 nations of man. So in this event, the whole panoply of pagan gods are being revealed as inadequate - only Yahweh has the power to control the storm.

Also, as Jonah offers his life for theirs, a powerful image is created of the entirety of the pagans nations being saved through the willing martyrdom of a Hebrew[92].

As such, there is here a wonderful prophetic foreshadowing of the accomplishment of Jesus on the cross.

Whilst continuing to pray, the sailors begin to jettison their cargo. Such an action indicates that they are totally convinced that their situation is a matter of life

---

[91] Stuart D. *ibid.*, p460
[92] Ben Hyrcanus E. *ibid.*, p67

and death. As Cary points out, their voyage was purely about commerce and profit (Mammon), yet when danger strikes and death is in view,

> ...all that is sacred to Mammon goes overboard –
> it is too heavy to carry, not worth keeping[93]

Where is Jonah, the prophet of the true God, at this moment? Is he practically encouraging and helping the sailors to jettison the cargo? Is he supporting them spiritually by reminding them that it is the spiritual which is of ultimate importance, that the material is only transitory? Is he operating like a prophet, encouraging their spiritual activity and instinct to pray? Is he leading them to a knowledge of the true God and helping them to direct their prayers to the One who can really help? Is he exercising his prophetic ministry in seeking a word from God about this event?

No. Instead, somewhat amazingly, Jonah is asleep!

In order to understand this state of affairs, we need to look at the results of sin. Jonah is in rebellion against God. One of the consequences of being in such a position is that all spiritual activity becomes distasteful and difficult. In the psalm attributed to David, where he confesses his adultery with Bathsheba and his complicity in the death of her husband, he says;

> I know my transgressions, and my sin is always before me [94]

Under God's chastening, David found that his mind was dominated by the memory of his sin. To such a degree that prayer became impossible for him. The joy of his salvation, his enjoyment of God's presence, was just a distant memory. Similarly, Jonah, even in the face of death, cannot bring himself to pray for God's help.

It will help us to understand Jonah's mental state if we think for a moment about just what he has had to go through to get to this point. He has put himself in direct opposition to God's will for his life. This prophet - who has spent his whole life reading God's word, praying to God, drawing closer to God, listening to God, speaking to others about God – has turned his back on God! He is without hope for the future. He knows that in his rebellion against God it is impossible that his life will have any further spiritual significance, meaning or usefulness. He is now heading for a distant pagan land, where he will live out his remaining years as an alien, without family or friends. He has no God, no ministry, no family, no hope, no future.

---

[93] Cary P. *ibid.*, p50
[94] Psalm 51:3 NIV

57

To get to this point Jonah has struggled with his conscience and with God for a significant period of time, perhaps even months. He is most likely in an anguished state of mind. Having finally made the intensely difficult and painful decision to rebel against God, having boarded the boat and made a start on his journey to exile, Jonah just collapses in a heap. The trauma, the stress, the mental anguish, the sleepless nights - all finally catch up with him and he collapses, mentally, physically and spiritually exhausted.

Jonah also gives the impression of being careless towards his own life, perhaps even suicidal. Certainly he seems not to care much whether he lives or dies. Given what he has recently been through, this is understandable.

All of which creates a rather emotionally dramatic scene. However, in the midst of all this high drama we have an almost comical incident - the pagan captain comes to tell the Jewish prophet to pray!

Jonah may be resigned to death but the captain is not. He wants to live! He scolds Jonah for being asleep and tells him to get praying. The captain wants everyone on board his ship to be praying to their god. He is not a man of great faith but at least he believes there is a **possibility** that something **might** happen. His prayer is based on a *maybe* (1:6), but in a storm even a *maybe* is better than nothing! So whilst Jonah the prophet sleeps, up on deck the pagan sailors are holding an ecumenical prayer service![95]

Here we also see the vital difference between the Jewish faith and the pagan religions. It was to the Jews that God had revealed Himself and His will. It was to the Jews that God had given the scriptures which had helped them to know Him and to understand something of His creation. Without this divine revelation all human religion is based only upon the ideas of men, vague conceptions and dreams. The Jews had had the privilege of knowing the one true God – their faith had solidity, and certainty.

> *You don't have to be a Christian to believe in a gracious god and pray for help,*
> *and unlike Christian theologians the Bible never entertains the bizarre belief that*
> *pagans do not believe in unearned divine mercy.*
> *The only problem with these pagans is that they don't know which god to call*
> *upon.[96]*

Jonah and his people had received revelation about the true God Yahweh; along with this revelation came the duty of sharing it with the world. Indeed, the first

---

[95] Murray P. A Journey with Jonah – The Spirituality of Bewilderment, Dublin: The Columba Press, 2002, p59
[96] Cary P. *ibid.*, p53

words of God when he selected Abram as the founder of a His chosen people contain this idea,

...and all peoples on earth will be blessed through you[97]

Sadly the Jews had largely neglected this duty to bless the world by sharing their revelation of God and this fact is the central concern of the book of Jonah.

Jonah finds himself outside Israel - the nation of God's special grace - but does this mean he is outside of the arena of God's activity? Does the failure of the Jews to spread their knowledge of God mean that God is completely unknown and inactive outside of Israel?

The response of the book of Jonah is categorical – No! Jonah discovers that God is also at work amongst the pagan nations. Certainly God reveals Himself less explicitly to them than He has done to the Jews, pagan faith lacks content and is based on 'maybes' rather than on concrete revelation; but nonetheless God is at work here - in the sea, in the storm, in the sailors.

Where can I go from your Spirit? Where can I flee from your presence? If I go up to the heavens, you are there; If I make my bed in the depths, you are there. If I rise on the wings of the dawn, if I settle on the far side of the sea, even there your hand will guide me, your right hand will hold me fast [98]

As Jesus was to teach his disciples,

My Father is always at His work [99]

There is neither a time, nor a place where God is not at work in some way. Often His work is hidden from us, but He is working nevertheless. For Jonah, this meant concretely there was no hope of his escaping from the presence of God; which ultimately he would come to appreciate as a great blessing.

There are two important truths contained in these verses.

Firstly, no situation is hopeless. Even in the most extreme situation, God is there and is always capable of turning things around. Jonah's future had never seemed more hopeless, socially, professionally, spiritually and physically. His ministry is over, his family abandoned, his country is far away, his reputation is destroyed and he is in the middle of a storm and about to be thrown overboard. Yet, in the

---

[97] Genesis 12v3b, NIV
[98] Psalm 139:7-10 NIV
[99] John 5:17 NIV

grace of God, an incredible turnaround is about to take place. It will be a painful experience, but it will lead to the most incredible ministry success, perhaps the most successful the world has ever seen. In a few days Jonah will preach in the greatest city in the world, to the worst people in the world and they will all turn to God! The story of this experience will then go on to inspire and nourish the faith of Jews, Christians and Muslims for nearly three thousand years!

All this can be summed up by saying that hope is the proper state of mind for the Christian. Even when, like Jonah, we find ourselves overtaken by sin, in rebellion against God and even despairing of our lives, there is always hope. Whilst we might be tempted to despair and to think about self-destruction, with God there is always a way back. Often it will be a painful way back. There will be often-times long-lasting consequences for our sin. But in God's grace and mercy restoration **IS** possible. And God will do everything He can to bring us back to Him.

Secondly, God is always with us. No matter how hard we try, we cannot take ourselves out of the presence of God. Jonah fled the area of God's special grace, the area of his self-revelation – Israel – but he found he couldn't leave God behind. If we distance ourselves from our Christian community it will not mean that we are outside the area of God's activity. We will just find ourselves, like Jonah, in the pagan world. A place where God is still active, but less well understood, often unrecognised and sometimes responded to in inappropriate ways. We can be certain that God will continue to be active carrying out His chastening activity in our lives and circumstances in order to bring us back to Him. His profound love for us will not permit Him to abandon us.

Notice that it was the pagan sailors who first recognised the activity of God in the storm; before even the Jewish prophet, Jonah, was aware of it. We see here another consequence of sin – our spiritual sensitivity is dulled. Sin affects our spiritual capacity to recognize God and His activity; it makes us deaf to the voice of God. But whether, like Jonah, we are aware of it or not, God is still actively working to bring us back to Himself.

Questions for Reflection and Discussion

1   Jesus said, "All things have been committed to me by my Father. No-one knows who the Son is except the Father, and no-one knows who the Father is except the Son and those to whom the Son chooses to reveal him.[100] What does this indicate to us about the nature of God's self-revelation in the Church and in the World? What differences do you think there are between these two areas of God's activity?

2   Can you think of a hopeless situation, like that of Jonah in the storm, that was turned around by God? Or a time when you were far away from God and He worked to bring you back to Himself?

3   What consequences can we draw for our own spiritual lives from God's activity in Jonah's life?

---

[100] Luke 10:22 NIV

10 – Whose Fault? (Jonah 1:7-9)

Then the sailors said to each other, 'Come, let us cast lots to find out who is responsible for this calamity.' They cast lots and the lot fell on Jonah.
So they asked him, 'Tell us, who is responsible for making all this trouble for us? What kind of work do you do? Where do you come from? What is your country? From what people are you?'
He answered, 'I am a Hebrew and I worship the Lord, the God of heaven, who made the sea and the dry land.'

Jonah 1:7-9, NIV

We noticed previously that it was the pagan sailors and not Jonah who first recognised the supernatural nature of the storm.

The sailors respond by trying to find out if someone has angered the gods. A contemporary superstition held that a runaway slave would bring bad luck to a ship[101]. So for them, the first logical step is to check that no-one on-board is in that situation. The Qur'an's version of the Jonah story seems to indicate this,

And, behold, Jonah was indeed one of Our message-bearers when he fled like a runaway slave onto a laden ship.[102]

The pagan sailors proceed quite logically to use supernatural means (the casting of lots) to identify the supernatural cause of the storm. This was the only way they had to communicate with the gods. We don't know exactly how this was done. One of the most common methods at this time was to use marked sticks or pebbles and to draw them blindly. Perhaps each person drew a lot in turn and the marked lot indicated the person responsible, or perhaps someone drew a lot in the name of each individual. Whatever the method, on this occasion the system worked, Jonah is indicated as the guilty party. In effect, their suspicions are confirmed, Jonah **IS** a runaway slave, he is a prophet running away from his Master, God.

The sailors then gather around Jonah and they fire a series of questions at him. In Semitic culture seven is the number of completeness, so this series of seven questions indicates a complete interrogation of Jonah and the facts concerning him. They ask him specific questions about his identity and about what he has done to bring about the divine displeasure. Verse 10 makes it clear that Jonah

---

[101] Mermer A. and Yazicioglu U. *An insight into the prayer of Jonah (p) in the Qur'an*, The Journal of Scriptural Reasoning, Number 3.1, June 2003, accessed at http://etext.lib.virginia.edu/journals/ssr/issues/volume3/number1/ssr03-01-e02.html on 07/12/12
[102] 37 :139

has already told them that he is running away from God - but he hasn't told them from which God.

For these pagan sailors, the gods were primarily local deities, based in a certain area and having power only over that place[103]. So much so that,

> Banishment from the territory of one god
> meant the transfer of a man's worship to another.[104]

Therefore the fact that Jonah indicated that he was running away from his god wouldn't cause them great concern. But their appreciation of the situation changes drastically when Jonah reveals to them that he is a Hebrew and tells them exactly which God he is running away from. He is running away from,

> Yahweh, the God of heaven who made the sea and the land.[105]

Now that is a very different thing indeed!

The Israelites had themselves struggled to fully appreciate the revelation of scripture of the omnipresent reality of Yahweh. This is evidenced during their captivity in Babylon. The great question for the people of God, now displaced from their homeland, was,

> How can we sing the songs of the Lord while in a foreign land?[106]

The people of Israel found the answer, as recorded in the following psalm,

> ...before the gods I will sing your praise[107]

In exile, the people of Israel learned that their God was above and beyond any geographic limitation, they learned to sing their praise of Him in a foreign land and in defiance of the gods that are no gods.

> ...the supposed guardians of foreign lands, were fading into powerless ghosts,
> like shreds of the night mists a summer dawn disperses,
> and that with their evanescence the whole wide world was Yahweh's land.[108]

---

[103] See 1 Kings 20:23
[104] Martin A.D. *The Prophet Jonah – The Book and the Sign*, London : Longmans, Green & Co., 1926, p41
[105] Jonah 1:v:9 NIV
[106] Psalm 137:4, NIV
[107] Psalm 138:1b, NIV
[108] Martin, *ibid*. p43

The pagan sailors discover that Jonah's God is an omnipresent reality, not a small local deity with local jurisdiction. Thus, as St John Chrysostom remarked, the real problem facing the ship is now unmasked,

> *...the most significant weight in the ship was not in its cargo*
> *but the sin of the prophet*[109]

In spite of the efforts made, the ship's true burden remained entire – Jonah. He burdened the ship not with the weight of his body but with the weight of his sin[110].

The sailors are now not only terrified of the storm, but of Yahweh too. Their previous knowledge of the divine had been confined to the polytheistic worship of localised, pagan deities. There was no real need to fear such little gods. Now they are face to face with the power of Yahweh, the universal God - the one who is limitless and awesome. They are also learning that this Yahweh is active in the lives of men. They find themselves unwittingly on the receiving end of Yahweh's displeasure and can only ask Jonah incredulously,

> *What have you done?* [111]

Questions for Reflection and Discussion

1   The sailors' understanding of God changed because of this event. The way in which we understand God has an enormous impact in how we evaluate our lives and our situations. How has your understanding of God changed over time? How have those changes altered the way in which you relate to God and understand His world?

---

[109] Chrysostom J. (tr. Christo G.G.) *On Repentance and Almsgiving* (The Fathers of the Church, Vol. 96), Washington: CUA Press, 1997, p62
[110] de Monléon Dom J. *ibid.*, p68
[111] Jonah 1 :10 NIV

11 - God Speaks Using the Vocabulary We Have (Jonah 1:7)

Then the sailors said to each other,
'Come, let us cast lots to find out who is responsible for this calamity.'
They cast lots and the lot fell on Jonah.

Jonah 1:7, NIV

We have to face up to a real problem here. In the laws that God gave to the people of Israel, the casting of lots and other pagan methods for divining were specifically banned.

Let no-one be found among you who sacrifices his son or daughter in the fire, who practises divination or sorcery, interprets omens, engages in witchcraft, or casts spells, or who is a medium or spiritist or who consults the dead. Anyone who does such things is detestable to the Lord, and because of these detestable practices the Lord your God will drive out those nations before you.
You must be blameless before your God.[112]

Yet here the sailors cast lots and God allows this banned practice to reveal to them the truth of their situation. Why?

In answering this question we have to consider the totality of the response which the sailors made to the situation in which they found themselves. The sailors behaved like good, honest pagans in this crisis. Their approach to the extreme circumstances was to try to do their best.

- They did all that they humanly could to save themselves. They tried to make for shore.
- They did their duty. They tried to save both men and cargo at first. This attempt having failed, they jettisoned the cargo in order to try to save human life.
- Once they recognised the supernatural nature of the storm they tried to plead with the divinity behind it. They each cried out to their own god.
- They used their only means of communicating with the divinity to try to identify who had angered the god(s). They cast lots.
- They approached the identified cause of the problem and asked for confirmation / explanation. They ask Jonah for information about himself and his God.

No-one could have asked for more from such men. They were courageous, dutiful and eager to communicate with, and to placate, the divinity they had unwittingly angered. Whilst their understanding and methods may leave a lot to

---
[112] Deuteronomy 18:10-13 NIV

be desired from a biblical viewpoint, their intentions and motivations are nonetheless commendable.

There seems to be a certain resonance between this situation and the Jewish rite for the choosing of the scapegoat on Yom Kippur[113]. In this ceremony lots were cast over two goats, one of which was designated the 'scapegoat'. This goat was symbolically loaded with the sins of the people of Israel and then driven out into the desert. This imagery was specifically applied to Jesus,

> *God made him who had no sin to be sin for us,*
> *so that in him we might become the righteousness of God.*[114]

It seems likely that there an intended resonance here with Jonah. He is presented as a scapegoat, indicated by lot and symbolically loaded with the sins of the sailors - taking on himself the sins of the Gentiles. Indeed, this is entirely logical, for as we see later, Jonah is a type or a 'foreshadowing' of Christ.

So what do we learn from this event? We learn that God's willingness to communicate with mankind is such that He is ready to speak to people using whatever means with which they approach Him. In other words, God speaks to us in the vocabulary we already have. These sailors did the best they could, they did all that they could reasonably be expected to do. Rather than condemning them for their superstitious pagan practices, God responds in grace and mercy. He responds to their prayers, (even though those prayers were misdirected), He overrules in their magic in order to guide them and to reveal to them the truth of their situation.

We can sum this up by saying that honest intent goes a long way with God **prior to revelation**. Before God reveals to us the specifics of His will for mankind, it seems that He is open to all honest approaches from those who seek Him, however confused and stumbling these approaches might be. This is in itself powerful evidence of God's grace and mercy, and gives us concrete proof of His desire to save all men[115].

Enns reminds us however, that God's intention is always more than simple communication,

> *...God always speaks in ways that the people understand,*
> *not simply to leave them there*
> *but to bring them along to a deeper knowledge of himself.*[116]

---

[113] Leviticus 14:7-10, 20-22
[114] 2 Corinthians 5 :21, NIV
[115] See 1 Timothy 2:1-7
[116] Enns P. *Inspiration and Incarnation*, Grand Rapids : Baker Academic, 2005, p102

Once revelation has been given we are constrained to live in its light. The prophet Amos expresses this clearly, where God speaking to Israel says,

You only have I chosen of all the families of the earth;
therefore I will punish you for all your sins [117]

The Bible shows us clearly that God is unremitting in His condemnation of magical, superstitious practices amongst His people; they should know better. For the people of God it is through the word of God and through the prophets of God, that God's will is to be sought; not through divination or magic. But for the pagans who have not yet received the same revelation as Israel, God seems willing to allow the use of dubious, or even completely wrong methods, in order that they serve as an **initial** means of communication. God speaks to us in the vocabulary we already have.

We see the same principle at work in the story of the pagan prophet Balaam, who was hired to curse Israel through magical means. Balaam was over-ruled by the Spirit of God and forced to pronounce a blessing rather than a curse upon God's people[118]. So we have the bizarre scenario of a pagan magician pronouncing God's word of blessing over Israel! We can also remember how God intervened when Saul went to consult the medium of Endor in order to speak with the spirit of the dead prophet Samuel[119].

Ultimately God is sovereign and controls all things, something expressed in Proverbs,

The lot is cast into the lap,
but its every decision is from the Lord[120]

With regard to knowing God's will, we are fortunate to live in a time where we enjoy the possession of the complete Bible. In the Old Testament we have God's historical self-revelation in the life of the nation of Israel. In the New Testament we have four accounts of God's greatest self-revelation in the person, life and work of Jesus[121]. Finally, we have the apostolic correspondence to the first Christian churches, written to help them understand and to live out their faith in Jesus.

---

[117] Amos 3:2, NIV
[118] Numbers 22 - 24
[119] 1 Samuel 28
[120] Proverbs 16:33, NI
[121] Colossians 2:9

67

Thus it is within our grasp to have an adequate understanding of God and of His will for us. This great privilege brings with it the duty of making use of it, of living in its light.

However, even for those who do not have access to the Bible, God is not silent. Several passages in scripture indicate that God has other means of revealing Himself to men and women. Some biblical texts tell us God reveals something of Himself through what He has created[122]. This is known as God's 'general revelation' in contrast to the 'special revelation' of the Bible.

So creation itself presents mankind with an 'eternal gospel'. This 'gospel' calls man to contemplate the evidence for a creator, and in response to;

Fear God and give him glory ...
Worship Him who made the heavens, the earth, the sea and the springs of water.[123]

'General revelation' has been defined as,

God's self-manifestation through nature, history, and the inner being of the human person. It is general in two senses: its universal availability (it is accessible to all persons at all times) and the content of the message (it is less particularized and detailed than special revelation).[124]

General revelation can point people towards the idea of God. Obviously, special revelation - the explicit information contained in the Bible - goes way beyond this in terms of clarity and content. Therefore telling those who have never heard about the Bible or its message is an absolute priority. However, it is a vital principle of scripture that **all** men have access to **some** knowledge of God, and are therefore able to choose how to respond to that knowledge[125].

The Bible doesn't reveal to us in any clear manner how a response to general revelation might save people. Scripture makes clear that salvation is possible **only** through the person and work of Jesus Christ[126]. In other words, any possibility of salvation that exists, exists solely because of Jesus.

---

[122] Psalm 19:1-6, Acts 14:16f, Romans 1:20
[123] Revelation 14:7 NIV
[124] Erickson M.J. *Christian Theology*, Michigan: Baker Books, 1994 (1983) p154-174. An interesting book looking particularly at what the human body can reveal to us about God is, Yancey P. & Brand P. *Fearfully and Wonderfully Made*, Michigan: Zondervan, 1987 (1984)
[125] See Romans 2:12-16
[126] Acts 4:12

In the Old Testament the Jews looked forward for their salvation, towards the coming Messiah[127]. As Christians, we look back at the Christ event for our salvation. How those who can only access general revelation (and can neither look forward to, or back to, Jesus) might be saved is a mystery. God does, however, make clear to us in the Bible that His saving work will never be completely understandable to human minds[128]. We need to live in the hopeful anticipation of the mystery of grace.

Empirical studies do however seem to reveal some outlines of this divine activity. Contemporary missiologists report finding people groups who have had no contact with the outside world, yet who have some ideas that are completely coherent with the Christian gospel. These ideas or prophecies often enable them to recognise the Christian God when they are told about Him[129]. So we do have clear grounds for the hope that God is at work in ways we do not fully comprehend, drawing people into relationship with Himself.[130]

Questions for Reflection and Discussion

1   What are the limitations of a general revelation gospel – such as that detailed in Rev. 14:6-7. What limitations do you see of having a faith that is based only on this gospel?

2   The fact that God limited his self-revelation to the nation of Israel has been called "the scandal of particularity"[131]. How do you respond to this statement? In what other ways does the Christian faith sometimes scandalise those outside of it?

---

[127] John 8:56; Hebrews 11:13, 26

[128] Isaiah 55:6-9

[129] See Richardson D. *Eternity in Their Hearts*, California: Regal Books 1984 (1981) and the story of Ahatsistcari, the famous Huron warrior chief and his conversion in 1642 Thwaites R.G. (ed.) *The Jesuit Relations and Allied Documents - Travels and Explorations Of The Jesuit Missionaries in New France 1610-1791*, Vol. XXIII 1642-1643, CLEVELAND: The Burrows Brothers Company, 1818, p25ff accessible online at http://archive.org/download/jesuits23jesuuoft/jesuits23jesuuoft.pdf.

[130] For a detailed treatment of the subject of the accessibility of salvation I recommend Tiessen T. *Who Then can be Saved?* Illinois: IVP, 2004

[131] Morris L. *I Believe in Revelation*, London: Hodder and Stoughton, 1976, p47

12 - What Should We Do? (Jonah 1:11)

The sea was getting rougher and rougher. So they asked him,
'What should we do to you to make the sea calm down for us?'

Jonah 1:11, NIV

Following the divine revelation about the supernatural nature of the storm and the reason behind it, we might expect that the storm would now be stilled. From a logical perspective the storm seems to have served its purpose. Through this storm God has not only given Jonah a clear indication that He means business, but God has also used the same event to reveal some truths about Himself to the Gentile sailors. We might expect that God would now still the storm to give Jonah and the sailors some time to respond to His action; Jonah by re-orienting himself towards Nineveh at the earliest opportunity, the sailors by re-orienting their worship towards the true God and becoming proselytes of the Jewish faith. However, counterintuitively, the storm continues. In fact it not only continues but becomes even more violent.

But something significant **has** changed. I believe that from this point on, the **purpose** of the storm is different. Up until now the storm has been a **chastisement**, a divine indication to Jonah of God's displeasure about his disobedience. From this point on the storm is not so much a punishment as a **preparation**.

This change is brought about by the responses made to the storm by the sailors and by Jonah. The sailors responded to the storm in an exemplary manner. Jonah too responds, after a little prompting by the Captain, with a prophetic proclamation about the true nature of God. Notice exactly how Jonah identifies himself.

I am a Hebrew and I worship the Lord, the God of heaven,
who made the land and the sea.[132]

At this moment Jonah is having a hard time in his relationship with God. He has been probably been struggling for a long period of time with God's command to go to Nineveh. This new revelation - that God cares for the Gentiles, even the monstrous Assyrians - is something that Jonah is having difficulty accepting. Jonah's faith is being shaken and his understanding of the nature of God is being stretched, but in this statement we see that his essential faith is still intact. He is a Hebrew and he worships Yahweh. Jonah might not **like** God very much at this moment in time, but he still **believes** in Him.

---

[132] Jonah 1:9 NIV

So Jonah and the sailors have both responded positively to the storm. They are reorienting their lives in the face of a new revelation about God. The storm's chastising purpose in the life of Jonah is accomplished; it can now begin its preparative function. It is important to always remember that when God chastens us it is always with our future in mind. In fact as we shall see, what Jonah is about to experience will be the foundation of the success of his future ministry.

Remember the question the sailors asked Jonah, "*What have you done?*" It seems that this was a question that Jonah was too ashamed to answer, for he says nothing in response to it. Now the sailors ask him another, "*What should we do to you to make the sea calm down for us?*"

In responding to this question, Jonah is put into a position where he begins to act as a prophet – for it is the function of prophets to communicate God's will to their fellow men. God has already manoeuvred Jonah into a situation where he was obliged to declare to the sailors the truth about the nature of God, to declare that He is;

Yahweh, the God of heaven who made the sea and the land [133]

Now God manipulates the situation in order to give Jonah an opportunity to function as a prophet; to proclaim the specifics of God's will in a particular situation. God seems to be making the point that His call on Jonah's life remains firm; to be a prophet to the Gentiles. Jonah is given another chance to embrace, rather than to reject, this calling.

Questions for Reflection and Discussion

1   When God sends a 'storm' into our personal lives or into the life of our church fellowship, what can we do to try to determine the nature and cause of the storm?

2   How can we ensure that we respond appropriately to the storms of life?

---

[133] Jonah 1:9 NIV

13 - One Way to Survive (Jonah 1:11-13)

The sea was getting rougher and rougher. So they asked him,
'What should we do to you to make the sea calm down for us?'
'Pick me up and throw me into the sea,' he replied, 'and it will become calm. I know
that it is my fault that this great storm has come upon you.'
Instead, the men did their best to row back to land.
But they could not, for the sea grew even wilder than before.
Jonah 1:11-13, NIV

It is interesting to notice that the situation the sailors were experiencing finds a parallel in the great city of Nineveh. The unfortunate sailors are on the edge of disaster, in a boat about to be torn apart by a violent storm. Even if they survive they will be financially ruined, since they have had to jettison their precious cargo. All of this has happened to them because a Jew, the prophet Jonah, has been disobedient to God.

In a similar fashion the Ninevites were also in a precarious situation. The message Jonah has for them is that they have just 40 days before they will be destroyed. So they too are hanging on the edge of disaster. Why are they in this position? At least in part, it is because the Jewish nation has failed to take to them the message of God.

We see in the opening chapters of the Bible, in Genesis, that the Jews were meant to be a blessing for the nations – specifically in sharing what God had revealed to them, His chosen people, about His nature and His will[134]. This was their primary calling right from the very beginning, when God first chose Abram.

The Lord had said to Abram,
'Go from your country, your people and your father's household to the land I will
show you.
'I will make you into a great nation,
and I will bless you;
I will make your name great,
and you will be a blessing.
I will bless those who bless you,
and whoever curses you I will curse;
and all peoples on earth
will be blessed through you.'.[135]

The prophecies of Isaiah had further developed this calling,

---

[134] See Genesis 12:3, 18:18, 22:18, 26:4, 28:14
[135] Genesis 12:1-3, NIV

I, the Lord, have called you in righteousness;
I will take hold of your hand.
I will keep you and will make you
to be a covenant for the people
and a light for the Gentiles,
to open eyes that are blind,
to free captives from prison
and to release from the dungeon those who sit in darkness. [136]

It is too small a thing for you to be my servant
to restore the tribes of Jacob
and bring back those of Israel I have kept.
I will also make you a light for the Gentiles,
that my salvation may reach to the ends of the earth. [137]

God wanted His people to tell others about Him! Gentiles are therefore not excluded from the plan of God for the world, but right at its centre. He wanted all peoples to be blessed by knowing Him as He really is, to experience His love, to live in Him, with Him and for Him.

However, the Jews had largely ignored the 'blessing for others' aspect of their chosen-ness. They had preferred to focus on their calling to be different from the Gentile nations, rather than to undertake the difficult task of going to these pagan nations with the revelation of the true God.

In many ways Jonah's story is a retelling of the story of the Jews and the Gentiles. It throws into clear relief the attitude Israel had towards the Gentiles, in stark contrast to God's intention.

So if the Ninevites are still living in ways which are contrary to the will of God, it is partly the Jews that are at fault. We could even say that Jewish national disobedience has placed in jeopardy a whole city (and by implication the whole Gentile world), just as Jonah's personal disobedience has placed in jeopardy a whole ship.

God places Jonah in circumstances which make real in his life the situation of his whole nation; the Gentiles are doomed and it is God's people who are partly at fault.

This way of reading the story of Jonah is reinforced by the Jewish tradition, related earlier, that there were representatives of the seventy nations of the

---

[136] Isaiah 42:6-7, NIV
[137] Isaiah 49:6-7, NIV

earth present on board the ship (the whole of humanity as then understood by the Jews). The ship therefore represents the whole world.

The 'world' is at sea, caught in a storm which it doesn't understand. The 'world' has no hope - save that someone comes to them to reveal the spiritual truth of their situation; to bring them safely through the storm. But God's 'agents of revelation' are asleep. They have failed in their task and everybody is paying the price.

As Christians today, we need to ask the hard question, does this image fit our situation? Before judging Jonah and the Jews, can we be sure that we are doing any better? We too have received a divine commission to take the message of Jesus to the nations,

> Then Jesus came to them and said, 'All authority in heaven and on earth has been given to me. Therefore go and make disciples of all nations, baptising them in the name of the Father and of the Son and of the Holy Spirit, and teaching them to obey everything I have commanded you.
> And surely I am with you always, to the very end of the age.[138]

This mission mandate is the continuation of God's original promise to Abram, that all the nations of the world would be blessed through him. How are we doing in this task? Concretely what are we doing individually and communally to fulfil this mission?

How many people today are in the same situation as the Ninevites and the pagan sailors? Caught in a storm they don't understand, without hope because the people of God have refused to share with them the good news of Jesus Christ?

It is often said of the Church that it is the only organisation that exists for the benefit of non-members. This statement certainly reflects a true understanding of the heart of the Church's mission. God calls together His people into the Church, not simply that they might enjoy fellowshipping together and worshipping Him; but that they might undertake His mission to the world.

Mission is certainly not limited to the verbal proclamation of the message of Jesus – even if that is an important part of it. A wide reading of Scripture shows us that mission is often simply a matter of living differently – living in a way that pleases God, creating a community which makes visible the love of God. It is by our lives, our communities which make visible this love through holiness, honesty, concern for justice, solidarity with the poor and with those who suffer;

---

[138] Matthew 28:18-20, NIV

it is by these means that God will accomplish His mission of drawing people to Himself.

This is what the Lord Almighty said:
"Administer true justice; show mercy and compassion to one another.
Do not oppress the widow or the fatherless, the foreigner or the poor.
Do not plot evil against each other" [139]

These are the things you are to do:
Speak the truth to each other, and render true and sound judgment in your courts;
do not plot evil against each other, and do not love to swear falsely.
I hate all this,' declares the Lord. [140]

If the people of God live in this fashion this will be the result;

And many peoples and powerful nations will come to Jerusalem to seek
the Lord Almighty and to entreat him.'
This is what the Lord Almighty says: 'In those days ten people from all languages
and nations will take firm hold of one Jew by the hem of his robe and say,
"Let us go with you, because we have heard that God is with you." [141]

If we live as we should, then this creates a plausibility structure for our message; the message of Jesus then becomes credible, convincing. Conversely, a failure to live as we should serves to undermine and invalidate our message; however well that message is presented.

Questions for Reflection and Discussion

1   Are the peoples of the world blessed by you? In what concrete ways does your church fellowship bless the peoples of the world, both locally and internationally?

2   Is your life, the life of your church community, something which makes the Christian message plausible?

---

[139] Zechariah 7:9-10, NIV
[140] Zechariah 8:16-17, NIV
[141] Zechariah 8:20-23, NIV

14 – The Communal Effects of Sin (Jonah 1:11-13)

The sea was getting rougher and rougher. So they asked him,
'What should we do to you to make the sea calm down for us?'
'Pick me up and throw me into the sea,' he replied,
'and it will become calm. I know that it is my fault that this great storm has come
upon you.'

Jonah 1:11-13, NIV

Jonah tells the sailors that the only way to calm the storm is to throw him overboard. He tells them to sacrifice him in order to turn away the anger of God. The technical term for such an action is 'propitiation'. This is one of the ways that the New Testament authors think about Jesus' death on the cross[142].

Here Jonah offers himself to save the lives of the sailors. We see here clearly a prefiguration of Christ, who offered Himself on the cross for our sin. Certainly the metaphor breaks down if stretched too far. It was Jonah's own sin that was the cause of the sailor's predicament. Whereas Jesus was guiltless but took on Himself the sins of the world,

God made him who had no sin to be sin for us,
so that in him we might become the righteousness of God.[143]

Jonah's statement here to the sailors reveals several things about him. Firstly, he has concern for these sailors and is prepared to sacrifice himself to save their lives. Perhaps Jonah is motivated by a sense of justice - it is simply not fair that these poor Gentiles have to suffer because of his sin. Secondly, we get the distinct impression that Jonah doesn't care much about his own life! There is little reason for us to doubt that Jonah fully expected to drown. He was ready, willing and expecting to die.

It is not clear from his statement if Jonah really expresses penitence or not. It's true that he admits that he is guilty before God. He acknowledges that it is his sin which has brought great danger upon these sailors. However, it is not clear that he repents in any way. It seems more likely that Jonah's attitude is one of obstinate stoicism. He knows that he is guilty of disobedience, but he is still not in agreement with God and His plan for Jonah's life. Jonah is prepared to accept whatever punishment God will dish out. Yet, and this is greatly to his credit, he wants to make sure that God's punishment falls solely upon him and not upon the innocent.

---

[142] Romans 3:25; 5:1, 10f; 2 Corinthians 5:18f, Colossians 1:20f; 1 John 2:2; 4:10; Hebrews 9:5
[143] 2 Corinthians 5:21, NIV

David expresses the same sentiment when God brings a plague upon the people of Israel because of David's lack of faith,

I am the one who has sinned and done wrong.
These are but sheep. What have they done?
O LORD my God, let your hand fall upon me and my family,
but do not let this plague remain on your people.[144]

Sadly, sin always has communal dimensions. Sin is never personal. Our choices and our actions, both positive and negative, will always have consequences for those who live with us.

- In David's case, 70,000 men died from the plague because of his sin.
- King Abimelech's royal household was struck with barrenness because Abraham sinned in passing off his wife Sarah as his sister[145].
- The whole population of the exodus (2,000,000 people) was punished because 3,000 of them had made and worshipped a golden calf idol[146].
- Achan, disobeyed God's clear instructions and this led to the army of Israel suffering a humiliating defeat[147].
- A New Testament Christian community experienced sickness because of their failure to confess their sins to each other[148].
- A New Testament Christian community experienced sickness because of their inappropriate manner of celebrating the Lord's Supper[149].

As 21st century Westerners, we often find this communal dimension of sin hard to comprehend. The society we live in has not only weakened the nature of family, and of community, but has also changed its structure. A few centuries ago, people lived in the same family group for the whole of their lives. Their identity was tied to that group and most of the key decisions in their lives were either taken for them by the group, or at least in consultation with the group.

The industrial revolution caused people to become more mobile. It became normal for people leave their traditional communities and go to live and work in cities. Gradually the family came to mean not the **extended** family of grand-parents, cousins, uncles and aunts etc., but the **nuclear** family - father, mother and children.

---

[144] 1 Chronicles 21:17 NIV
[145] Genesis 20:17f
[146] Exodus 32
[147] Joshua 7
[148] James 5:16
[149] 1 Corinthians 11:29-30

In recent decades the explosion of cohabitation and the massive increase in divorce, have weakened still further the sense of belonging and of family.

This sociological change has dramatically changed the way in which we think about ourselves. Nowadays, we tend to think of ourselves primarily as individuals. This change is also reflected in our spirituality. We talk about a **personal** saviour, a **personal** conversion, a **personal** spiritual life. However, until fairly recent times, religious faith was not so much thought of as a personal matter but as a communal – even national decision. It was the King who would often decide on the religion of his people.

Certainly there is a very real personal element to Christian faith. We all have to make our individual response to God, and to live out a personal love relationship with Him. Otherwise our religious observance is merely an empty, outward show of religious conformity. However, we mustn't lose sight of the fact that individual religious convictions are always lived out **in community**.

What God desires are not isolated individuals who live in relationship with Him, but redeemed communities who make present His love and His truth in the world.
'A new command I give you: love one another.
As I have loved you, so you must love one another.
By this everyone will know that you are my disciples, if you love one another.[150]

Our relationship with God is therefore both **personal** and lived out in the context of a **community** of faith. Above, we considered some New Testament examples which clearly show the communal consequences of individual sin[151]. These New Testament passages, along with the examples from the Old Testament given above, make clear to us that God holds the group accountable for what goes on inside it. Where the members of a group tolerate sinful behaviour, that group **as a whole** will be judged by God.

So the same process of chastening that we have seen active in the life of Jonah – making him aware of his sin and bringing him to repentance – will also apply to groups. The same love that drives God to intervene in our lives individually, to prevent our bad choices and weaknesses, will also cause Him to reach out to erring communities. God loves us too much to allow us to put in peril our spiritual life and our participation with Him in His project for saving the world.

This communal way of dealing with people may seem strange to us, given our individualistic cultural context. However, we shouldn't let our culture determine

---

[150] John 13:34-35, NIV
[151] James 5:16 and 1 Corinthians 11:29-30

our theology, rather we must let the Bible determine our theology and allow that to speak prophetically into our culture. Western individualism, where every man lives for himself and has no responsibilities towards his neighbours, is in **no way compatible** with an authentic Christian faith. We need to preach this prophetic message in our churches and find ways of modelling radical, loving community to a splintered world.

Questions for Reflection and Discussion

1   How do you respond to this reality of the communal consequences of personal sin? How do you live out this reality of communal responsibility?
2   It says in Romans,

> *... in Christ we who are many form one body,*
> *and each member belongs to all the others.* [152]

What are the implications in your life of the fact that you **belong** to your fellow believers, and that they **belong** to you? How can we live this unity?
3   We have looked at how sin affects not only individuals but also their community. In what ways does our obedience to God affect our community?

---

[152] Romans 12 :5, NIV

15 - The Pagan Sermon (Jonah 1:11-14)

The sea was getting rougher and rougher. So they asked him,
'What should we do to you to make the sea calm down for us?'
'Pick me up and throw me into the sea,' he replied, 'and it will become calm.
I know that it is my fault that this great storm has come upon you.'
Instead, the men did their best to row back to land. But they could not, for the sea
grew even wilder than before. Then they cried out to the Lord,
'Please, Lord, do not let us die for taking this man's life. Do not hold us
accountable for killing an innocent man, for you, Lord, have done as you pleased.'

Jonah 1:11-14, NIV

We might think that these desperate, pagan sailors, whose boat is about to sink, would immediately respond to Jonah's offer of self-sacrifice and quickly throw him over the side. But the sailors, to their great credit, do not immediately follow Jonah's directions. Instead they try to do everything within their power to escape from the storm by their own means. They row with all their might to try to get the ship to land - but the storm just gets stronger. In fact God increases the violence of the storm for a third time - it must have been of an incredible ferocity by this point.

Saint Francis of Assisi wrote in his instructions to his disciples,

let all the brothers preach by their works [153]

Which made the point that it is our lives, in particular our choices and actions, that are often the most convincing proclamation of the gospel. By their actions here, the pagan sailors certainly preach a powerful sermon. In fact, they do exactly what Jonah (and the Church) should be doing. They are demonstrating kingdom values; showing a real, costly and practical concern for those in difficulty.

Jonah was doomed to die because of his wickedness, yet they do all they can to save him. Nineveh was also doomed to destruction because of her wickedness. But do we see Jonah answering the call to help her by bringing God's message? Not at all! The sailors are thus a powerful rebuke to Jonah (and to the Jewish nation). The 'so-called' pagans are shown demonstrating the kind of attitude towards others that the people of God should have.

---

[153] Assisi F. *Regula non bullata or Earlier Rule (1221,)* Chapter XVII, accessed online at http://www.francis-bible.org/writings/witings_francis_earlier_rule_1.html#regula_non_bullata on 15/01/13

Two particular aspects of the sailors' behaviour speak prophetically to the people of God.

Firstly, these Gentile sailors value Jonah's life as a sacred thing. Jonah, by contrast, cared nothing about the destruction of a whole city.

We have to recognise that the church has no monopoly on righteous behaviour. There are many people of other religions, or of none, who live exemplary lives characterised by justice, sharing and love. This should be a challenge to us as Christians to live lives that truly express a sacrificial love for our fellow man. As we have already noted, this is at the same time a powerful means of communicating the gospel message and also something which makes our preaching credible.

> Live such good lives among the pagans that, though they accuse you of doing wrong, they may see your good deeds and glorify God on the day he visits us. [154]

Secondly, these sailors also teach us about gentleness towards those who fall into sin. These sailors knew that Jonah was a delinquent prophet; they knew that he was on the run from God. However, they did not despise him for his sin and weakness, even though it had brought them into mortal peril. Rather, they were considerate and respectful towards him. Instead of reproaching him for his failures they did all they could to help him.

Often the Church has a hard time behaving like these noble pagans. Someone once said that the Church is the only army that shoots its own wounded. Those who fall into sin often experience judgement, condemnation and rejection from their brothers and sisters in the Church. When what they should find is mercy, forgiveness and grace. This is a horrible state of affairs, 'hellish' in the true sense of the word.

Of course we have to treat sin seriously. The Church must do all it can to help its members lead godly lives and this must sometimes include confrontation and even discipline. However, it is also clear from scripture that people have to be treated gently and lovingly too.

> Brothers and sisters, if someone is caught in a sin,
> you who live by the Spirit should restore that person gently.
> But watch yourselves, or you also may be tempted.
> Carry each other's burdens, and in this way you will fulfil the law of Christ. [155]

---

[154] 1 Peter 2:12, NIV
[155] Galatians 6:1-2, NIV

*Opponents must be gently instructed, in the hope that God will grant them
repentance leading them to a knowledge of the truth,
and that they will come to their senses and escape from the trap of the devil,
who has taken them captive to do his will.*[156]

We can also see a general life principle in this story. The more we are willing to be humble, to judge and condemn ourselves rather than others, the more likely we are to experience mercy from both God and man. Jonah had openly confessed his failure and sin to the pagan sailors. He had confirmed his responsibility for the dreadful situation they were in. He had even offered his life in an attempt to save theirs. In so doing, Jonah wins the respect and mercy of the sailors. They don't rail at him and abuse him. They don't throw him immediately into the raging sea. Instead, they do all they can to avoid taking his life.

There is something appealing, refreshing and winsome about someone who owns up to their faults; someone who shows humility and real repentance. A friend of mine once told me about a day when he made a serious mistake at work. He knew that he was going to be in real trouble as the works' foreman was a fiery and short-tempered man. He was dreading the inevitable show-down and the torrent of abuse that would be publicly showered on him. Suddenly he saw the foreman storming across the factory floor towards him. He knew that the game was up, that his big mistake had been discovered.

My friend decided to pre-empt the situation. Before the foreman could even open his mouth, my friend said, "*Look, I've made a terrible mistake. I am really sorry. It is entirely my fault. I just want to apologise.*"

The foreman was dumbfounded. He didn't know what to say. In all his factory-floor experience this had never happened to him before. He had expected denial, defiance, explanations, excuses, and blame-shifting. My friend's humility and honesty completely baffled him. He didn't know how to react. Eventually he just mumbled something and walked off. In fact, not only did my friend avoid a public 'tearing a strip off', but from this point on that foreman treated him with new-found respect and their relationship was transformed.

---

[156] 2 Timothy 2:25, NIV

Questions for Reflection and Discussion

1   How does your standard of behaviour and the standard of behaviour of your local church measure up to the standards of behaviour of those outside the church?

2   How do you respond to this life lesson about the advantages of owning up to mistakes, rather than hiding, denying, and justifying them? In what ways can we as individuals 'own up' to our failure and sin? Corporately how do local church fellowships admit their mistakes and short-comings?

16 - A Desperate Act (Jonah 1:14-15)

Then they cried out to the Lord, 'Please, Lord, do not let us die for taking this man's life. Do not hold us accountable for killing an innocent man, for you, Lord, have done as you pleased.' Then they took Jonah and threw him overboard, and the raging sea grew calm.

Jonah 1:14-15, NIV

Finally, in the face of their helplessness and realising Jonah's sacrifice is their only hope for survival, the sailors are obliged to follow his instructions. But they don't do this lightly. Before they set themselves to carry out the monstrous act of taking a man's life, they pray to God.

And not just any God! Whereas in verse 5 each man had cried out to his own god (the Hebrew word '*elohim*' is used indicating the pagan gods, the local divinities), now they cry out to the LORD or 'Yahweh', the name of God revealed to Moses[157]. Now they are convinced that the only God controlling their situation is *Yahweh*. Before, their strategy had been to pray to any god they could think of – just in case. But now only *Yahweh* is invoked.

The sailors want to explain to *Yahweh* what they are about to do to His prophet. They want to explain that this is not their choice. They believe that it is *Yahweh* Himself who has guided them to this act, and they want to ask for *Yahweh's* forgiveness in advance.

The sailors seem to be as scared of taking Jonah's life as they are of the storm. Taking anyone's life is always a fearful thing, never mind the life of a prophet – someone especially precious to God.[158]

He allowed no one to oppress them; for their sake he rebuked kings:
'Do not touch my anointed ones ; do my prophets no harm.'[159]

Precious in the sight of the Lord is the death of his faithful servants.[160]

A Jewish legend holds that the sailors were so hesitant to take the life of Jonah that they did not immediately consign him to the waves. Rather they lowered him towards the water by ropes under his arms.

---

[157] Exodus 3:13-14
[158] See Revelation 6:9, 12:11, 17:6, 18:24, 19:2, 20:4
[159] 1 Chronicles 16:21-22, NIV
[160] Psalm 116:15, NIV

In the first instance they lowered him up to his knees and the storm abated. However, as soon as they drew him back into the ship, the storm returned. They tried this exercise twice more.

The second time they lowered him in as far as his navel, and the last time they lowered him into the sea as far as his neck. However, each time that they lifted him back into the ship the storm returned. Realising that nothing less than Jonah's total abandonment was required; they finally and very reluctantly, consigned him wholly to the waves[161].

Whilst these Gentile sailors quail before the act of taking the life of one of God's prophets, the people of God themselves often had an altogether different attitude.[162]

Jerusalem, Jerusalem, you who kill the prophets and stone those sent to you[163]

These pagans excel the Jews in another way. Looking again at our text for today, we notice that it is in fact the sailors (just like the captain previously) who acknowledge the sovereignty of God - 'You have done as you pleased'. They declare that God is sovereign over His creation and free to do as He likes. This forms a delicious irony as these Gentiles are declaring a theological truth that Jonah has yet to accept – that God is sovereign!

In fact, Jonah's biggest problem is with this very issue. He is deeply disturbed by the idea that God can do what He wants with regard to the Ninevites. Jonah is scandalised that God wishes to extend His grace to them. As far as Jonah is concerned **God has no right to act in this way**.

The Gentiles, however, declare the truth, however uncomfortable it may be – that God has the **right** to do exactly as He chooses. God is sovereign over His creation.

We know that God is holy and just. So we can exclude the possibility that He will act in any way that is unjust or unfair. If we struggle to understand His actions and His choices, that is **our** problem. Faced with the absolute sovereign rights of God over His creation, our only appropriate response is humble acceptance; cherishing the hope that His mercy might reach out to its maximum extent in our world.

---

[161] Ginzberg L. *ibid.*, p248
[162] Also see 1 Kings 19:1f for a demonstration of the treatment of prophets in an incident that occurred only about 50 years before the story of Jonah.
[163] Matthew 23:37, NIV

85

Thus whilst Jonah is trying to thwart the will of God for the world, and in particular the people of Nineveh, the sailors and the captain accept God's right to act in whatever way He chooses and throw themselves upon His mercy.

It is both strange and wonderful to see that although Jonah had fled Israel – the place where God's presence was most recognized and His voice most heard - God simply responds by using pagans to proclaim the truth about Himself to Jonah!

Questions for Reflection and Discussion

1   The sailors prayed to *Yahweh* because they were convinced that only *Yahweh* was able to help them in their situation. When we face a difficult situation it is our understanding of God – His nature, His relationship with His creation – that determines if we will pray and how we pray. Reflect on a difficult situation that you have previously faced in your life. Did you pray about it? If so, how did you pray about it, what did you pray for? What does this tell you about your understanding of the nature and activity of God?

2   Have you accepted God's sovereign right to act in any way He wants in your life? Are there areas of your life over which you retain control? Are there places that you still declare to be 'off limits' to God?

17 - The Sailors' Conversion (Jonah 1:15-16)

Then they took Jonah and threw him overboard, and the raging sea grew calm. At this the men greatly feared the Lord, and they offered a sacrifice to the Lord and made vows to him.

Jonah 1:15-16, NIV

And so the sailors throw Jonah overboard. Throughout the whole of chapter one, the verb 'to throw' (*hiphil*) is used repeatedly. God has 'thrown' a storm (1:4), the sailors have 'thrown' the cargo overboard (1:5) and now they 'throw' Jonah. The rebellious prophet is thrown away like useless cargo.

This is an interesting reversal of the Noah story. In the flood, God's chosen people ride safely above the waves whilst the pagan nations drown in the depths below. Here, the pagan nations are praising and worshipping God whilst the prophet of Israel sinks to the bottom of the ocean! It is no longer the chosen few who are saved; rather the chosen one gives his life to save the many.[164] Again, we cannot but help see a foreshadowing of Jesus in this incident.

As soon as Jonah hits the water, calm descends. This sudden calm was as terrifying to the sailors as the storm had been. They realise that they are in the presence of *Yahweh* Himself, the living God, He who made the land and sea and who controls everything.

These poor sailors seem to have spent their whole time being terrified. Firstly, it was the storm (v5). Then they are terrified by the realisation that Jonah is running away, not from a local divinity, but from the God of heaven who created the sea and land (v10). Then they have to face up to the prospect of killing an innocent man, one who is a servant of *Yahweh* (v14). Finally they are terrified by the revelation of the power of God in calming the storm (v16).

Interestingly we see the same reaction of fear amongst the disciples after Jesus stills a storm,

He got up, rebuked the wind and said to the waves, "Quiet! Be still!"
Then the wind died down and it was completely calm.
He said to his disciples, "Why are you so afraid? Do you still have no faith?"
They were terrified and asked each other,
"Who is this? Even the wind and the waves obey him!"[165]

---

[164] Cary P. *ibid.*, p72
[165] Mark 4:39-41, NIV

It seems that fear is a natural human response to the manifestation of the power and presence of God in our midst.

However, the sailors don't remain simply in an attitude of fear, rather they respond to *Yahweh* with acts of worship. Their worship was no doubt partly rooted in simple gratitude for their survival through the storm, but it also seems clear that it goes beyond that.

These are no longer simply Gentiles who believe in a multitude of gods all acting within specific geographical limits. Through this experience they have come to encounter *Yahweh*, the God of heaven, the one who made, and who has demonstrated that He still controls, the land and sea.

Their worship does not simply look backwards, thanking God for what He has done in saving their lives, but it looks also to the future. They make vows about their future behaviour - a promising sign about the genuineness of their conversion. They seem to want to enter into a relationship with *Yahweh*.

A vow is an engagement to do something in the future and is evidence of our intent We are told that the sailors came to 'fear the Lord'. Timmer notes that,

> *This can hardly mean something less than whole-hearted conversion to Yahweh: the phrase "to fear/revere God" in the Hebrew Bible consistently describes those who have, and maintain, a healthy relationship to Yahweh.* [166]

Often in a crisis people will make vows to God. These vows take the form, 'God if you do this, then I will do that'. There is nothing wrong with such prayers; they can be a sincere expression of our intense desire that God might act[167]. However, making a vow **after** divine help has been received is an altogether a nobler and more genuine expression of our gratitude towards God.

It is important to note that these sacrifices the sailors made would probably not have taken place on board ship,

> *In all the religions of the ancient Near East ...*
> *sacrifices took place at shrines of temples*[168].

So the sailors must have gone to a Yahwistic shrine[169], or more likely to the Temple at Jerusalem in order to fulfil their vows of sacrifice.

---

[166] Timmer D. *ibid.*, p15
[167] See Acts 18:18
[168] Stuart D. *ibid.*, p464
[169] See 2 Kings 14:4, 15:4 16:2-4 ; Hosea 4:13

The Midrash has them going to Jerusalem and converting to Judaism,
which is only spelling out an implication strongly suggested in the story itself.
It also indicates that the place to fulfil vows was the Temple in Jerusalem[170]

Rabbi Eliezer quotes this tradition,

They returned to Joppa and went up to Jerusalem
and circumcised the flesh of their foreskins, as it is said,
"And the men feared the Lord exceedingly;
and they offered a sacrifice unto the Lord ."
Did they offer sacrifice ?
But this (sacrifice) refers to the blood of the covenant of circumcision,
which is like the blood of a sacrifice. And they made vows every one to bring his
children and all belonging to him to the God of Jonah ;
and they made vows and performed them, and concerning them it says,
"Upon the proselytes, the proselytes of righteousness".[171]

In a round-about way, this is a vindication of Jonah's ministry. He had communicated God's truth regarding the situation to the sailors and he prophesied that the storm would cease if they threw him over the side. The sailors have seen that prophecy fulfilled. This experience has confirmed to them Jonah's prophetic credentials and given weight to his proclamation about *Yahweh*. This experience has brought them to a point of conversion. So, even in his disobedience, Jonah is successful in the mission to which God has called him; to be a prophet to the Gentiles!

These sailors experience the presence of God powerfully in the silence after the storm. This experience of 'God in the silence' is not unique to these sailors. If we remember the story of Elijah,

The Lord said, 'Go out and stand on the mountain in the presence of the Lord,
for the Lord is about to pass by.'
Then a great and powerful wind tore the mountains apart and shattered the rocks
before the Lord, but the Lord was not in the wind. After the wind there was an
earthquake, but the Lord was not in the earthquake. After the earthquake came a
fire, but the Lord was not in the fire. And after the fire came a gentle
whisper. When Elijah heard it, he pulled his cloak over his face and went out and
stood at the mouth of the cave.
Then a voice said to him, 'What are you doing here, Elijah?'[172]

---

[170] Magonet J. *The Book of Jonah and the Day of Atonement*, Service International de Documentation Judeo-Chrétienne (SIDIC), XVIII 1985/1, pp4-8
[171] Ben Hyrcanus E. *ibid.*, p72f
[172] 1 Kings 19:11-13, NIV

As for the sailors, it is in the silence that follows the violence, that the presence of God is revealed. Here we have more than a hint that the essential nature of God is gentle and loving. Whilst He can and does use acts of power and violence in order to serve His purposes, they do not represent His essential nature. Rather God's primary characteristic is love.

> *Whoever does not love does not know God, because God is love...*
> *And so we know and rely on the love God has for us.*
> *God is love. Whoever lives in love lives in God, and God in them.* [173]

Also note the immediacy of the cessation of the storm. As soon as God's purposes are served, He dispenses with the storm;

> *For I take no pleasure in the death of anyone, declares the Sovereign LORD.*
> *Repent and live!* [174]

> *As surely as I live, declares the Sovereign LORD, I take no pleasure in the death of*
> *the wicked, but rather that they turn from their ways and live.*
> *Turn! Turn from your evil ways! Why will you die, O house of Israel!* [175]

Persistence in disobedience is therefore foolish. All we do is merely extend the duration of God's chastening activity. The wisest thing we can do is immediately repent and obey. God will not prolong our suffering a single second beyond its usefulness.

The sailors' example also reminds us that true worship looks in two directions. We look back to our knowledge of God, revealed through history and through our own previous experience, but we also look forward. We resolve to live differently.

The Catholic mass concludes with the priest exhorting the congregation to *'Go in the peace of Christ'*, to which the congregation responds, *'We give thanks to God'*. This is an important reminder that our worship does not conclude at the end of the service, but that it should be merely the **foundation** and the **fuel** for a life of worship.

> *Therefore, I urge you, brothers, in view of God's mercy, to offer your bodies as living*
> *sacrifices, holy and pleasing to God—this is your spiritual act of worship.* [176]

---

[173] 1 John 4:8, 16, NIV
[174] Ezekiel 18 :32, NIV
[175] Ezekiel 33 :11, NIV
[176] Romans 12 :1, NIV

Real worship is whole life worship.

Questions for Reflection and Discussion

1   Is the essential nature of God as gentle and loving the picture of God presented in the local church to which you belong?

2   Does your worship of God **look both ways**? Is it based upon what you know and have experienced of God in the past and does this understanding and experience provide a foundation and an incentive for you to live differently from this point forward?

3   Concretely, how can we worship God with the totality of our life?

Ionah : the second part - Pride and Anger

Pride and anger weighing me down
Closed my eyes and outstretched my arms
Slowly sinking into the abyss
Down to the darkness where I would not be seen

Waiting, created especially for me
A fish, Leviathan of the Depths
Swallowed me down in one massive gulp
There I languished in its belly pulp.

I breathe, I ponder and meditate
Wondering and conscious, eating fish
Concentrating hard on my immediate fate
How long would I be served this humbling dish?

Crying out to my God for help
Repenting of my foolish pride
Ready to do what I was supposed
I saw the light and the way.

A. P. McIntyre   2012.

18 - Three Days in Hell (Jonah 1:17)

Now the Lord provided a huge fish to swallow Jonah,
and Jonah was in the belly of the fish three days and three nights.

Jonah 1:17, NIV

As Jonah falls into the water he fully expects to die by drowning - God however, has something else in mind. Poor Jonah is about to experience something even worse! Instead of being swallowed by the sea, he is swallowed by a sea monster.

There has been great debate about the plausibility of this event. People have studied the anatomy of all the known fish and sea mammals of a sufficient size. They have tried to work out which species might have been used and how it could have happened; there do seem to be certain species capable of such a feat.

But is this really the point? This story is presented to us as an event that is both miraculous and prophetic. By definition, a miraculous event is one which surpasses the normal human experience of what is possible. A prophetic event is something designed by God in order to reveal a spiritual truth to us.

From a logical perspective, if we believe in the all-powerful God that the Bible presents to us, such a God is capable of anything. So why is one miraculous event more problematic than another? If God wants a sea monster capable of swallowing a man and keeping him alive for 30 hours or so[177], He is certainly capable of creating one!

Note that the text specifically says that God 'provided' a great fish, a word otherwise translated as 'prepared'. Dom Jean de Monléon remarks that if such an animal already existed, God would not have needed to 'prepare' one[178].

In this sea monster, we see God using one of the largest and most impressive creatures on the planet to do His will. Later on we will see God use a worm – one of His smallest and least significant creatures. This teaches us several lessons. Firstly, that the whole of creation is under the sovereign command of God, from the smallest element to the grandest. Nothing escapes His divine control.

In Near Eastern mythology the primeval forces of chaos are often symbolised by three monstrous beasts. The sea-dwelling mythical monster was known as

---

[177] In Jewish culture a day begins in the evening at sunset, and any part of a day is counted as a day. Thus although Jesus was placed in the tomb late Friday afternoon and rose from the dead on Sunday morning,(36 hours or so later) he was counted as being dead for three days. This the minimum time that Jonah might have been inside the sea monster is the same.
[178] de Monléon, Dom J. *ibid.*, p76

'Leviathan'[179], the land beast was 'Behemoth' and the monster of the air was known as 'Ziz'[180].

The Genesis creation story tells us that these great forces were the first beings to be created by God[181]. The Genesis story is, however, radically different to the creation myths of the other Near Eastern cultures. In the other stories, these monsters are seen as elemental forces of chaos; forces which have to be **overcome** before order can be established. In stark contrast, the Genesis account shows God first establishing peace and order and then **creating** these great and marvellous forces[182].

Indeed, Psalm 104 presents the mighty and terrifying Leviathan as the plaything of God,

How many are your works, Lord!
In wisdom you made them all;
the earth is full of your creatures.
There is the sea, vast and spacious,
teeming with creatures beyond number—
living things both large and small.
There the ships go to and fro,
and Leviathan, which you formed to frolic there.[183]

So in the light of this background, the first hearers of the Jonah story might well understand the choice of a monstrous fish as demonstrating God's absolute power over this elemental force of chaos known as Leviathan[184]. The story would therefore show that even the mighty Leviathan was merely one of God's creatures and His to command.

Secondly, there is a particular Jewish resonance in this image of being 'swallowed up' – that of exile.

The people of Israel were 'swallowed up' by Egypt – only to emerge 400 years later, intact, their identity as the Chosen People of God reinforced and reaffirmed.

---

[179] See Job 3:1, 41:1-12, Psalms 74:13-14, 104:26, Isaiah 27:1
[180] Burrows D.P. *ibid.*, p42
[181] Genesis 1:21
[182] Cary P. *ibid.*, p75
[183] Psalm 104:24-26, NIV
[184] Ellison H.L. *ibid.* p375.

Similarly, the people of Israel and Judah will soon be 'swallowed up' by the Babylonian empire with the fall of Jerusalem in 586 B.C. They will be deported to Babylon, an exile which will last 70 years and from which only Judah will return.

> *Nebuchadnezzar king of Babylon has devoured us,*
> *he has thrown us into confusion,*
> *he has made us and empty jar.*
> *Like a serpent he has swallowed us*
> *and filled his stomach with our delicacies,*
> *and then has spewed us out.* [185]

However, this experience of being 'swallowed up', although terrifying in prospect, will actually prove to be a safe abode,

> *...a place where one can build a house, plant a garden,*
> *and raise children (Jeremiah 29:5-6)* [186]

It must be said, that ordinarily, nations do not survive exile; they do not return to their homelands. But, amazingly, Judah returns. Had they not done so, it would have been the end of the Jewish nation. There could therefore not have been a Jewish Messiah, Jesus Christ, and in consequence, no salvation for the world [187].

God's plans seemingly hang by a thread; His people swallowed up and all but snuffed out; all seems lost. Yet, as Jonah will discover in the belly of the monster, our perspective on the divine plan is seldom valid. In reality there is no danger, there is no threat, God cannot be stopped, He cannot be thwarted, things are going according to plan, and He will accomplish His purposes.

Thus, regardless of when one thinks the book of Jonah was actually written – before or after the Babylonian exile – Jonah's experience of being swallowed up by this terrifying sea monster has importance for the Jewish understanding of their national history. Either it is a prophetic promise that the coming exile will merely prove to be God's means of assuring Israel's survival and an experience from which the nation will subsequently emerge safe and sound; or it is a reflection upon God's miraculous saving and keeping of the nation throughout the Babylonian exile.

Thirdly, as we note God's use of the greatest and the smallest of His creatures in Jonah's story, we need to learn the lesson that each of them is necessary; each

---

[185] Jeremiah 51:34, NIV
[186] Cary P. *ibid.*, p76
[187] *ibid.*, p86

has a capacity that the other lacks. The monster could not do the worm's job and the worm could not do the monster's.

This reminds us of Saint Paul's teaching about the variety that exists in the Church; a variety designed by God to promote interdependence. No-one can 'go it alone' in terms of our relationship with God – we need each other.

> *There are different kinds of gifts, but the same Spirit distributes them. There are different kinds of service, but the same Lord. There are different kinds of working, but in all of them and in everyone it is the same God at work.*
> *Now to each one the manifestation of the Spirit is given for the common good.* [188]

Fourthly, there is a stark contrast in the immediate and total obedience of the sea monster compared with the prophet's disobedience.

> *Unlike the prophet, the fish responded promptly, as soon as it knew God's will.* [189]

Whilst we can only speculate about the kind of relationship God has with the animal kingdom, it is clear that they respond immediately to His prompting; an example we can all learn from!

Getting back to our story, we need to take a look at the sea itself in more detail. In Jewish culture, the sea is always a symbol of swallowing up and of death. The surrounding nations also regarded the depths of the ocean as personifying the power that fought against the deity[190].

> *The gods had created order by defeating the forces of chaos;*
> *but these had been tamed, not abolished, and so remained a constant threat.*
> *The embodiment of these lawless and chaotic forces was the sea.* [191]

Indeed, the Jews were very reticent about the sea in general. Their attitude towards it was so negative that heaven is specifically described as having no sea.

> *Then I saw 'a new heaven and a new earth', for the first heaven and the first earth had passed away, and there was no longer any sea.* [192]

---

[188] 1 Corinthians 12:4-7, NIV
[189] Ellison H.L. *ibid.*, p378
[190] Thompson J.G.S.S 'Sea' in *The Illustrated Bible Dictionary – Volume 3*, Leicester: IVP, 1980.
[191] Ellison H.L. *ibid.* p370
[192] Revelation 21:1, NIV

We can understand this better if we know that the Jews thought the dead resided in a place that was surrounded by a river called the Torrent of Destruction[193].

> *The cords of death entangled me;*
> *the torrents of destruction overwhelmed me.* [194]

This place of the dead is called *Sheol*. It was thought to be situated deep under the earth and to be separated from the land of the living by locked doors.

> *Have the gates of death been shown to you?*
> *Have you seen the gates of the deepest darkness?*[195]

As well as being the name of a place, Sheol was also thought of as a huge and insatiable monster; one whose belly can never be filled,

> *Therefore Sheol has enlarged itself*
> *and opened its limitless jaws —*
> *and down go their nobles and masses,*
> *along with their noise and revels.* [196]

So for Jonah, being thrown into the sea means he enters the realm of chaos. He is shown as being **doubly** dead. Not only is he swallowed by the sea, he is also swallowed by the terrifying primeval force of chaos. Perhaps there is here a reference to Jonah's contemporary, the prophet Amos, who uses the following metaphor,

> *Though they dig into hell,*
> *From there My hand shall take them;*
> *Though they climb up to heaven,*
> *From there I will bring them down;*
> *And though they hide themselves on top of Carmel,*
> *From there I will search and take them;*
> *Though they hide from My sight at the bottom of the sea,*
> *From there I will command the serpent, and it shall bite them;*[197]

Amos was commissioned by God to prophesy divine judgement upon the people of Israel. They had failed to live up to the requirements of the Covenant. Instead of living in a holy and righteous way, they had become a people who paid only lip service to God whilst living complacent, self-obsessed lives. Their faith was only a matter of external forms and words. Inescapable judgement is about to come

---

[193] See 2 Samuel 22:5ff and discussion by Jacques Ellul *ibid.*, p42
[194] Psalm 18:4, NIV
[195] Job 38:17, NIV
[196] Isaiah 5:14, Complete Jewish Bible see also Habakkuk 2:5
[197] Amos 9:2-3, NKJV

upon them - A judgement that will reach them even though they hide in the very depths of the ocean.

It is difficult not to see in this a parallel with the Jonah event. Jonah, a Jew, who is in rebellion against God, who has failed to live up to the terms of the Covenant, discovers that even at the bottom of the sea God can still reach him.

However, there is also a striking contrast here. For the Jews of Amos' time, God's ability to reach them in the deepest part of the earth was a symbol of the inescapability of God's judgement. For Jonah, however, God's ability to reach him at the bottom of the sea **is his only hope of salvation**.

Given the cultural and biblical references outlined above, it is clear that this image of Jonah falling to the bottom of the sea is cleverly worked and carefully thought out. Even the time period, three days, is significant. In the Sumerian myth *'Inanna's descent to the netherworld'* three days is given as the time needed to make the journey from the land of the living to the dwelling place of the dead[198].

It is therefore highly probable that this three day period represents a Semitic convention. So Jonah is symbolically making a journey from the underworld (2:2) back to the land of the living (2:10). He therefore represents a person, judged by God, swallowed by death and who finds himself imprisoned in Hell. Jesus seems to regard the story in this way. Prophesying about His coming death Jesus will say,

> *For as Jonah was three days and three nights in the belly of a huge fish,*
> *so the Son of Man will be three days and three nights in the heart of the earth*[199].

Jonah is on his way back to life, a foreshadowing of Jesus' own victory over death. Although Jonah has been swallowed up and is symbolically dead and in Hell, this is not to be the end of his story. Through the drama of the previous hours of the storm, and now in the depths of the sea, God is reaching out to Jonah – and Jonah is on his way back to God.

One of the earliest symbols which designated Christian identity was the fish. Is it possible to see in the Jonah story of 'the fish that saves' a reason for this choice? The Greek word for fish – *icthus* - was used as an acrostic for *Iesus Christos Theos Uios Soter* (Jesus Christ, Son of God, Saviour). Was the story of Jonah was in view when this choice of the fish symbol was made?

---

[198] Black, J.A., Cunningham, G., Fluckiger-Hawker, E, Robson, E., and Zólyomi, G., *Inana's descent to the nether world: translation*, (173-175)
[199] Matthew 12:40 NIV

The sea monster is transformed from a terrifying agent of chaos into an expression of the powerful grace of God that reaches into the most extreme places in order to save. The God of the Bible is,

...the one who meets you at the bottom when it seems you have been swallowed up by some monstrous evil, even by death itself.[200]

Indeed, the Christian hope is sometimes expressed as a reversal of this 'swallowing' metaphor.

When the perishable has been clothed with the imperishable, and the mortal with immortality, then the saying that is written will come true:
'Death has been swallowed up in victory.'
'Where, O death, is your victory?
Where, O death, is your sting?'[201]

For the Christian, it is not death that swallows life, but God's life that swallows death! In related imagery Saint Paul describes the new glorified bodies that Christians will have after their resurrection.

For while we are in this tent, we groan and are burdened,
because we do not wish to be unclothed
but to be clothed instead with our heavenly dwelling,
so that what is mortal may be swallowed up by life.[202]

All that is mortal, transient, prone to decay and death, will one day be 'swallowed up' by life; consumed, removed and taken away. What a glorious hope!

Jonah, in this most extreme of locations - the bottom of the sea - and at this most extreme of moments - when all hope seems lost - discovers that even here God's grace is at work.

To Jonah is revealed the startling dimensions of the grace of God. Not only does God reach out in grace to the horrific and bloody Assyrians in Nineveh, He also reaches down to the bottom of the sea and even into Hell itself. Such is the wild nature of God's unstoppable grace!

---

[200] Cary P. *ibid.*, p77
[201] 1 Corinthians 15:54-55, NIV
[202] 2 Corinthians 5:4, NIV

Questions for Reflection and Discussion

1   Does this truth - that God's grace is capable of reaching those who are most in rebellion against Him, and in the most extreme circumstances - have significance for your life of faith?

2   We have seen that the smallest and the largest creatures can be used by God in His projects. What are the consequences for you as a disciple of Jesus and your participation in the projects of God?

Jonah – The Mouth of Death

The mouth of death was my escape.
God sought me, as it were, in hell
And swallowed me for three days' spell
In acid, meant to cleanse my soul.
From death to death, God's gracious goal
Leads back to Nineveh and life.
And on the way, as with a knife,
One razor tooth slashed through my face
And gave me this sweet sign of grace.[203]

[203] Piper J. *Jonah – Part 1*, accessed online at http://www.desiringgod.org/resource-library/poems/jonah-part-1 on 01/02/13

19 - Jonah Prays (Jonah 2:1)

From inside the fish Jonah prayed to the Lord his God.

Jonah 2:1, NIV

This must have been a terrifying experience for Jonah. He is in total darkness, cramped up, inside the moving body of a great fish. If he was lodged in the belly of the fish, then he would probably be experiencing burns from the gastric acid present there and, unless God supernaturally intervened, Jonah would probably be physically scarred for life. Indeed, we might well imagine that he would be left both physically and psychologically scarred by this experience.

It is here, at this most terrifying point in the story, that Jonah first prays. Since God's first communication with Jonah we have not heard him pray. Jonah has been stoically silent towards God. The storm did not make him pray. The Captain could not make him pray. The revelation of his being the cause of the storm could not make him pray. The threat of death by drowning could not make him pray. Even when every single man on that ship was on his knees in prayer crying out to God, still Jonah would not pray! This gives us some idea of the character of the man. He is not a man easily moved, or whose opinion is easily changed. He is as hard as flint.

Maybe it was pride that made him so stubborn. Maybe he feared losing face before the sailors more than he feared death. Avoiding shame is a powerful motivator in Semitic and Asian cultures – something that is often difficult for Westerners to understand. Some of the parables of Jesus seem opaque to us for this very reason[204]. But Jonah has already told the sailors that he is fleeing from God. It is possible that he fears 'losing face' by having to publicly admit his error and repent.

Whatever the reason, Jonah has set himself against God. He has steadfastly refused to buckle even under the most intense pressure. But now, lost from sight, and in the dreadful silence of the undersea world, hidden for three days inside the body of the great fish, now, finally, Jonah prays.

Some other Biblical characters have found themselves praying in strange places. Joseph found himself praying in a pit[205], Jeremiah in a cistern[206], David in a cave[207], but perhaps Jonah's situation is the most bizarre of all, inside a monstrous fish, under the waves. However, these bizarre places where people have prayed

---

[204] See Luke 11:5-13
[205] Genesis 37:24
[206] Jeremiah 38:6, 9
[207] 1 Samuel 2 2 :1

teach us an important spiritual lesson - no place is too strange to be inappropriate for prayer. In this most terrifying and unpleasant place, Jonah finally turns back to God.

There is an interesting feature of the Hebrew text in this section. In 1:17 (note that in some versions this is the first verse of chapter 2) the word for the 'insides of the fish' is masculine; whereas in 2:2 the Hebrew word for the 'insides of the fish' is feminine. This unusual change is important because it opens up a wonderful translation possibility for the second usage. For in the feminine, this word, elsewhere translated 'belly', can also be translated 'womb'[208].

Which is a wonderful touch, for here in the belly of the great fish - a place where Jonah expected only to be eaten, to be consumed, to die - in this very place God is about to create new life. Something new is about to be **born** in Jonah. As he lives through what he no doubt feels are the last moments of his life, he finally turns back to God. At this point, nothing left to lose, swallowed by the fish, Jonah finally swallows his pride, he accepts God's sovereignty and he prays.

Questions for Reflection and Discussion

1   What strange places have become places of prayer in your life and experience?
2   What extreme circumstances has God used to bring you, or your church fellowship, to your knees in prayer? What 'whales bellies' have become 'wombs' that birthed something new in you?

---

[208] Calmet Dom, *La Sainte Bible avec Commentaire*, Tome XI, Arras : Sueur Charrey, 1896, p350

20 - Jonah's Prayer (Jonah 2:1-10)

From inside the fish Jonah prayed to the Lord his God.
He said: 'In my distress I called to the Lord, and he answered me.
From deep in the realm of the dead I called for help, and you listened to my cry.
You hurled me into the depths, into the very heart of the seas,
and the currents swirled about me; all your waves and breakers swept over me.
I said, "I have been banished from your sight; yet I will look again towards your
holy temple."
The engulfing waters threatened me, the deep surrounded me;
seaweed was wrapped around my head.
To the roots of the mountains I sank down; the earth beneath barred me in for
ever.
But you, Lord my God, brought my life up from the pit.
'When my life was ebbing away, I remembered you, Lord,
and my prayer rose to you, to your holy temple.
'Those who cling to worthless idols turn away from God's love for them.
But I, with shouts of grateful praise, will sacrifice to you.
What I have vowed I will make good. I will say, "Salvation comes from the Lord."'
And the Lord commanded the fish, and it vomited Jonah onto dry land.

Jonah 2:1-10, NIV

Jonah's prayer, such as it is presented to us in here, is obviously a well-polished and finely-crafted literary creation. As such, it is most probably a later reworking of the heart of Jonah's exchange with God at the time. This is evidenced by the fact that it also contains Jonah's later reflections on the completed event. This prayer is presented in poetic form, as a praise psalm. Indeed, we can recognise many expressions, phrases, and ideas that are taken directly from the book of Psalms.

The structure of Jonah's psalm shows an inverted parallelism (a chiastic form), which, as we have already noted, is a common form in Semitic literature. Following the conventions of this literary structure, the poem, or prose, reflects around a mid-point. This mid-point contains the key incident or the main point of the story[209].

The structure of Jonah's psalm can be represented as follows;

---

[209] A great book which explains the different forms of Semitic literature, and then applies these to wonderful effect to the parables of Jesus is, Bailey K.E., *Poet and Peasant and Through Peasant Eyes* (Combined Edition), Michigan, William B. Eerdmans, 1983 (1976, 1980)

A	In my distress I called - *Yahweh* answered.
B	From the depths of *Sheol* I called. - You heard my cry.
C	You hurled me into the deep. - Into the very heart of the seas.
D	The currents swirled about me. - Waves and breakers swept over me.
E	I have been banished from your sight.
E'	Yet I will look again towards your holy temple
D'	Engulfing waters threatened me and the deep surrounded me. - seaweed was wrapped around my head.
C'	To the roots of the mountains I sank down. - The earth barred me in.
B'	From the pit. - You brought up my life.
A'	As my life was ebbing away, I prayed. - My prayer rose to you in your holy temple.

Here the key point is the central two phrases (E and E'). In the first of these Jonah admits his condition before God - banished because of his disobedience, alienated and excluded. In the second he expresses his desire to turn back to God, to be reconciled with Him. He also declares his hope, his faith in God, that reconciliation is still possible. Even in the belly of a sea monster, even at the bottom of the sea, even at the very gates of hell, Jonah believes God's grace may yet be accessible.

Questions for Reflection and Discussion

1   Jonah's prayer makes the point that **no** situation is hopeless when God is involved. There is always hope, even if that hope is only the hope of the life to come. Reflect on how this truth should impact your way of dealing with, and praying in, **hopeless** situations.

2   How do you respond to the remarkable accessibility of God's grace? What does that change about how you view the world?

21 - Prayer and Rescue (Jonah 2:1-10)

Prayer in Distress (Stanzas A - A')

A   In my distress I called to the Lord, and He answered me.

A'   When my life was ebbing away, I remembered you, And my prayer rose to you, to your holy temple.[210]

Previously, we saw the entire ship in distress, here we see only Jonah. Jonah is honest enough to acknowledge that it was only in extreme distress, and in the face of impending death, that he is finally brought to prayer. Although the **prospect** of death has not shaken him from the path of disobedience, as he finally faces the **reality** of it, his resolve breaks. Maybe it was the very natural fear of death, or maybe it was the thought of facing his maker still in a state of disobedience? Whatever his motivation, Jonah repents and makes an about-turn.

The quality of God's grace and mercy is such that, regardless of how mixed our motivation might be, as soon as we turn to God, God turns to us. Jonah had rebelled against God over a period of days, weeks or even months, yet it took just one tiny moment of prayer and God moves to save him.

Counting the number of words in the book of Jonah we find that stanza A' is at the exact centre. A construction which serves to give emphasis to this phrase as the key summary of the truth revealed.

Rescued from Hell (Stanzas B - B')

B   From the depths of the grave (Sheol) I called for help, and you listened to my cry.

B'   But you brought up my life from the pit, O Lord my God.[211]

Sheol, as we saw above, was the Hebrew place of the dead, a shadowy place where somehow conscious existence continued. The word 'pit' is a metaphor for the grave. It is important to recognise that the Hebrew idea of death was very different to our own. For us death occurs at a specific moment in time when certain vital functions cease. However, in Hebrew thinking,

Any form of weakness or misery suffered in life is considered to be the intrusion of death into the sphere of life ... Death is thus understood to be more a process than an event. It is a deterioration or, to use the imagery of the psalm, a "sinking". The greater distress in which a person finds himself the more the reality of death that person experiences.[212]

---

[210] Jonah 2:2a, 7 NIV
[211] Jonah 2:2b, 6b NIV

Following this understanding we see that Jonah is presenting himself in his prayer as someone who is **dead and buried**. He presents his extreme circumstances as a death experience. So his subsequent deliverance can be understood as a 'resurrection'.

As we have previously seen the word used to describe the belly of the fish, *beh'ten*, also carries the sense of 'womb'. Thus the text gives us our first clue that this is not going to be the end of the story. Jonah is not about to experience death, but rebirth. This is why Jonah's experience is often seen in scripture as a prefiguration of the death and resurrection of Jesus[213]. It is also why the early Christians used the image of Jonah as the main representation of their hope of resurrection from the grave.

The hope of eternal life was only a vague and shadowy concept in the Old Testament[214]. There were only a few prophetic texts that could be interpreted as speaking of it,

> *I will deliver this people from the power of the grave;*
> *I will redeem them from death.*
> *Where, O death, are your plagues?*
> *Where, O grave, is your destruction?*[215]

As can be imagined, the Jews thought and talked much about this subject. Two distinct groups developed; those who believed in life after death and those who did not. In His ministry, Jesus gave new teaching on this subject.

> *Just then a man came up to Jesus and asked,*
> *'Teacher, what good thing must I do to get eternal life?'*
> *'Why do you ask me about what is good?' Jesus replied.*
> *'There is only One who is good.*
> *If you want to enter life, keep the commandments.'*[216]

Here Jesus affirms the possibility of life after death; something that He will continue to express throughout His teaching[217].

> *But when you give a banquet, invite the poor, the crippled, the lame, the blind,*
> *and you will be blessed. Although they cannot repay you,*
> *you will be repaid at the resurrection of the righteous.'*[218]

---

[212] Fretheim T.E., ibid., p100
[213] See Matthew 12:39-41
[214] e.g. Psalm 133:3, Daniel 12:2
[215] Hosea 13:14, NIV
[216] Matthew 19:16-17, NIV
[217] Matthew 22:23ff, 24:31 ; Luke 20:27-34 ; John 5:28, 6:39-54 etc.
[218] Luke 14:13-14, NIV

The story of Jonah is therefore very significant, in that, some six centuries before the time of Jesus and His new teaching on this subject, it gives us a symbolic prefiguration of the Christian hope of eternal life. Following a purely logical expectation, the psalm of Jonah should end at v6a; with Jonah dead, buried, in hell. But instead we find a,

> ...radical discontinuity in the psalm;
> verse 6a in no way leads to or even remotely suggests verse 6b[219]

God's unpredictable, surprising, wild grace breaks in. Symbolically dead and in hell, Jonah discovers that even here he is not separated from the grace of God. As St Paul will later confirm, for those who die in God there is nothing which can separate them from His love – not even death[220]. This promise of eternal life and the resurrection of the dead is to become a central feature of the Christian faith; a development that is symbolically foreshadowed in Jonah's deliverance.

Jonah's rebellion may have brought him down to the dwelling place of the dead but God's grace will not leave him there. We have at this turning point the wonderful image of God as a grave robber! This element of the story of Jonah has been understood by some as a foreshadowing of the harrowing of Hell by Christ. This theological belief understands Christ as having descended into Hell during the time between His death and resurrection, in order to liberate the righteous dead[221]. What a wonderful image and metaphor for the Christian hope in the face of death![222]

The image of Jonah's rescue was adopted by early Christian art as a powerful motif for both salvation and the resurrection of the dead. It came to be one of the most popular images to be painted on the catacomb walls - the burial chambers of the early Christians. In fact, for certain scholars, the image of Jonah safely landing on the shore after his sea-monster voyage is **the essential image** for the early Christians[223]. This is confirmed by Barclay-Lloid's observation that the story of Jonah,

> ...was depicted more frequently and in more episodes than any other Old
> Testament subject[224]

---

[219] Burrows D.P. *ibid.*, p66

[220] Romans 8:38-39

[221] See 1 Peter 3:9, 4:6; Ephesians 4:8-10, Revelation 1:17-18

[222] See 1 Corinthians 15:21-26, 42-57; 2 Timothy 1:10; Hebrews 2:14; Revelation 1:18, 21:4

[223] Louis Réau, *Iconographie de l'art Chrétien*, Vol II, Ancien Testament, Paris, France, p417, cited in Murray P. *ibid.*, p33

[224] Barclay-Lloid J.E. *The Prophet Jonah in Early Christian Art*, Service International de Documentation Judeo-Chrétienne (SIDIC), XVIII, 1985/1

For the first Christians, Jonah became a precious symbol of hope. Living in difficult circumstances, under persecution and threatened with death, the early Christians took heart from Jonah's story. They were encouraged to hope and believe that God's salvation often comes in the most remarkable way. Who indeed, in the height of the horrors of the Roman persecutions, could have foreseen that the whole Roman Empire would convert to Christianity under Constantine in the 4th century?!

Jonah was also a powerful symbol of the resurrection of the dead. His image was an expression of the hope that the martyred Christians, those who had written their testimonies in blood, would one day experience God's resurrection.

Jesus will show concretely in His resurrection what Jonah shows only symbolically. Jesus' resurrection is the central element of Christian faith, for it showed definitively that the enemy, death, is now defeated.

> *But if it is preached that Christ has been raised from the dead, how can some of you say that there is no resurrection of the dead? If there is no resurrection of the dead, then not even Christ has been raised. And if Christ has not been raised, our preaching is useless and so is your faith ...*
> *For if the dead are not raised, then Christ has not been raised either.*
> *And if Christ has not been raised, your faith is futile; you are still in your sins.*
> *Then those also who have fallen asleep in Christ are lost.*
> *If only for this life we have hope in Christ, we are of all people most to be pitied.*
> *But Christ has indeed been raised from the dead,*
> *the first fruits of those who have fallen asleep.*[225]

Thus, for those who put their faith in God, death is no longer a 'full-stop' but only a 'comma'.

---

[225] 1 Corinthians 15:12-14, 16-20, NIV

Questions for Reflection and Discussion

1   Reflect on the implications of the following text.

> *For I am convinced that neither death nor life,*
> *neither angels nor demons,*
> *neither the present nor the future,*
> *nor any powers,*
> *neither height nor depth,*
> *nor anything else in all creation,*
> *will be able to separate us from the love of God*
> *that is in Christ Jesus our Lord.*
>
> Romans 8:38f NIV

2   What other images of salvation and resurrection do you find helpful?

22 - Buried Alive (Jonah 2:1-10)

Buried Alive (Stanzas C - C')

C   You hurled me into the deep, into the very heart of the seas.

C'   To the roots of the mountains I sank down; the earth beneath barred me in forever.[226]

Jonah describes himself as being in the deepest and the most inaccessible places on earth - the deepest part of the ocean, the deepest part of the earth. Again this emphasises the hopelessness of his circumstances, and the fact that he considers himself to be irrecoverably lost; which only goes to reinforce the dramatic nature of God's deliverance.

In his prayer psalm Jonah uses imagery directly drawn from the book of Psalms;

> *Do not let the floodwaters engulf me*
> *or the depths swallow me up*
> *or the pit close its mouth over me.*[227]

David also used this metaphor to express a moment of extreme danger that he had lived through,

> *The waves of death swirled about me;*
> *The torrents of destruction overwhelmed me.*
> *The cords of the grave coiled around me;*
> *The snares of death confronted me.*[228]

It is a truism that the more extreme the danger faced, the more glorious the eventual deliverance. We see in Scripture that God often allows circumstances to become extreme before He acts. In the story of the Exodus, for example, God could easily have moved the heart of Pharaoh in response to Moses' first request. However, right from the start, God warns Moses that this is not going to be the case, rather the reverse.

> *But I will harden his (Pharaoh's) heart so that he will not let the people go.*[229]

God explains the reason for this later on,

> *But I will harden Pharaoh's heart, and though I multiply my miraculous signs and wonders in Egypt, he will not listen to you. Then I will lay my hand on Egypt and*

---

[226] Jonah 2:3a, 6a NIV

[227] Psalm 69 :15, NIV

[228] 2 Samuel 22:5-6, NIV

[229] Exodus 4:21b NIV. See also 7:3; 8:15, 32; 9:12, 34; 10:1, 20, 27; 11:10; 14:4, 7, 17

with mighty acts of judgement I will bring out my divisions, my people the Israelites. And the Egyptians will know that I am the Lord when I stretch out my hand against Egypt and bring the Israelites out of it.[230]

In other words God is going to use Pharaoh's refusal to create **an arena for the revelation of His existence and His glory** – for both the Egyptians and the Jews. The plagues, the signs and wonders of the exodus, will all serve to build the faith of the people of God and will take them to a new level in their appreciation of His power and majesty. By these prodigious acts God will also reveal Himself to the Egyptians and the surrounding nations.

Questions for Reflection and Discussion

1   Are there difficult or worsening problems in your life? How does it affect your attitude to them when you consider that God could be working in them to create an arena for the demonstration of His glory?

2   Jonah finds the words to describe his circumstances and to pour out his heart to God from his knowledge of the Psalms. What are the implications of this for us?

---

[230] Exodus 7:3-5, NIV

23 - Preparing the Corpse for Burial (Jonah 2:1-10)

Preparing the Corpse for Burial (Stanzas D - D')

D   ... the currents swirled about me; all your waves and breakers swept over me.

D'   The engulfing waters threatened me, the deep surrounded me; seaweed was wrapped around my head.[231]

These phrases highlight the awful nature of Jonah's ordeal. He describes his disorientation and terror. He gives us a graphic image of being tossed about by the raging seas, tangled up in seaweed and totally helpless. In Semitic culture corpses were wrapped in cloths rather than placed in coffins. We see this referred in the book of Job;

> Bury them in the dust together;
> shroud their faces in the grave.[232]

So having one's face wrapped is an image of preparation for burial. Jonah presents himself as a corpse being prepared for the grave.

There are many scriptural incidents when, figuratively speaking or even literally, the corpse is being prepared for burial, then God breaks into the situation and turns it all around. God seems to really enjoy snatching victory from the jaws of defeat.

Think of Abraham and Isaac. Isaac is Abraham's only descendant. Abraham was the man God had named 'Great Father' – the man to whom God had promised that he would become the father of many nations. Yet we find him about to sacrifice his only son on an altar; the knife is poised in the air. Isaac is symbolically a corpse being prepared for burial, yet God breaks in, stays Abraham's hand, and gives Isaac back to him, as if from the dead.

Or we can think of Elijah,

> Then the word of the Lord came to him: 'Go at once to Zarephath in the region of Sidon and stay there. I have instructed a widow there to supply you with food.' So he went to Zarephath. When he came to the town gate, a widow was there gathering sticks. He called to her and asked, 'Would you bring me a little water in a jar so I may have a drink?' As she was going to get it, he called, 'And bring me, please, a piece of bread.'

---

[231] Jonah 2:3b, 5 NIV
[232] Job 40:13, NIV

*'As surely as the Lord your God lives,' she replied, 'I don't have any bread – only a
handful of flour in a jar and a little olive oil in a jug. I am gathering a few sticks to
take home and make a meal for myself and my son,
that we may eat it – and die.'*[233]

Elijah follows God's clear instructions and what does he find? The region to
which he is sent has been struck by famine. His supposed hostess is completely
out of food and, with her son by her side, has resigned herself to a slow death by
starvation! Elijah is starving too. They are just three corpses being prepared for
burial.

But God breaks in and their meagre supply of food is miraculously multiplied.
They are symbolically brought back from the dead. This resurrection metaphor is
further hammered home in a later incident when the woman's son becomes ill
and dies. Elijah prays over his dead body and he is raised to life. (Which makes
for an interesting side-note to our story, as a Jewish tradition holds that this very
person, the resurrected son, is actually Jonah himself! [234]).

There are many more such incidents in scripture, times when things seemed
over, finished, failed, dead and buried. Yet God breaks in, breathes new life into
the corpse, and demonstrates His power and His glory in a dramatic turnaround
of events.

In any seemingly hopeless situation our response should always be that of
Ezekiel.
*The hand of the Lord was on me, and he brought me out by the Spirit of
the Lord and set me in the middle of a valley; it was full of bones. He led me to and
fro among them, and I saw a great many bones on the floor of the valley,
bones that were very dry.
He asked me, 'Son of man, can these bones live?'
I said, 'Sovereign Lord, you alone know.'...
Then he said to me, 'Prophesy to the breath; prophesy, son of man, and say to it,
"This is what the Sovereign Lord says: come, breath, from the four winds and
breathe into these slain, that they may live."'
So I prophesied as he commanded me, and breath entered them;
they came to life and stood up on their feet – a vast army.*[235]

Only God knows what is possible in any situation.

And with God anything is possible.

---

[233] 1 Kings 17:8-12, NIV
[234] Sasson J.M. *ibid.*, p86
[235] Ezekiel 37:1-3, 9-10, NIV

Questions for Reflection and Discussion

1   What incidents are you aware of in your experience where God broke in just as the 'corpse was being prepared for burial'?

2   Are there any situations in your life that seem hopeless to you? Why do you feel they are hopeless, and what does that say about your understanding of God?

24 -Turning Towards the Temple (Jonah 2:1-10)

Turning Towards the Temple (Stanzas E - E')

E   I have been banished from your sight;

E'   yet I will look again towards your holy temple[236]

This is the great turning point in the story, emphasised by its central placement in this chiasm. In this verse we have a description of the result of Jonah's disobedience - he is banished from God's sight. But it is the second phrase which is the most important; here he shows both his change of heart and his hope of grace.

Jonah finally admits **where he is** before God. He admits to himself that he is banished from the presence of God because of his sin and disobedience. But Jonah then expresses **where he wants to be**. His desire is to repent, to be restored into God's presence. He makes a mental and spiritual 'about-turn'. He metaphorically **turns towards the temple**.

In Jewish religious practice the temple was understood to be a privileged place for experiencing God's presence on earth. So in the same way that Muslims pray towards Mecca, the Jews would always pray facing towards the temple[237].

In terms of the Covenant between God and His people, Jonah is still in trouble. Even though he has decided to turn away from his rebellion, in his extreme circumstances he cannot comply with what the religious laws prescribed – that he should offer a sacrifice to show his penitence. Trapped inside the monstrous fish, Jonah can change nothing in his outward behaviour to prove his change of heart. He can make no public sign of contrition and repentance. All Jonah can do is pray. Will this be enough?

The Bible makes clear that God's glory is most evidenced by His grace and mercy. We often underestimate the wonder of this grace and mercy. We get used to the idea of the availability of forgiveness and reconciliation. We get into a situation where grace becomes banal, easy and cheap.

We need to remember what it cost God to make His grace available to us. It required the incarnation, the cross, Christ's death and resurrection. There is nothing easy or lightweight in God's provision of His great grace. It is truly **amazing**.

---

[236] Jonah 2:4 NIV

[237] See 2 Chronicles 6:20, 21, 26, 29, 32, 34, 38

Such is the wondrous nature of this grace that all it takes to re-establish Jonah in his relationship with God, to reconcile him, to readmit him into God's presence, is his repentance. All he has to do is to turn towards the temple.

Who is a God like you,
who pardons sin and forgives the transgression
of the remnant of his inheritance?
You do not stay angry for ever
but delight to show mercy.
You will again have compassion on us;
you will tread our sins underfoot
and hurl all our iniquities into the depths of the sea.[238]

Jonah is at the bottom of the sea, but following his repentance, there is only one thing that he will leave there – his sins - forgiven, forgotten, forever.

As a Jew, and especially as a prophet, the temple had been the most important place in Jonah's life. It was here that the worship of God was focussed. It was here that the sacrifices were offered. It was here that acts of praise and worship were carried out before God. It was here that vows were made and fulfilled. It was here that the Jewish people came to hear God's word taught and explained and where the prophets came to declare what God was saying to the nation. In turning towards the temple, Jonah re-centres his life on God; he recommits himself to an involvement in the communal life of faith.

Certainly, as we shall see later, Jonah's repentance is not complete. Note that in his psalm, Jonah makes no lamentation for his sin; in fact the only sin he mentions is the one of idolatry – a sin that Gentiles, rather than Jews, were guilty of[239]. So whilst Jonah's prayer is completely pious and humble, as we shall see later, his heart is still resistant and recalcitrant. Sweeney is of the opinion that,

Perhaps he is truly repentant ... but he is still angry[240]

Jonah's prayer, facing death and in great distress, foreshadows Jesus' prayer in Gethsemane. As Jonah prepares himself for his 'passion' he comes to the point where he abandons himself to God, giving himself over to God's grace and mercy. Jonah prepares himself for the service of God by abandoning his own will. Jesus will express the same sentiment,

---

[238] Micah 7:18-19, NIV

[239] Kennedy, *ibid.*, p33

[240] Sweeney M.A. The Twelve Prophets Vol. 1, Collegeville, 2000, p318, cited in Dray S. Facing the Powers – A Biblical Framework for those Facing Political Oppression , Carn Brae Media, 2013, p44

Father, if you are willing, take this cup from me;
yet not my will, but yours be done[241]

This change of heart of Jonah, this reorientation of his life, is all that it takes to move him from the experience of God's judgement into the experience of God's favour. Muslim piety focusses on Jonah as an example of perfect repentance,

...as a result of his supplication, the stormy sea calmed down, and the fish became
a vehicle for Jonah (p), carrying him to the "shore of salvation".
That is, with the command of the Merciful Creator
the creation that seemed hostile to him was put into his service[242]

For Christians too, this idea that a simple act of repentance should be able to effect such a profound reversal forms one of the key mysteries at the heart of our faith. This staggering notion of the incredible grace and mercy of God which reaches out towards repentant people is the very centre of Christianity. It is of such importance that it is even expressed in church architecture.

Since at least the 10th century almost all church buildings have had cockerels mounted upon their roofs. This is in reference to St Peter and his denial of Christ[243]. We are told that during Jesus' arrest and trial St Peter denies three times that he knows Him. We might imagine that this behaviour would have significant consequences for St Peter, and certainly for his position as leader of the Apostles.

But this is not the case. Following His resurrection, Jesus simply asks St Peter *"Do you love me?"*. This question is repeated three times – once for each denial. St Peter confirms his love for Jesus and is reconfirmed and re-instated as leader of the Church.

In the light of this incident the cockerel became a powerful Christian symbol of the grace and forgiveness of God. The cockerel above our churches proclaims to the world that if you ever need forgiveness, if ever you need a second chance, if ever you need to find a place where you can receive grace, mercy and forgiveness – here is where you can find it. It is under the sign of the cockerel, amongst the people of God, where the failures, the no-hopers, and the broken can find the opportunity to start again, to be forgiven, to be restored and renewed.

---

[241] Luke 22:2, NIV
[242] Mermer A. & Yazicioglu U., *ibid.*, p3
[243] See John 18:27, Matthew 26

For Christians who often fail, mess up or, like Jonah, rebel against God, it is a great encouragement to know that our future is not determined by our past failures, but rather by our present choices. Up to this point Jonah has been making wrong choices. He has followed his own ideas and his own desires, which have led him to the edge of disaster. He is now at death's door at the bottom of the ocean. What can turn all this around? What can take him from this point to a successful international ministry? One thing - his chosen direction. All he has to do is to turn towards the temple.

Questions for Reflection and Discussion

1   How well does your local church fellowship resemble a community of grace and of the second chance?

2   Reflect on and thank God for any **second chances** that God and His Church have given you in the course of your Christian experience.

25 - Jonah's Testimony (Jonah 2:8)

Those who cling to worthless idols forfeit the grace that could be theirs.

Jonah 2:8, NIV

The word translated idols here literally means *'empty ones'*. There is a reference here to the two-pronged tragedy of idolatry. Not only is idolatry futile - idols are not gods and they cannot help - but idolatry also prevents us from coming to know the grace and mercy of the true God, one who really exists, who is both powerful and who cares for us. These idols, these *'Worthless ones of emptiness'* (a literal translation of the Hebrew phrase) not only leave us helpless but also ensnare us and keep us away from God.

Jonah has been worshipping an idol too. Jonah's idol has been his misunderstanding of the nature of God. Jonah has created an idol of his own theology - a theology that tries to impose limits on the nature and the scope of the grace of God.

When God revealed His true nature to Jonah and thereby exposed Jonah's mistaken understanding of grace, Jonah preferred to cling to his idol, rather than to embrace the truth. Jonah's words reveal the folly of such behaviour. What has Jonah achieved through his actions? He is hurt - physically, spiritually, and emotionally. He has even put the lives of others at risk - the sailors and the Ninevites. His behaviour has made him miss out on experiencing God's presence in his own life.

For all these reasons the Bible condemns idolatry fiercely[244] and often mocks it mercilessly[245]. Sadly, for the people of Israel, idolatry was always a major temptation. The surrounding nations all worshipped idols; it was a constant fight to stand apart from this kind of activity.

But what is idolatry for us, today, in the 21st century?

Idolatry is properly defined as the putting of anything else in the place of pre-eminence that rightfully belongs to God. As such, idolatry it not necessarily solely concerned with physical objects – the classic understanding of idolatrous practices.

Modern idolatry rarely, if ever, involves the actual worship of objects, rather it expresses itself in behaviours where things like financial gain, the pursuit of power, the priority of pleasure, or even our family, to take first place in our lives.

---

[244] See Exodus 20:4; 32:7ff
[245] See Isaiah 41:7; Jeremiah 10:5

Which highlights the complicated nature of idolatry; idols can often be 'good' things. There is nothing wrong in wanting to advance in one's professional life, there is certainly nothing wrong in wanting the best for one's family. The error of idolatry is not in the concern itself but in the priority that we allow it to assume. An idolatrous priority displaces God from the centre of our lives.

The problem of idolatry is that it denies the truth about God. It says God isn't the most important thing in human life. It pushes God from His rightful place and replaces Him with something else – anything else – and, as a consequence, contaminates the whole of a person's life.

Mankind's chief glory and significance is fulfilled in giving to God our willing worship, flowing out of our appreciation and love for Him. Idolatry squeezes something else into this place that should be reserved for God. It thereby diminishes human value and significance.

Instead of existing for the noblest purpose possible - to glorify God - we settle for something empty, vain. Contemporary examples of idolatry result in trading the glory of living in a relationship with God, of being involved in His eternal projects, for what amounts to an 'amassing of trinkets', or merely 'having a nice time', or whatever else. Idolatry not only slights God, but degrades man.

They have mouths, but cannot speak,
eyes, but they cannot see;
they have ears, but they cannot hear,
noses, but they cannot smell;
they have hands, but they cannot feel,
feet but they cannot walk;
nor can they utter a sound with their throats.
Those who make them will be like them,
and so will all who trust in them. [246]

Questions for Reflection and Discussion

1   How can we know if our priorities are correctly ordered and that God has number one place in our lives?

2   What things are temptations to idolatry in your life?

---

[246] Psalm 115:4-9, NIV

26 - Jonah's Resolution (Jonah 2:8-9)

Those who cling to worthless idols
turn away from God's love for them.
But I, with shouts of grateful praise, will sacrifice to you.
What I have vowed I will make good.
I will say, "Salvation comes from the Lord."

Jonah 2:8-9, NIV

Reflecting on his amazing, terrifying experience, Jonah finishes his psalm with a shout of praise, worship and commitment. This experience has led him to appreciate the vast difference between the idols of the pagans and *Yahweh* the living God. Jonah has had first-hand knowledge of a God who can control the storm, who can beckon the greatest monsters on the planet to do His bidding, a God who effortlessly guides the lives of men.

Jonah has begun to see a little of the immense majesty and glory of God and to respond to this new revelation with obedience, which he confirms with an oath. His personal experience of the grace and mercy of God *in extremis* has led him to a place of thanksgiving and song. Not only this, he makes a vow. In this Jonah is a model of what the normal response to a 'grace' experience should be - gratitude, thanksgiving, sacrifice and vow.

Gratitude shows our humility. We acknowledge our helplessness and God's kindness.

Thanksgiving demonstrates our conviction about God being the source of our help.

Sacrifice gives concrete physical expression to our thanksgiving.

Vows show our determination to live in a different way in the light of grace received.

Jonah responds to the experience of God's grace and mercy in the same way that the sailors did, with a vow of commitment (1:16). Those who profess to be followers of God should be at least as grateful for His grace and mercy as those who do not yet claim such allegiance.

However we are left with some unanswered questions. We know that Jonah made a vow, but what did he vow to do, exactly – to go to Jerusalem, to make a sacrifice? What promise(s) did he make?

We don't have any information about this. Perhaps his vow was simply to do what God had commanded him to do — to go to Nineveh. Vow making was an important aspect of Jewish spirituality and there were specific regulations given by God about it[247].

The practice of making vows also continued in the New Testament church, particularly amongst those from a Jewish background[248]. A vow was basically a voluntary promise made to God. Sometimes it was made in hope of some help from God, of the form, "if You do this, I'll do that". At other times it was made as a spontaneous act of gratitude for grace received.

There is a quote attributed to Thomas Goodwin, an English Puritan preacher and theologian of the 17th century, which says,

> *Great blessings that are won with prayer are worn with thankfulness[249]*

Jonah's response to mercy received - gratitude, thanksgiving, sacrifice and vow - is a good model to adopt. We **should** live lives of thankfulness.

> *Rejoice always, pray continually, give thanks in all circumstances;*
> *for this is God's will for you in Christ Jesus[250]*

> *Let the peace of Christ rule in your hearts, since as members of one body you were called to peace. And be thankful. Let the message of Christ dwell among you richly as you teach and admonish one another with all wisdom through psalms, hymns, and songs from the Spirit, singing to God with gratitude in your hearts. And whatever you do, whether in word or deed, do it all in the name of the Lord Jesus, giving thanks to God the Father through him.[251]*

No human being has ever had as much to be grateful for as a Christian. Thankfulness is the proper attitude towards God - He who gives us everything we have and are[252]. If we cannot be thankful towards God, then we can be thankful to no-one!

---

[247] See Leviticus 7:16, 22:21; Numbers 6:2ff
[248] See Acts 18:18, 21:24
[249] Goodwin T. *The Works of Thomas Goodwin, Vol. III*, Edinburgh : James Nichol, 1890, p389
[250] 1 Thessalonians 5:16-19, NIV
[251] Colossians 3:15
[252] See Psalm 104

Questions for Reflection and Discussion

1   How high is your 'thankfulness quotient'? How well does thankfulness characterise the nature of your local fellowship?

2   Jonah presents to us a good model of how we should respond to the experience of the goodness of God in our lives – gratitude, thanksgiving, sacrifice and vows. Have you ever responded to an experience of God's grace in this way?

27 - The Key Truth (Jonah 2:9)

Those who cling to worthless idols
turn away from God's love for them.
But I, with shouts of grateful praise, will sacrifice to you.
What I have vowed I will make good.
I will say, "Salvation comes from the Lord."

Jonah 2:9, NIV

This statement of Jonah's - Salvation *comes from the Lord* - is the key to the whole book. This statement is the foundational truth on which all the rest relies. Whether we like it or not, salvation is all of God. We do not control it. We do not often understand it. It is a wild grace.

Although this section has shown us that Jonah can celebrate God's salvation when it comes to him, his subsequent behaviour shows that he still has great difficulty in accepting the idea that God's grace might come to other people, people like the Ninevites. This is still outrageous to Jonah. We will see later the enormous extent of his outrage.

But Jonah's chastisement has accomplished its purpose – Jonah has repented and set himself on the path of obedience. And so God commands the great fish to vomit him out onto the shore.

The image painted here is rather disgusting! Somewhere on the Mediterranean coastline, Jonah finds himself back on dry land - covered in fish vomit and more dead than alive! He must have caused quite a stir amongst any people who witnessed his arrival!

As we saw earlier, whilst obedience brings blessing, disobedience has consequences too. Jonah's disobedience has probably left him scarred for life; perhaps broken in health, possibly psychologically damaged. Sin is never trivial, never without consequences. At the very least, it prevents us from experiencing God's presence and blessing and it disqualifies us from being involved in His purposes. At worst it brings us into a place of chastening; an experience which will be difficult and may well leave permanent scars. But which is nonetheless a blessing, as through it God will bring us back to Himself.

Jonah's escape form the fish definitely qualifies as a miracle. But we need to remember that miracles, such as Jonah's escape from death, are never conclusive proof of God's existence for those who witness them. For example, many of the people of Israel who saw the plagues of Egypt, the Red Sea crossing, the pillar of fire and of cloud - these people still subsequently doubted and rebelled against God's instructions.

Similarly, although Jesus healed hundreds of people, cast out many demons, even raised several people from the dead, He was still ultimately rejected by the majority of the nation of Israel. Miracles do not prove anything - they merely witness to the truth. Only those who look with eyes of faith will see the truth that the miracle confirms.

Another thing about miracles is that they all point to the resurrection of Jesus as **THE** miracle. Impressive healings, or mighty acts, bring only temporary relief. Those Jesus raised from the dead subsequently died, those He healed no doubt got sick again. But the resurrection of Jesus is definitive, permanent, without possibility of changing; it is the solid foundation of the Christian faith and hope.

That is why St. Paul can say;

> *... if Christ has not been raised, our preaching is useless and so is your faith.* [253]

The resurrection proves that Christ has conquered death; that there is an eternal hope for mankind. And so Jonah's experience, pointing forward to this event, takes on an enormous significance. This is why resurrection, that which Jesus named **the sign of Jonah**, is so important.

No surprise then, that in the catacombs where the first Christians were buried, this image of Jonah being ejected from the great fish was frequently painted on tombs as a symbol of the resurrection. It is a powerful image of God's ability to take us safely through death and Hell and to bring us finally into his presence. [254]

Indeed, von Orelli described it as,

> *'the Easter-sign of Jonah',* [255]

---

[253] 1 Corinthians 15:14, NIV
[254] Murray P., *ibid.*, p32f
[255] Von Orelli C. *ibid.*, p1

Figure 3 - Jonah Vomited Out[256]

The above fresco, from the catacombs of Saints Marcellinus and Peter in Rome, shows such an image of Jonah being vomited out of the sea monster.

So Jonah is saved but, as we will later see, he is not yet converted. His heart and mind still refuse to accept the vision of divine grace and mercy that he is being encouraged to adopt. His experiences in the storm and with the sea monster have merely convinced him that, while he can continue to protest, he cannot continue to run[257].

Given the genuinely mixed-up nature of Jonah's feelings, Dray amusingly asks,

Does the fish vomit up Jonah because it is literally sick of his hypocrisy?[258]

---

[256] http://www.vatican.va/roman_curia/pontifical_commissions/archeo/inglese/documents/ rc_com_archeo_doc_20011010_cataccrist_en.html accessed 20/07/12

[257] Bruckner J.K. *Jonah, Nahum, Habakkuk, Zephaniah – NIV Application Commentary*, Grand Rapids : Zondervan, 2004, p86 cited in Dray S. *ibid.*, p51

[258] Dray S. *ibid.*, p54

Questions for Reflection and Discussion

1   What 'sin scars' are you aware of (in your own life or the life of your local fellowship) that are due to errors or bad choices? What can we do in the light of these? How does the reality of these scars affect your walk with God?

2   Given that the resurrection is the central event in human history, how well is this centrality expressed in your own Christian life and that of your local fellowship?

Ionah : the third part - Long and Dusty Road

Hands sinking into wet sand, mouth full of salty kelp
Head thumping from breath held too long
Limbs weary from swimming in deep blue sea
Smelling of fish and oceanic pulp

Sun baked skin covered in salty sheen
Tattered clothes flapping like flags
Blown by heat-filled air as I walked the road
To the city of magnificence and wealth.

I stood a while, watching the gates
Open and close as traders and merchants
Came and went about their daily trade
With no thought, or care about their fate.

A raggedy man was I as I stepped inside
Would they listen and laugh, or stone me dead?
Do they deserve this truth I bring?
Do I care if they worship and sing?

A. P. McIntyre   2012.

28 - Take Two (Jonah 3:1-2)

Then the word of the Lord came to Jonah a second time:
'Go to the great city of Nineveh and proclaim to it the message I give you.'

Jonah 3:1-2, NIV

God speaks to Jonah a second time. Ever since Jonah's flight from God, all communication has been from man to God. The sailors prayed to God. Then, inside the sea-monster, Jonah finally prayed to God. But God, apart from directing the outcome of the sailors' lot-casting, has said nothing. Now, as Jonah turns back to God, the communication lines are open again and God speaks.

We know that our ability to communicate with God is blocked by sin. The Bible contains many scriptures which show this link;

if my people, who are called by my name,
will humble themselves and pray
and seek my face and turn from their wicked ways,
then I will hear from heaven, and I will forgive their sin and will heal their land. [259]

But your iniquities have separated you from your God;
your sins have hidden his face from you, so that he will not hear. [260]

Then they will cry out to the Lord, but he will not answer them.
At that time he will hide his face from them because of the evil they have done. [261]

So if we ever find that communication with God seems difficult, one of the first things we should do is to examine our conscience, to see if we have offended God or sinned in some way.

Jonah, having resolved the issue of his disobedience (though not all of his theological issues) now hears God speak a second time, telling him to go to Nineveh.

The first time God had told Jonah,

Go to the great city of Nineveh and preach against it,
because its wickedness has come up before me [262]

---

[259] 2 Chronicles 7:14, NIV
[260] Isaiah 59:2, NIV
[261] Micah 3:4, NIV
[262] Jonah 1:2, NIV

Jonah had gradually discovered that God intended to bring the Ninevites to repentance and into the experience of His grace and mercy. This second communication of God's assignment for Jonah is worded in a different manner, which is significant.

> Then the word of the Lord came to Jonah a second time:
> 'Go to the great city of Nineveh and proclaim to it the message I give you.'

God's mission now seems more open-ended. Jonah is told to go to Nineveh and to proclaim the message that he **will** be given. The fact that Jonah's assignment is not explicitly laid out ahead of time revels that Jonah is being invited into an activity of **partnership** with God. God does not give him the whole picture **up-front**. Rather God invites Jonah to walk with Him, to work in dependence upon Him, to declare His message, as and when God will give it to him.

God thereby places Jonah in a position where he will need to maintain close fellowship and intimate contact with God, in order to be in a position to receive instruction each step of the way, to understand what God wants him to do and say.

This verse speaks of the necessity of relying on God. Jonah is invited to go to Nineveh and to deliver the message that God **will** give him. This requires **faith**, the ability to trust that when the moment comes, God will give Jonah something to say. Jonah must prove his faith.

We see this same model in the call of Abram;

> The Lord had said to Abram,
> 'Go from your country, your people and your father's household
> to the land I will show you.'[263]

The destination is not given in advance. Abraham is simply invited to leave with God, to trust God to show him the way.

The same principle is expressed in the Exodus, where the Israelites have no detailed information before-hand about their route to the Promised Land. What they do have is the promise of the presence of God with them, manifested in the pillar of cloud by day and the pillar of fire by night.

---

[263] Genesis 12:1, NIV

By day the Lord went ahead of them in a pillar of cloud to guide them on their way
and by night in a pillar of fire to give them light, so that they could travel by day or
night. Neither the pillar of cloud by day nor the pillar of fire by night
left its place in front of the people. [264]

This dependence upon God is a divine principle, and we see it most perfectly expressed in the life and ministry of Jesus. For Jesus makes very clear His total dependence upon God the Father[265].

I tell you the truth, the Son can do nothing by himself;
he can only do what he sees his Father doing, because whatever the Father does
the Son also does. For the Father loves the Son and shows him all he does. [266]

Here we have Jesus' *modus operandi*. He concentrates on His relationship with the Father and seeks to discern the Father's activity in His life and circumstances. Jesus becomes involved only when He discerns that the Father is at work, such discernment is His cue to get involved Himself.

This being so, one of the keys to a successful Christian life is the ability to discern where and when God is at work. The capacity to do this grows and develops in a Christian over time. However there are some key indicators that help us to discern where God is at work.

One of these key indicators is when we see people being drawn to God, opening up to Him. Jesus tells us that any person who is actively seeking God is doing so **only** because God is at work in their lives.

No one can come to me unless the Father who sent me draws them,
and I will raise them up at the last day. [267]

We can therefore interpret such a phenomenon as an infallible evidence of God at work.
Another key indication is a conviction about sin.

When he comes (the Holy Spirit), he will prove the world to be in the wrong about
sin and righteousness and judgment[268]

---

[264] Exodus 13:21-22.
[265] In this section I follow closely the model developed in Blackaby H. & King C., *Experiencing God – Knowing and Doing the Will of God*, Tenessee: Lifeway Press, 1990.
[266] John 5:19-20a, NIV
[267] John 6:44, NIV
[268] John 16:8, NIV

The Holy Spirit reveals to us the truth about our sin, our need for righteousness and the judgement we will ultimately face. Whenever we see someone convicted about their sins, sensing that they have thereby offended God and feeling the weight of this, we know for certain this is **only** because God is at work in their lives.

Discerning the activity of God always begins in prayer. We need to pray daily that God will reveal to us what He is doing around us. We should also be paying attention to those we meet each day. Are there signs that someone is beginning to seek God? Is this person expressing a sense of their sinfulness, sharing regrets for past mistakes? All of these are indications that God is at work. Our job is then to respond to this invitation to join God in what He is doing.

To return to or text, we see that Jonah's experience expresses the reality of the normal Christian life. All of God's invitations to us will require us to step out in faith, not knowing the end, in confidence, trusting Him to show us the way forward moment by moment. We must understand that God's primary goal in any mission that He might give us, is not to accomplish **something**, but to draw **us** closer to Himself.

Questions for Reflection and Discussion

1   In this section a model of the Christian life has been developed. This model presents the life of discipleship as an adventure towards the unknown, in relationship with God. From your knowledge of the Bible do you agree with this model? Are there examples from your own life, or the life of your local fellowship, where God has led you in this way?

2   Certain infallible signs of the activity of God have been mentioned. Using these indicators, do you think God is working in the life of someone you know? If so, what can you do to join God in what He is doing?

29 - Jonah Obeys (Jonah 3:3)

Jonah obeyed the word of the Lord and went to Nineveh.

Jonah 3:3a, NIV

The whole of the trauma and suffering of the previous two chapters has been brought about by four words, *But Jonah ran away*[269]. The rest of the book, and the amazing work of salvation amongst the Ninevites, all flow directly from two words - *Jonah obeyed*.

Jonah's obedience was costly for him. To get to Nineveh he had to undertake a 600 mile (870 km) overland journey. This would have taken him weeks, if not months. We also need to remember Jonah's likely physical and psychological state, after his near-death experience. For someone who had just been through all that Jonah has experienced, it was a tough challenge. However, Jonah obeyed and went to Nineveh, the city to which God had sent him.

In the first part of our story we have seen that disobedience is costly. Now we see that obedience is costly too. Jonah has embarked on a long and difficult journey, leaving behind family, friends and homeland. He is being sent to the capital city of a hostile nation, a notoriously violent and bloodthirsty people.

The great difference between obedience and disobedience is not so much in the experience that they lead us to (they can both be unpleasant) but in their results. Jonah's disobedience led to;

- A breakdown in his relationship with God.
- His being side-lined from involvement in God's activity.
- Jonah and those around in him being put in mortal danger.
- Serious financial loss for many people.

Jonah's obedience, though also costly, will lead to;

- A greater revelation of the character and the ways of God.
- To a deepening in Jonah's relationship with God.
- To an incredible involvement in the work of God.
- To the transformation of an entire city.

So the question is not so much whether or not we are willing to accept discomfort, but rather *do we want our pain to be profitable?*

---

[269] Jonah 1:3 NIV

Questions for Reflection and Discussion

1   Are you committed to costly obedience in order that the projects of God might be advanced?

2   Are there any areas of your life where you need to make changes; are there priorities that need to be changed, situations that need to be addressed, things that need to be done?

30 - Forty More Days (Jonah 3:4b)

Forty more days and Nineveh will be overthrown.

Jonah 3:4b NIV

So Jonah makes it! The long treacherous journey is over – he arrives in Nineveh and begins to preach his message of impending doom.

We need to remember that prophetic proclamation was part and parcel of everyday life in the ancient world. Prophets, seers and magicians were present in all areas of national life. Wherever treaties were being negotiated, policies set, the future planned; recourse was always made to the gods; which in turn meant the involvement of prophets[270].

Some prophets were itinerant, going from place to place as they prophesied. This was such a normal occurrence that a certain protocol had been developed and had to be followed. Any visiting prophet would first present himself to the city officials at the entrance to the city, or at a checkpoint along the main highway leading to the city. His credentials would be investigated and a decision made. Was this prophet to be welcomed? If so, how, and by whom?

Jonah would certainly have had to follow this protocol. Given the exceptional nature of his story, it is highly likely that advance word of him would have reached Nineveh long before his actual arrival, and this may help to explain the rapid acceptance of his message and the peoples' immediate response.

What kind of a city was Nineveh? We are told later that it had 120,000 *'people who cannot tell their right hand from their left'*. This could be interpreted to be simply a statement of the spiritual blindness of the entire population of 120,000. But generally speaking, in Semitic convention this phrase indicates children who are not yet of an age to be morally responsible,

...human beings, not knowing the difference of right and left, therefore children of the tenderest age, who as yet have done no wrong,[271]

It is there stated to have contained 120,000 persons who "could not discern between their right hand and their left,"—a figurative expression usually understood of young children. As these are, in any place, commonly reckoned to form one-fifth of the population, Nineveh must have contained 600,000 inhabitants.[272]

---

[270] Wiseman D.J. *ibid.*, p43f
[271] Von Orelli C. *ibid.*, p181
[272] Anonymous *The Buried City of the East – Nineveh*, London : National Illustrated Library, 1851, p29

This seems to fit with archaeological evidence for the size of the administrative district comprising Nineveh, Rehoboth Ir, Calah and Resen[273].

We are also told that it took three days to visit the city. It is not clear if this refers to the actual time needed to walk around the city itself or the larger administrative area. The total circumference of this administrative area was around 60 miles (96 km). In Jonah's time, a day's journey was thought to be 20 miles (32 km). So this would agree with the 'three days' journey description of its size.

Alternatively, three days could be a description of the protocol for prophetic proclamation. This would indicate that a day was required for the presenting of credentials and their verification, a day to accomplish one's business, and then a day to take one's leave.

Regardless of the choice one makes, it is clear that Nineveh was a great city and a significant population centre. In 612 B.C. Nineveh was destroyed and was subsequently lost from sight for almost 2,500 years. This disappearance caused many to doubt the Bible's accuracy on this point. How could such an enormous city disappear so completely, leaving not the slightest trace? It seemed improbable, and so the Bible was considered unreliable.

However, in the 1840's, a British archaeologist, Sir Austen Henry Layard, was excavating around Mosul in Northern Iraq and discovered Nineveh[274]. The size of the city he discovered corresponded exactly with the Biblical data, making Nineveh the largest city in the world at that time.

So Jonah arrives at this immense city of Nineveh, the world power centre of its day, and begins to speak his message. It is interesting to note what Jonah's message **did not** contain. There is neither any strident presentation by Jonah of his prophetic 'credentials', nor any explanation of who *Yahweh* is – His character, His nature, His past revelation to the Jews. There is neither any statement of the central Jewish belief that there is no god but *Yahweh*.

In fact, Jonah's message is rather ambiguous. In both Hebrew and Assyrian the word translated 'overthrown' could equally be translated 'have a change of heart'[275]. So as far as the Ninevites were concerned, Jonah just tells them that in 40 days something major is going to happen. Exactly, what form this event will take is not made clear. There is therefore an inherent possibility that the die has not yet been cast – there is a period of decision before the final outcome is set.

---

[273] See Genesis 10:11f
[274] See Layard A.H. *Nineveh and its Remains (2 vols.)*, London: Routledge and Kegan, 1970 (1849)
[275] Stuart D. *ibid.*, p489

In fact we see that this is often a characteristic of God's dealings with mankind,

If at any time I announce that a nation or kingdom is to be uprooted, torn down and destroyed, and if that nation I warned repents of its evil, then I will relent and not inflict on it the disaster I had planned. And if at another time I announce that a nation or kingdom is to be built up and planted, and if it does evil in my sight and does not obey me, then I will reconsider the good I had intended to do for it.[276]

It is interesting to compare Jonah's message to the Ninevites with the message that Daniel delivered to another pagan king;

Renounce your sins by doing what is right,
and your wickedness by being kind to the oppressed.
It may be then that your prosperity will continue[277]

Again, there is no detailed critique of pagan religion, nor any presentation of the central elements of the Jewish faith. God's first concern is with the poor and the oppressed – something we see not only here but throughout scripture.

Religion that God our Father accepts as pure and faultless is this:
to look after orphans and widows in their distress
and to keep oneself from being polluted by the world.[278]

Jonah's message to the Ninevites was a simple, stark statement - 40 days and the city would be turned upside down – whatever that might mean.

But why 40 days?

The number 40 appears very often in scripture. There is a clue to its significance in the practices of ancient Egypt. The Bible tells us that the mummification process for Joseph's body took 40 days[279]. In Egyptian culture this time period came to be seen as the time during which the soul was separated from the body. And, by extension, the period during which it was determined whether or not a deceased person might enter the gates of eternity.

This Egyptian understanding seems to have spread widely and become a Semitic convention. Its meaning gradually developed to that of a period of transition, a time during which one's future destiny was settled.

---

[276] Jeremiah 18:7-10, NIV
[277] Daniel 4:24b, NIV
[278] James 1:27 NIV, see also Exodus 23:6, 9 ; Leviticus 19:9-10, 33-34; Deuteronomy 14:28, 15:3-15, 24:14-15; Isaiah 3:14-15; 10:1-4; Psalm 82:1-4; Proverbs 14:31, 17:5, 19:17, 21:13, 22:9, 28:27
[279] Genesis 50:2f

Thus forty here probably takes on the sense of the duration from the going out of one condition until the entry into another; it seems often to end with some sort of a conversion ... And so Nineveh has forty days to exit its condition of sinfulness and to enter a condition of salvation from God's punishment [280]

There are two groups of 40 periods in the Bible. The first are times of testing, where God gives people time to repent. The second group are times when faith is needed in order to recognise something that is hidden.

---

[280] Burrows D.P. *ibid.*, p99f

Times of Testing (Time to Repent)	Times of Faith (God's Kingdom is Established, but in a Hidden Way)
The Flood - The rain fell for 40 days and 40 nights. (Genesis 7:12)	The Flood – In the 40 days after the rain ends, Noah attempts to find out the state of the earth (Genesis 8:6)
Moses - After murdering an Egyptian Moses fled and spent 40 years as a shepherd in Midian. (Acts 7:30)	Moses - When the Covenant with God was confirmed, Moses spent 40 days in the presence of God on Mount Sinai. During this time he was supernaturally sustained (Exodus 24:18)
The Promised Land - 40 years of desert wandering is imposed on the people of Israel, following their refusal to trust God and enter the land. During this time they are supernaturally sustained. (Numbers 14:34f)	The Promised Land – The spies took 40 days to look over the land that God had promised to give to his people (Numbers chapters 13 and 14)
Elijah's Flight - Fleeing Jezebel, and fearing for his life, Elijah undertook a supernaturally sustained, 40 day journey to Horeb, the Mountain of God. (1 Kings 19)	David and Solomon - Both these kings, (whose reigns are prophetic of the reign of the coming Messiah), reigned for 40 years. (1 Kings 2:10f; 11:42)
The Temptation of Jesus - Jesus spent 40 days fasting and praying and being tempted by the Devil prior to beginning his ministry. He is supernaturally sustained during this time. (Matthew 4)	The Resurrection and the Ascension - For 40 days after his resurrection Jesus continues to appear to the disciples, then he ascends into heaven. (Acts 1:3)

Table 2 - 40 day periods in the Bible

The Times of Testing-
We mustn't forget that in these 40 – day periods of testing there was **always** a favourable outcome;

> *Noah is saved, Moses becomes leader of God's people, Israel enters Palestine, Elijah returns when he learns that there are seven thousand men who have not bowed the knee to Baal, Jesus overcomes temptation and angels minister to him. We know of no instance where the forty days or years do not lead to salvation.*[281]

This is an amazing testimony to God's grace and to His ability to transform human lives. Anytime we experience these faith-stretching experiences, we can be sure that God has the ability to bring things to a positive conclusion.

The Times of Faith-
The second series of 40 - day periods are times when people are challenged to live by faith and not by sight.

> *It is the time when God's Kingdom is set up on earth in a way which is hidden but beyond dispute for those who have eyes to see. It is the time of a new humanity with Noah, obedient to the Lord's will. It is the time of God's taking possession of his people by giving them the laws on Sinai. It is the time of the hidden and symbolical but nonetheless true and certain possession of the land of Canaan by the envoys of God. It is the time of the prophetic affirmation of the reign of Jesus Christ in David and Solomon; these two figures of Jesus Christ both reveal and conceal his reality. Finally, it is the time of the presence on earth of the glorious and risen body of the Lord who will return in this body to establish his reign*[282]

During such times the authority, rule and reign of God can seem to be a figment of our imagination. In times like these the people of God have to face the challenge to be guided by faith and not by sight[283].

Questions for Reflection and Discussion

1   Do you remember **times of testing**, when God was inviting you to repent, or **times of faith**, when you were challenged to live by what you knew to be true, rather than trust the evidence of your own eyes?

2   Reflect on the amazing truth that the Bible shows every time God puts his people through a **time of testing** it ends positively. Why is this? What effect should this truth have on us?

---

[281] Jacques Ellul, *ibid.*, p90f
[282] Jacques Ellul, *ibid.*, p91f
[283] 2 Corinthians 5:7 NIV

31 - A City Turns to God (Jonah 3:4-5)

On the first day, Jonah started into the city.
He proclaimed: "Forty more days and Nineveh will be overturned."
The Ninevites believed God.
They declared a fast, and all of them, from the greatest to the least, put on sackcloth.

Jonah 3:4-5, NIV

For some people the most amazing thing in the story of Jonah is his being swallowed by a monster fish and surviving! Others would say that the most incredible event in the book is the response of the Ninevites, related in the verses above. We have here nothing less than a description of the most effective evangelistic activity in the whole of scripture. Nothing else even comes close!

Even Jesus never had such a massive response to His ministry. The largest group Jesus ever preached to was the crowd of 5,000 thousand men (thus a total of approximately 10,000 - 15,000 people)[284]. At this event Jesus preached to them all day. In fact it got so late that the disciples started to worry that the people wouldn't have time to get home before nightfall; a serious situation that provoked the miracle of the feeding of the 5,000. But even after Jesus had preached all day and then performed an amazing miracle, it is clear that only a small fraction of the crowd became genuine disciples.

In the New Testament Church the most successful evangelistic event is the preaching of St Peter on the Day of Pentecost. Here, following the miracle of the Apostles speaking in foreign languages, St Peter preaches a fairly long sermon and around 3,000 people are saved[285].

We can see that these two events are as nothing in comparison with Jonah, who gives an eight word sermon (only 5 words in Hebrew!) and a city of possibly 600,000 comes to repentance! This is by far and away the most incredible evangelistic success in the whole of Church history!

Other factors make the success of this evangelistic effort even more incredible;

- The preacher doesn't want to preach. Jonah is forced to go to Nineveh against his will.
- The preacher despises his audience. Jonah and his people have suffered at the hands of the brutal Assyrian military machine; he is hardly likely to have feelings of warmth and compassion towards them.

---

[284] Mark 6:30-44
[285] Acts 2:14-41

147

- Jonah's hearers are hostile to the Jewish nation. They have dominated them and successfully held them in subjection over many years.
- Jonah's hearers are violent, sadistic people who delight in cruelty and torture.
- Jonah's hearers are not even monotheistic. They are a polytheistic people who practice idolatry, witchcraft and all kinds of superstitious practices.
- The message that Jonah is told to preach is not even clear. He doesn't even mention whether there is a possibility of avoiding the coming judgement. Jonah just tells them that in forty days the city of Nineveh will be 'overturned'.

It would be hard to design a scenario for evangelism that was less likely to succeed than this!

When God sent Moses to speak to pagan Pharaoh, He gave him the power to perform certain miraculous signs in order to convince Pharaoh that God had sent him. Moses could turn his staff into a snake and then back again, he could make his hand leprous and then restore it, he could also turn water into blood[286].

Jonah, however, has no such impressive acts to perform.

Jonah offered Nineveh no sign but himself[287]

So what was it that so convinced the Ninevites that they believed Jonah's message? A message that told them that a God they didn't know about and didn't worship was, for some unspecified reason, going to punish them? We will explore this further in our next sessions.

Questions for Reflection and Discussion

1   Reflect on your own experience of evangelism. What unforeseen successes and unexpected disappointments have your experienced? What conclusions can you draw from this?

2   Why do you think that God did not give Jonah the ability to do miracles in order to convince the Ninevites?

---

[286] Exodus 4:1-9
[287] Cary P. *ibid.*, p80

32 - God's Unseen Preparation (Jonah 3:5)

The Ninevites believed God. A fast was proclaimed,
and all of them, from the greatest to the least, put on sackcloth.

Jonah 3:5, NIV

From the information presented to us in the book of Jonah, there is nothing that can explain Jonah's astonishing success. From a purely rational perspective Jonah's mission seems doomed to failure. It just can't be successful.

However, some background information gives us clues which make Jonah's success far more understandable. These factors reveal a God who has been at work preparing not only Jonah, but Nineveh too. Certain elements in both ancient Assyrian culture and in Nineveh's recent history have prepared them to receive Jonah and his message. All this has been done by God without Jonah's knowledge and helps to explain why his mission was so spectacularly successful.

Factor 1 - Recent History - Signs in the Sky

In the introduction to our study, we saw that if Jonah was the historical figure identified in 2 Kings 14, then it was likely that he came to Nineveh around 760 to 750 B.C.[288].

We know that around this time (784-745 B.C.), and in particular during the reign of *Asher-Dan* III (771-754 B.C.), the Assyrian empire was at a low ebb. Things would turn around after the ascension to the throne of *Tiglath-Pilezer* III in 745 B.C., but for the moment Assyria was struggling. They were militarily and economically weakened and only just managing to repulse the tribes on their mountainous border.

As a result of this weakened status, the kings of Assyria undertook few military expeditions during this period, and the ones they did attempt were often unsuccessful.

This historical reality is shown by the revolt of the country of *Namri* and the city of *Gozan* at this time. Even towns in the immediate vicinity of Nineveh were intermittently in revolt against it. In fact, the king's sovereignty was limited to little more than a day's journey from the capital[289], and this may be the reason that the ruler of Nineveh is called 'King of Nineveh' and not 'King of Assyria'. His currently fragile grip on power is also shown by the fact that the decree he

---

[288] Limburg J., *ibid.*, p28
[289] Kennedy, *ibid.*, p18

makes to the people is not only in his own name, but is also made in 'the name of his nobles'[290].

As well as these military difficulties, Assyria had also experienced a total solar eclipse in the year 763 B.C. Such events were always seen as an augur of catastrophe and disaster. Just how seriously such events were taken is made clear from 70 or so clay tablets which were discovered at Nineveh and which contain amongst them a series called *Enuma Anu Enlil*[291]. Along with astronomical records of celestial events, these tablets also record the astrological predictions about what sort of events were thought to follow an eclipse.

> *...the king will be deposed and killed and a worthless fellow will seize the throne; the king will die, rain from heaven will flood the land. There will be famine; a deity will strike the king and fire consume the land; the city walls will be destroyed*[292]

Indeed, Wiseman cites evidence from Babylonia that these predictions were taken with such seriousness, that kings would even appoint a substitute king until the danger period was over[293].

> *A total eclipse is to be a time of solemn fasting when the king hands over the throne to a substitute king (of Nineveh) until the danger passes*[294]

In the recent history of Nineveh, the validity of these beliefs would have seemed to have been confirmed by the fact that several years of flooding and famine had followed the solar eclipse of 763 B.C.

To make matters worse, probably in association with the flooding and famine, plague fell upon the area, either continually or recurrently, in the period 765-756 B.C.[295]

To further complicate the social climate in Nineveh there had recently been a significant and rather revolutionary religious upheaval. *Adad-Nirari* III (811-783 B.C.) seeking to bring the Babylonian and the Assyrian peoples together in a cohesive empire, made an attempt to harmonise the religions of the two peoples. He forbade the worship of the many new gods that the Assyrians had

---

[290] Lawrence P.J.N. *Assyrian Nobles and the Book of Jonah*, Tyndale Bulletin, No.37, 1986, p130.
[291] A new book is currently in preparation regarding these solar eclipse tablets Rochberg F. *The Solar Eclipse Tablets of Enuma Anu Enlil : Samas Tablets 31-36*, Leiden: NINO
[292] Cited in Wiseman D.J. *ibid.*, p46
[293] *ibid.*, p47
[294] *ibid.*
[295] Stuart D. *ibid.*, p492

introduced into the Babylonian pantheon and established the worship of one god, *Nabu,* as the state religion. Rogers notes,

> *The policy, strange as it was, met with a certain success,*
> *for Babylonia disappears almost wholly for a long time as a separate state*
> *and Assyria alone finds mention.*[296]

So in addition to economic, health and political crises, there was also a religious crisis, or at least a movement of deep religious questioning and confusion.

As contemporary Westerners, when we encounter difficulties – be they social, economic or political – they are for us, first and foremost, technical problems. It is therefore to science and technology that we look for solutions.

But this is a very recent change in human outlook. Throughout history, up until the 17th and 18th centuries, **every** problem was primarily a **religious** problem. It was the gods who controlled everything. When crops failed, people turned to the gods. When illness struck, they turned to gods. When violence broke out internally or externally, they turned to the gods. So every problem they experienced was, first and foremost, a religious problem.

Thus for the Ninevites, their difficulties would be understood as symptoms of a religious problem. Their sacrifices are no longer working. Their prayers are not being answered. Their priests seem to have lost their influence over the gods. How can this be understood?

Their empire was on the decline, they were no longer the uncontested super-power of the day. They had seen a powerful omen of doom in the sky - a full solar eclipse. Several years of bad weather had followed, leading to flooding and famine. Their king had forbidden the worship of most of their gods and imposed a state cult of the god *Nabu.* The people have been crying out to this god to help them, but to no avail. They were no doubt starting to ask themselves searching existential and theological questions. Does our god hear? Can he answer? Is he real?

Factor 2 - Felt Need – A god who can control the weather

The Ninevites' recent history had made them ask questions about the reality and power of their gods. They have been suffering for an extended period due to the vagaries of the climate. The natural order seems to be in chaos, and their gods appear to be powerless to re-establish balance.

---

[296] Rogers R.W. *A History of Babylonia and Assyria – volume II*, New York: Eaton and Mains, 1900, p25f.

Into this situation comes Jonah, with a story of a God who sends storms and quiets storms at will; a God who simply uses the weather as a tool to accomplish His purposes. Here is a God who is powerful in the area where they most need help. Here they are, suffering from flooding and famine, and Jonah tells them about a God who can control the weather.

Factor 3 - Cultural Resonance
A - The God Who Uses a Fish
From a religious perspective, Jonah's testimony was specifically designed to get the people of Nineveh's attention. Their most ancient beliefs, dating from around 2000 B.C., concerned *Anu, Enlil* and *Ea,*

> *...the triad of divine powers who precede the creation of the active gods.*
> *They stand as it were above and behind "the great gods"*[297]

Of these three, *Ea* was considered to have been the creator of man[298].

Interestingly, with regard to Jonah, *Ea*

> *...is the god of the waters ... Pictured as half-man, half-fish,*
> *he is shar Apsi the 'King of the Watery Deep'*[299]

In the following millennia these early beliefs developed into a polytheistic pantheon of gods and goddesses, who - in contrast to the original triad - were active in human history and accessible to man.

The Assyrians worshipped *Dagon*, a god often represented symbolically as having the body of a man and the head of a fish. They also worshipped *Ishtar*, who was also often represented as a fish.

Ishtar was also known as *Ninua* and the city of Nineveh was named after her. In Assyrian cuneiform script the name of *Ishtar*, or *Nina*, is represented by the sign of a fish and the name of Nineveh was this symbol of *Nina* within an enclosure[300].

---

[297] Jastrow M. Aspects of Religious Belief and Practice in Bablylonia and Assyria, New York : G.P. Putnam, 1911, p247
[298] Spence L. *Myths of Babylonia and Assyria*, New York : Frederick A. Stokes Co., 1916, p86
[299] Jastrow M. *ibid.*, p87
[300] See Wiseman D. J., 'Nineveh' in Douglas J. D. (ed.) *The Illustrated Bible Dictionary - Part 2*, Leicester: IVP, 1980, p1089. See also Speiser E. A., 'Nineveh' in Buttrick G. A. (ed.) *The Interpreter's Dictionary of the Bible – Vol. 3*, New York: Abingdon Press, 1962, pp551-553

The very name Nineveh, according to popular etymology, means "place of the fish", and the cuneiform pictogram for the city shows Nina, representing an enclosure with a fish inside[301]

The development of this cuneiform is from an more ancient hieroglyph,

Figure 4 - Hieroglyph for Nineveh[302]

...which is clearly the outline of a two-storied building, with a fish on the lower floor.[303]

The cuneiform logographic development is derived from a combination of two elements,

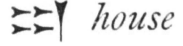 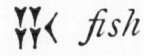

Figure 5 - Cuneiform Components of Nineveh

These two elements are combined to give the cuneiform for Nineveh, which has the meaning, 'The House of the Fish'[304]

---

[301] Feldman LH, *Studies in Josephus' Rewritten Bible*, Leiden: Koninklÿke Brill NV, 1998, p412.
[302] Image from Ball C.J. 'Babylonian Hieroglyph's in Anonymous *Proceedings of the Society of Biblical Archaeology Vol. XX, Twenty-eighth session, January-December 1898*, London : Society of Biblical Archaeology, 1898, p9
[303] ibid.
[304] *ibid.*, p10

Figure 6 - Cuneiform for Nineveh 'The House of the Fish'[305]

More recent studies also confirm this derivation,

Figure 7 - Logogram for Nineveh[306]

The enclosure has also been understood as symbolising the uterus of the goddess Nina / Ishtar. If this is the case, then Jonah being rescued from the 'womb' of the great fish has a specific resonance[307]. He could be thought of as the 'offspring' of Nina.

The fact of Nineveh being known as the 'House of the Fish' or 'fish-town' is strong evidence that the worship of the fish-god was significant.[308]. Archaeological evidence supports this popularity of this cult at Nineveh,

Nineveh, where the discovered sculptures tell that the fish-god must have had many followers.[309]

The following image, witnesses to the presence of this cult in Nineveh. It may either represent the fish-god or, perhaps more likely, shows one of the cultic-priests in his piscine vestments.

---

[305] *ibid.,* p9

[306] Miller D.B. & Shipp R.M. *An Akkadian Handbook,* Winona Lake: Eisenbrauns, 1996, p95 (Sign 200).

[307] Wiseman D.J. *ibid.,* p35

[308] Merrill E.H. *The Sign of Jonah,* Journal of the Evangelical Theological Society, vol. 23, no. 1, March 1980, pp27.

[309] Simpson W. *The Jonah Legend,* London : Grant Richards, 1899, p137

Figure 8 - A Priest of the Fish-God[310]

Given, the meaning of the name Nineveh and the importance of the fish-cult it is easy to imagine the interest that would be aroused when Jonah recounts his story. A story in which he speaks about how *Yahweh* used a monstrous fish to serve his purposes. Straight away his story has religious connotations for them.

Shemesh points out the irony this creates in the Jonah story,

> *Jonah tries to flee in the opposite direction, to get as far as possible from 'fish-city' and avoid performing his mission. But the Lord intervenes and sees to it that he ends up inside a fish all the same*[311]

---
[310]   Maspero G. (tr. McLure M.L.) History of Egypt Chaldea, Syria, Babylonia and Assyria – Volume III, London: Grolier Society, 1903-1906, p17
[311]   Shemesh Y. And Many Beasts (Jonah 4 :11) : The Function and Status of Animals in the

So after hearing Jonah's story, the Ninevites would know that whoever this *Yahweh* is, if He uses a monstrous fish to do His bidding, then He is probably more powerful than their fish goddess *Nina*.

B – The myth of Oannes

We can see God that shows an incredible degree of care in preparing the Ninevites to hear Jonah's story and also in preparing Jonah to be a powerful witness to them. God goes to the trouble of arranging to send Jonah to Fish-City by fish!

However, there is an even more amazing cultural preparation that we discover in the mythology of the Assyrians. In 273 B.C., *Berossus*, a Babylonian priest recorded the mythological history of Babylonia and her origins. These tales were probably first told around two or three millennia BC, although the versions *Berossus* cites seem to date from the 7th century B.C.[312]

Sadly, this work is now lost to us and only survives in fragments cited by other ancient authors. What we find in these fragments is of great interest for us and our study of Jonah.

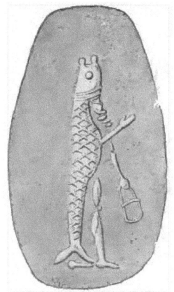

Figure 9 - Oannes[313]

Book of Jonah, The Journal of Hebrew Scriptures, Vol. 10, Art. 6, 2010, p12
[312] Maspero G. *ibid.*, p18
[313] *ibid.*, p3

Berossus' writing contains a story about *'Oannes'*. In this myth *'Oannes'* comes out of the sea. He has 'the shape of a fish blended with that of a man'[314]. He is what is generally classed as a 'culture god'[315]. Spence calls him, *'The Babylonian god of wisdom'*[316]

This *Oannes* instructs the primitive people of Chaldea. Through his teaching they become civilised and begin to develop learning and culture,

> *...he gave them insight into letters and sciences, and arts of every kind.*
> *He taught them to construct cities, to found temples, to compile laws, and*
> *explained to them the principles of geometrical knowledge.*
> *He made them distinguish the seeds of the earth,*
> *and shewed them how to collect the fruits;*
> *in short, he instructed them in everything which could tend to soften manners*
> *and humanize their lives* [317]

As a result, he has been named 'the god of pure life'[318]. In fact it is considered likely that the figure *Oannes* is none other than the biblical character Noah, and that Noah's saving of mankind through the waters of the flood has been corrupted into the idea of a mythical fish-man[319].

Given that *Oannes* and Jonah are the same word in Assyrian[320], we can see how Jonah and his story would immediately have had a striking significance for the Ninivites. Jonah 'comes out of the sea', he has lived inside 'the body of a fish', he tells them he has 'something to teach them' which comes from God. All of which are perfectly designed to resonate with a people who know and believe the story of *Oannes* !

And, as Merrill notes,

> *...since Luke specifies that Jonah was a sign to Nineveh that experience in the fish*
> *must have been communicated to the Assyrian capital and have become to the*
> *Ninevites a sign that Jonah was a divine messenger. Such a sign would be*

---

[314] Cory I.P. 'Berossus from Apollodorus', *Ancient Fragments*, Charleston: Bibliobazaar, 2008, (1832), p60
[315] Simpson W. *ibid.*, p129
[316] Spence L. *ibid.*, p25
[317] Cory I.P. *ibid.*, p56
[318] Sayce A. Hibbert Lectures 1887 : Lectures on the Origin and Growth of Religion, London : Williams and Norgate, 1898, p392
[319] *ibid.*, p15
[320] Simpson W. *ibid.*, p160f

particularly convincing to a people whose aetiology taught them that their city had been founded by a fish-god (Oannes).[321]

Factor 4 - The Right Messenger - A Prepared Prophet:

Jonah himself is designed to attract attention. He probably looks like the living dead, having spent 3 days inside the belly of the fish. Whilst it is possible that God miraculously saved him from harm (as he saved Daniel and his friends in the story about the fiery furnace[322]); it is equally possible that Jonah would have been scarred for life, (as Jacob was, following his wrestling with God or an angel[323]).

It may well be that Jonah's experience of deliverance from the great fish is what makes the Ninevites believe his message. Certainly there is a real sense in which Jonah **is** the message.

Jonah's own testimony holds out the hope that God's grace and mercy are accessible. If God's grace could reach out and save a rebellious prophet inside a sea-monster at the bottom of the ocean, then that same grace can reach even the most rebellious people, should they repent[324].

St Paul also had a body that was scarred and marked. In his case it was following the path of obedience, rather than disobedience, that led to these 'battle scars',

Finally, let no-one cause me trouble, for I bear on my body the marks of Jesus.[325]

Both Jonah and St Paul's stories show that God can use our scarred and broken bodies as an authenticating sign for our message.

But there is another sense in which Jonah **is** Nineveh. God has prepared Jonah by taking him step by step through exactly the same journey the people of Nineveh will have to take. Jonah's identification with Nineveh is reinforced by the fact that in Hebrew, the two names are comprised of the same letters[326].

---

[321] Merrill E.H. *ibid.*, pp29f

[322] Daniel 3

[323] Genesis 32, 2 Corinthians 11:24

[324] Jeremais J., Iwnas in *Theological Dictionary of the New Testament – vol. 3*, Grand Rapids : W.B. Eerdmans, 1964, pp406-410. See also Merrill E.H. *ibid.*, pp23-30

[325] Galatians 6:17 NIV

[326] Glardon T. *Ces Crises Qui Nous Font Naître*, Génève : Labor et Fides, 2009, p19

Jonah   Nineveh

Figure 10 - Hebrew for Jonah and Nineveh

We can see in the following table the similarities between Jonah himself and the people of Nineveh.

Jonah has been wilfully disobedient to God.	Nineveh is living in disobedience to God.
Jonah came under God's condemnation and chastening.	Nineveh is threatened with destruction by God.
Jonah repented.	Nineveh fasts and repents.
Jonah was saved by grace.	Nineveh is pardoned by grace.

Table 3 - Parallels between Jonah and Nineveh

Jonah and his story are perfectly designed to catch the Ninevites' attention. He has been in the same situation as them but he has experienced God's gracious rescue and stands before them safe and sound. In the wisdom and power of God, Jonah's rebellion has not only failed to thwart God's plans, but actually been the means of preparing Jonah for his mission and is the basis of its success!

In conclusion we can say that the above four factors have made the people of Nineveh receptive to Jonah and his message. Jonah may only have preached an eight word sermon, but when they asked him 'Who are you?' 'Where do you come from?' 'How did you get here?' 'Who gave you this message for us?' and 'Why did you come here?' Jonah's testimony knocked them side-ways.

If we find Jonah's story impressive, imagine the effect on the Ninevites! They are a people who worship a fish God, who were currently in dire economic straits and politically weakened, who had seen portents of disaster in the heavens, and who were undergoing deep religious confusion.

Allied to this, we have their mythological origins story about *Oannes* and the physical impact of a Jonah who is scarred and marked by his adventures. All of this worked to produce in them an incredible receptivity to Jonah's message.

This divine cultural preparation that enables a people to receive God's message is not an isolated phenomenon. The missiologist-anthropologist, Don Richardson, has identified many examples where pre-existing religious mythology has prepared pagan peoples to receive the gospel of Christ; a phenomenon Richardson has named "The Melchizedek Factor"[327]. To give a European example, there are powerful parallels between the Odin myth and the crucifixion of Christ,

> *Odin dies hanging on the World-Tree, as does Christ.*
> *Whilst on the Tree, Odin is 'wounded with a spear' as is Christ.*
> *Odin hangs for 'nine full nights', a multiple of three reflecting the three days between Christ's crucifixion and Resurrection.*
> *Odin thirsted in his agony, as did Christ (John 19:28).*
> *Odin screamed at the moment of truth,*
> *just as Christ 'cried with a loud voice' (Matthew 27:46).*
> *Above all, Odin was sacrificed to Odin, 'myself to myself'.*[328]

So strong are these parallels one might be tempted to say the Norse myth has been influenced by Christian typology, however,

> *all aspects of Odin's sacrifice listed above are far too deeply embedded in Teutonic mythology to be anything but native to Northern paganism long antedating the arrival of Christianity.*[329]

These parallels are believed to be the reason why northern Europe was converted to Christianity with amazing rapidity[330]. The historical Christ-event was seen to be a profound fulfilment of the pagan myths which had divinely foreshadowed this reality.

From our perspective, it is clear that God had been preparing the Ninevites to receive Jonah and his message for hundreds, if not thousands, of years.

---

[327] Richardson D. *Eternity in their Hearts*, Ventura : Regal Books, 1981, p32
[328] Tolstoy N. *The Quest for Merlin*, London : Hamish Hamilton, 1985, p180
[329] ibid.
[330] *ibid.*, p181

However, Jonah was ignorant of all this. He could not have possibly imagined the response he would receive from the Ninevites. He may well have expected to be killed, or at least beaten up - he certainly knew about the Assyrians and their cruelty. He also knew about their paganism. He knew about the power of the Assyrian nation in comparison to the nation of Israel. But what Jonah didn't know was that God had been preparing the ground. Jonah was going to preach perhaps the most successful sermon in the whole Bible – and all that would be needed would be eight words. But these eight words would turn around a city.

Whatever difficult situation we find ourselves in, it is always good to remember **there may be facts that we do not know**. It is always possible that God has been working in the background in a way that we aren't aware of. God seems to enjoy surprising people.

Sarah was surprised to learn that she was going to have a child in her old age - so surprised that she laughed out loud![331]

Zechariah, a humble country priest, was surprised that the lot fell to him to go place incense on the altar in the temple. He was even more surprised when he met an angel there and heard that he was going to be a father in his old age. He was even more astounded to learn that his son would be the one to prepare the people to receive the coming Messiah![332]

Our God is a God of surprises!

I will always remember a church weekend that my wife and I participated in. We had been tasked with looking after the children whilst the main sessions were taking place. To be honest, as is often the case in children's work, I felt side-lined. I felt like I was missing out and resented not being part of all that was going on. Plus we had a small baby at the time and looking after our own baby, as well as running a children's holiday club, was quite tough.

We had decided to use a holiday club workbook called 'The J Team'[333] which included the use of a catchphrase as part of the programme. Whenever the words 'The J Team' were spoken the children were encouraged to shout out, 'I wish I could be in it!'

To make our work even more challenging, we had to meet in a room next to the kitchen. So while we were trying to do some of the quieter activities with the children we would hear the cook crashing around and making noise with his

---

[331] Genesis 18:12
[332] Luke 1:8-23
[333] Graystone P. *The J Team – Holiday Club Programme*, Milton Keynes : Scripture Union, 1990

machines etc. It was hard work. We didn't enjoy it very much but we nevertheless tried to do our best.

Several weeks later, during a Sunday evening service, the pastor announced that someone was going to give a testimony. A man I recognised as the cook from the weekend stood up in front of the congregation and announced that he had recently become a Christian.

He said that during the church weekend he hadn't been to any of the meetings, as he had always been working preparing the meals. He had, however, seen and heard everything that went on in the children's club! He said that he had seen my wife and I show such love towards the children that it had changed his heart. He had listened to our talks to the children, and our simple presentation of the message of Jesus, and he had decided to become a Christian. He then looked at Sharon and I, who were sitting open-mouthed by this time! He said, I have only one thing to say, 'The J Team - I wish I could be in it!'

Incidents like that make me laugh, cry and also fill me with hope! Our God is certainly a God of surprises! Through this experience I learned that the Holy Spirit can work through 360°. Even if we tend to focus our attention on those who we have in front of us, we should never forget that God might be at work behind our back! Who knows what God might be doing through the circumstances of our lives? Who knows what fruit God will cause to grow from the often poorly sown gospel 'seed' that we haphazardly cast around? We must always have faith, and hope, and take heart that the power is in the seed, not in the sower.

Questions for Reflection and Discussion

1   How do you respond to the idea of the background preparation of God in the Ninevites culture and recent history? What implications might this have for our own obedience to the missions God might give us?

2   Have you experienced the 'background preparation of God' in your own or someone else's life? What factors did God arrange in order to strengthen our capacity to respond?

33 - A Sincere Belief (Jonah 3:5-6)

The Ninevites believed God.
A fast was proclaimed, and all of them,
from the greatest to the least, put on sackcloth.
When Jonah's warning reached the king of Nineveh, he rose from his throne,
took off his royal robes, covered himself with sackcloth and sat down in the dust.

Jonah 3:5-6, NIV

We are told that the Ninevites believed Jonah's message. They showed the genuineness of their belief by their actions - they fasted, put on sackcloth and sat in ashes. This may sound like bizarre behaviour to us, but for them it was a cultural convention which expressed deep sorrow.

Note that the whole of society participated. From the greatest of the lords to the least of the servants, they all believed Jonah's message. They all tried to do whatever they could to express their sorrow before God, in an attempt to turn away the prophesied destruction.

As I mentioned in the introduction, whilst at Bible college I was powerfully impacted by the statement, *'The scriptures you really believe are the ones you obey'*. I subsequently discovered many scriptures that, following this criteria, I didn't really believe. I might have **said** that I believed them, **intellectually** I might have held them to be true, but the reality was that these truths weren't being put into **practice** in my daily life. I then had to make a choice, to believe authentically, putting into practice what these Scriptures said, or to start to pull apart my Bible, removing the things that I didn't like.

The whole thrust of Christian discipleship is to get us to **live out** what **we say** we believe. Do we believe, as it says in the Bible, that God wants us to care for the poor, the outcasts, the prisoners, the foreigners? If we do, how are we living that out? Do we believe that our spiritual welfare is more important than our financial welfare? If so, how are we prioritising this?

There are many other scriptures Christians often manage to avoid obeying;

- Confess your sins to one another[334]
- Accept him whose faith is weak without passing judgement on disputable matters[335]
- Choose rather to be cheated by a fellow Christian, than to go to law and thus bring dishonour on the Christian gospel[336]

---

[334] James 5:16
[335] Romans 14:1

- Forgive one another as Christ has forgiven you[337]
- Give weekly to the church, proportionate to your income[338]

This is to cite just a few examples.

This 'application failure' is a serious problem for two reasons;

Firstly, it means that the model of the Christian life that we present to the watching world is flawed and inauthentic.

Secondly, as we have discovered above, disobedience takes us out of the place of blessing and usefulness in God's kingdom activity, and can lead to our chastening as we come under the curse of God.

In contrast, the Ninevites demonstrate a fully authentic response to the message of God. However, whilst the general population has received and responded to Jonah's message, the King has yet to hear of it. This is a significant moment. What will the leadership's response be?

Kings of the time enjoyed great power, prestige and privilege. They were often seen as semi-divine beings and were sometimes even worshipped by their subjects[339]. Their status was regularly reinforced by the proclamation of their achievements and victories. Everything was done to make them appear as super-human and infallible. We can imagine that it was very easy for these kings to start believing their own propaganda, to become prideful and arrogant[340].

We find here, however, a king who is as broken, confused and as much searching for an answer, as his subjects. The chaos of recent years, which has brought the nation to its knees, has also humbled and broken the king. He too is open and receptive to Jonah's message. His response, as that of his subjects, seems to be immediate. As Luther noted, this is all the more surprising given that he did not actually hear Jonah's message first-hand, he only heard a report of it![341]

It is interesting to see how the king reacts to the news he received;

---

[336] 1 Corinthians 6:1-8
[337] Colossians 3:13
[338] 1 Corinthians 16:2, Malachi 3:8ff
[339] See Daniel 6:6f
[340] See Daniel 4:28ff for an example of an eastern king full of pride and seeing himself as almost divine. In this instance, this is followed by divine judgement and a lesson in humility.
[341] Limburg J. *ibid.*, p120

He rose from his throne:
The throne was the king's seat of power. It symbolised his authority and his control over his subjects. Rising from his throne is therefore a public affirmation made by the king to show his sense of his own powerlessness to resolve this crisis. It is also a step of action. He will not remain seated and immobile but will be pro-active and take a true leader's role amongst his people.

He took off his royal robes:
These robes were a symbol of the king's grandeur and glory. His appearance set him apart from his people. The robes spoke of his wealth as well as his pomp. In taking off these robes he both humbles himself and expresses his solidarity with his people; perhaps even admitting that it is under his leadership his people have come to the brink of this disaster.

He covered himself with sackcloth:
Not only did he choose to deprive himself of his grandeur and pomp, he also expressed his grief at the situation by choosing to suffer physical discomfort before God. He enters into a period of ascetic discipline – voluntary self-denial and discomfort entered into for religious reasons. By this act he expresses to God the seriousness of his sorrow and repentance. Dom Jean de Monléon notes,

> *'What the royal purple couldn't do, sackcloth achieved;*
> *where the crown failed, ashes succeeded'*[342]

He sat down in the dust:
Again, he goes further than simple self-denial of luxury, he undertakes an even more significant act of humility and contrition before God. He hereby gives spiritual leadership to his people. To those, who were not sure how they should respond to Jonah's message, he shows the way.

The genuineness of our sorrow for sin, and the authenticity of our concern for others, should be seen in our lives as well as heard in our words. God's judgement is hanging over the city of Nineveh, and the king shows graphically his concern for his city and its population. He is a leader who loves his people.

We see that the first step towards reconciliation with God is humility. The Bible shows us that pride is at the root of nearly all sin. It was the cause of the fall of the angels[343] and it was the cause of the fall of man[344]. It is for this reason that God is so harsh with it,

---

[342] de Monléon J. Dom *ibid.*, p101 (my translation)
[343] See Isaiah 14:12-15
[344] See Genesis 3:5f

God opposes the proud but gives grace to the humble [345].

In Jonah's story, it was only when he owned up to the folly of following his own thoughts, the empty idols of his own imagining, that his restoration began[346].

The key attitudinal change that we need to pray for, both for others and for ourselves, is humility before God. Jesus expressed this in a very clear way;

> *... whoever exalts himself will be humbled,*
> *and whoever humbles himself will be exalted* [347]

Jesus gave us the ultimate example of this in His incarnation and His death on the cross, emptying Himself of His divine glory and becoming both a sacrifice and a servant[348].

As we have seen the Gentile sailors act in an irreproachable manner, so also the king of Nineveh does all that anyone could ask of him. He expresses his own penitence and calls for the whole city to do the same.

Questions for Reflection and Discussion

1   How do you react to the statement, 'The only Scriptures that you really believe are the ones you obey?' In the light of this, what Scriptures are you struggling to believe?

2   We see, in the king's response, an example of great leadership that would ultimately save his people from disaster. Have you experienced great leadership in your life? Have you ever been a leader in some context? If so, how was that experience for you, were you a good leader?

---

[345] James 4:6, see also Proverbs 3:34 and 1 Peter 5:5
[346] See Jonah 2:8
[347] See Matthew 23:12, Luke 14:11
[348] See Philippians 2:6-11

34 – Holistic Repentance (Jonah 3:7-9)

This is the proclamation he issued in Nineveh:
'By the decree of the king and his nobles:
Do not let people or animals, herds or flocks, taste anything; do not let them eat or
drink. But let people and animals be covered with sackcloth. Let everyone call
urgently on God. Let them give up their evil ways and their violence.
Who knows? God may yet relent and with compassion turn from his fierce anger
so that we will not perish.'

Jonah 3:7-9, NIV

The king's command to repent includes the domestic animals. Such was to be the intensity of this corporate repentance and intercession, that even the animals were called to fast and pray, and to be clothed in sackcloth!

The Talmud explains the mechanics of this event,

Concerning the Ninevites it is written [Jonah 3:8]:
"But let man and beast be covered with sackcloth."
How was it done?
They separated the suckling animals from their mothers and said:
"Sovereign of the Universe! If Thou wilt not have mercy upon us,
we will not have mercy upon them."[349]

Imagine the scene! The young, suckling animals crying out for their mothers and the mothers crying out for their young. In the work attributed to Rabbi Eliezer the Great, it is stated that this process was not just confined to the domestic animals, but extended to the human population too,

What did they do ? The men were on one side, and the women on the other, and
their children were by themselves ; all the clean animals were on one side, and their
offspring were by themselves. The infants saw the breasts of their mothers, (and
they wished) to have suck, and they wept. The mothers saw their children, (and
they wished) to give them suck. By the merit of 4,123 children more than twelve
hundred thousand men (were saved)[350]

Mixed together, the cries of the animals and of the people rise towards God.

---

[349] Rodkinson M.L. (ed. and tr.) *The Babylonian Talmud Vol. 1-10,* Second Ed., Boston: Boston New Talmud Publishing Company 1918 [1903], p2174
[350] Friedlander G. *ibid.,* p342f

A Jewish legend states that the Ninevites held their infants heavenward, and with streaming tears, cried to God to hear their prayers for the sake of their innocent babes[351].

The inclusion of domestic animals in the activity of prayer might seem very strange to us. In our culture we tend not to see animals as 'spiritual beings', we view them largely as soul-less and so without spiritual significance. This was not the view of the Ninevites, neither is it the view of the Bible. We will read later that God expresses a specific concern for the animals of Nineveh[352].

Animals were often included in the communal actions of ancient peoples. Citing *Herodotus* (Histories 9.24), Ellison reminds us that the Persians, after the death of *Masistius*,

> *...shaved their heads, cut the manes of their horses and mules* [353]

For ancient man, the link between humans and the animal kingdom was not merely biological, or utilitarian, but also spiritual. If we look closely at the Bible, we note that God has an on-going interest in the animal kingdom. When God makes his covenant with Noah after the flood, it was a covenant not only with the humans but also with the animals;

> *Everything that lives and moves about will be food for you.*
> *Just as I gave you the green plants, I now give you everything.*
> *'But you must not eat meat that has its lifeblood still in it. And for your lifeblood I will surely demand an accounting.* **I will demand an accounting from every animal.** *And from each human being, too, I will demand an accounting for the life of another human being.*
> *'Whoever sheds human blood, by humans shall their blood be shed;*
> *for in the image of God has God made mankind.*
> *As for you, be fruitful and increase in number;*
> *multiply on the earth and increase upon it.'*
> *Then God said to Noah and to his sons with him: 'I now establish my covenant with you and with your descendants after you and with every living creature that was with you – the birds, the livestock and all the wild animals, all those that came out of the ark with you – every living creature on earth. I establish my covenant with you: never again will all life be destroyed by the waters of a flood; never again will there be a flood to destroy the earth.'...*
> *I will remember my covenant between me and you* **and all living creatures of every kind.** *Never again will the waters become a flood to destroy all*

---

[351] Ginzberg L. *ibid.*, p255
[352] Jonah 4:11
[353] Ellison H.L. *ibid.*, p383

168

life. Whenever the rainbow appears in the clouds, I will see it and remember the everlasting covenant between God
*and **all living creatures of every kind on the earth.'***

Genesis 9:3-11, 15-16, NIV

This passage is extremely interesting, for on the one hand God gives mankind the right to eat animals (remember that in the origins story mankind's diet was vegetarian until after the Fall). On the other hand, God reminds mankind that this permission does not diminish the inherent value of these animals; neither does it confer 'object' status upon them. They are still beings, valued by God and enjoying a relationship with Him.

...they do not exist solely to be exploited by human beings;
their lives have an independent rationale.[354]

This same point is reinforced by God's speech to Job during which God states His concern for, and involvement in, the lives of many different animals[355]. The common factor shared by many of these animals in this list is that they are wild animals. As such, man can neither dominate them nor derive any benefit from them, therefore,

...they have their own raison d'être, wholly independent of human beings.[356]

This being the case, the partnership between men, God, and the animals, made in the time of Noah was natural. Indeed, it may well be that God's choice of the ark as the means of saving the animal kingdom was deliberate. Perhaps he was trying to teach Noah and his sons about their intimate link with the animal world.

Noah and his sons had to grasp their relationship with the rest of living beings by being the means of their preservation.[357]

Perhaps our own contemporary struggles to save many species of animal from extinction could be viewed in the same light. Might this be God's way of helping us remember our connection (biological and spiritual) with the animal kingdom; of causing us to take more seriously our God-given responsibility to manage the earth (Genesis 2:15-20)?

---

[354] Shemesh Y. *ibid.*, p25
[355] Job 39-41
[356] Shemesh Y. *ibid.*
[357] Ellison, H.L. *ibid.*, p389

Whilst God's covenant with Noah permitted the taking of animal life for human food purposes, it also contains an inherent warning that this shouldn't lead to indiscriminate slaughter.

Life is still inherently precious – **ALL** life. The covenant placed serious obligations upon all parties. Man was charged with certain obligations about the taking of animal life. The animals were also charged with this same obligation with respect to the killing of other living beings. These are obligations to which God will call us all – animals and man - to give account.

This view of animals, as beings who live in relationship to God, didn't end at the time of Noah. In the Ten Commandments animals are also included in the observance of the Sabbath along with people.

> *...but the seventh day is a Sabbath to the Lord your God. On it you shall not do any work, neither you, nor your son or daughter, nor your male or female servant, nor your animals, nor any foreigner residing in your towns.* [358]

Here we see that the Bible presents a vital spiritual connection between the animal kingdom and man. It seems that man cannot be in an authentic relationship with God without that relationship also involving the animal kingdom in some way. Similarly, when the Bible tries to explain what heaven will be like, it does so in terms of a restored harmony between animals and man, and between the animals themselves;

> *The wolf will live with the lamb, the leopard will lie down with the goat, the calf and the lion and the yearling together; and a little child will lead them.*
> *The cow will feed with the bear, their young will lie down together,*
> *and the lion will eat straw like the ox.*
> *The infant will play near the hole of the cobra,*
> *and the young child put his hand in the viper's nest.*
> *They will neither harm nor destroy on all my holy mountain, for the earth will be full of the knowledge of the Lord as the waters cover the sea.* [359]

There are further biblical references which hint at the relationship between animals and God and their sense of their dependence upon him[360]. Indeed Psalm 104 states that all the animals,

---

[358] Exodus 20:10, NIV
[359] Isaiah 11:6-9 NIV see also 65:20-25
[360] See Job 38:41 and Psalm 104:21. Jonathan Balcombe's books *Pleasurable Kingdom*, Hampshire: MacMillan, 2006 and *Second Nature*, New York: Palgrave MacMillan, 2010 although not written from a Christian perspective have much to teach us about the emotional life of animals. His exploration of the ethical and moral sense of animals also has interesting implications for their spiritual capacities.

... look to you to give them their food at the proper time. [361]

Perhaps these texts are a challenge to us and to our 21st century understanding. However the Bible reveals a spiritual dimension to the animal kingdom and the fact that creation has a holistic nature. Some Christian thinkers see the New Age movement as a challenge to the Church to rediscover these lost elements in her own tradition[362]. For the Bible, the animal kingdom has real spiritual significance, the spiritual fate of mankind and animal-kind are always presented as being vitally inter-linked.

As an example of this we can consider the prophetic message of Habakkuk. In this prophecy God tells the Babylonians that they are finally going to understand the shamefulness of their conduct. This shameful activity is described in terms that includes the maltreatment of animals, the destruction of the land itself, of human beings and of their societies,

> *The violence you have done to Lebanon will overwhelm you,*
> *And your destruction of animals will terrify you.*
> *For you have shed man's blood; You have destroyed lands and cities*
> *And everyone in them.* [363]

We see that the Bible presents the fact of there being a deep relationship between man and his environment. The Babylonians' sin included the destruction of the forest of Lebanon, the destruction of animals, as well as violence towards people. Sin mars every aspect of our existence - not only human lives and human society, but also the animal kingdom and the environment. It is therefore a logical corollary that redemption must also extend to these same areas.

As the story of Jonah has shown us, God involves the animal kingdom in His activity. We have already seen God use a monstrous fish; later we will see Him use a worm! Other Bible stories also show God using animals in supernatural ways. Ravens were used by God to bring food to the prophet Elijah, who was on the run from the king.[364] Jesus used a fish to provide a coin to pay the temple tax

---

[361] Psalm 104 :27, NIV
[362] Two books that explore this topic are, Bradley I. *God is Green*, London: Darton, Longman and Todd, 1990 and Campolo T. *How To Rescue The Earth Without Worshipping Nature*, Nashville, Thomas Nelson, 1992
[363] Habakkuk 2:17, NIV
[364] See 1 Kings 17:4

for himself and his disciples[365]. Moses' staff turned into a snake[366] and Aaron's into a serpent[367].

There are examples in the Bible of God using animals to execute divine punishment. Several of the plagues of Egypt involved the animal kingdom; she-Bears were God's agents of punishment for the children who were disrespectful to his prophet Elisha[368], hornets are used by God to drive out the enemies of Israel[369].

One story that seems to indicate a real spiritual capacity in animals is that of Balaam's donkey. In an amusing irony, the donkey was able to discern things in the invisible, spiritual realm that the world-renowned prophet could not![370].

Shemesh notes,

Sometimes animals serve as a portent by acting contrary to their nature:
the dogs that refrain from howling on the night before the Israelites' departure
from Egypt (Exodus 11:7), the lion that does not mangle the body of the man of
God or kill his donkey (1 Kings 13:28),
and the lions that do not touch Daniel (Daniel 6:22f).[371]

He also reminds us of the Philistines' attempt to discern the will of God concerning the captured Ark of the Covenant. They placed it on a cart drawn by cows,

...who, contrary to their nature, took the road to Beth Shemesh,
lowing as they went but turning neither to the left or right,
even though they had been separated from their calves (1 Sam. 6:12)[372]

All of these examples show that in the Bible the animal kingdom is often involved in the work of God. The story of Jonah highlights the involvement of animals in the spiritual activity of God and of man, for it is a story,

...in which animals play a prominent role, both as obedient servants of God and as
members of a community who are partners in repenting
and possibly also in shouting to the Lord [373]

---

[365] See Matthew 17::27
[366] Exodus 4:3
[367] Exodus 7:8-12
[368] 2 Kings 2:24
[369] See Exodus 23 :28; Deuteronomy 7 :20
[370] Numbers 22:22ff
[371] Shemesh Y. And Many Beasts (Jonah 4 :11) : The Function and Status of Animals in the Book of Jonah, The Journal of Hebrew Scriptures, Vol. 10, Art. 6, 2010, p5
[372] ibid.

Both the largest animal (the great fish) and one of the smallest (the worm) are part of God's teaching team for Jonah. Thus the animals, from least to largest,

...are all His creatures and consequently His servants and agents. Only the prophet Jonah, who is God's official messenger, tries to evade his mission.[374]

Although we have no biblical data informing us exactly 'how' animals relate to God, it seems evident that they do so in some way. We read in scripture that the whole of creation is eagerly awaiting the revelation of the 'sons of God' i.e. a redeemed and glorified humanity and hence its own subsequent liberation and renewal[375]. As the divinely appointed 'king' over creation, man's destiny is inextricably linked with that of the animals. Since both experience the result of man's sin and fall from grace, when salvation comes to man, the animals will benefit as well. Exactly what these benefits will be is as yet unclear, but we know they will be significant.

In conclusion, we need to hold in tension the biblical pre-eminence of man as God's highest and noblest act of creation, with the inherent value of the animal kingdom and man's interconnectedness with it. It is true that mankind bears the image of God in a special way and is tasked by God with a headship role over the whole creation[376]. But we also need to affirm the truth that the **whole creation** is **valued and sustained** by God and lives in **constant relationship** with Him.

It is not therefore incongruous to include the creation in human acts of worship. The inclusion of the animals in the Ninevites' prayers for mercy is wholly valid. Indeed, since the animals did not 'fall' by their own sin or choice, it may be that they are 'naturally' more open to God than we are. Perhaps their prayers count with God even more than ours do?

Questions for Reflection and Discussion

1   How do you respond to the idea of holistic repentance, that the animals are included in the call to prayer and fasting?
2   Is the biblical view of the animals' relationship with God something you have considered before? How do you think we should treat animals in the light of their spiritual relationship with God?

---

[373] ibid.
[374] *ibid.*, p13
[375] Romans 8:19-22
[376] Genesis 1:26

35 - Pagan Prayer (Jonah 3:7-9)

This is the proclamation he issued in Nineveh:
'By the decree of the king and his nobles:
Do not let people or animals, herds or flocks, taste anything; do not let them eat or
drink. But let people and animals be covered with sackcloth. Let everyone call
urgently on God. Let them give up their evil ways and their violence.
Who knows? God may yet relent and with compassion turn from his fierce anger
so that we will not perish.'

Jonah 3:7-9, NIV

The King encourages his people (and his animals) to pray for deliverance from the coming judgement based on the 'Who knows?' principle. His logic is this - We expect disaster - We have no other hope – So why not throw ourselves on the mercy of this newly-revealed God - Who knows what He will do?

This approach expresses a belief in the sovereignty of God. It acknowledges that God cannot be manipulated (as happens in sorcery) He can only be implored. We cry out to Him, acknowledging our guilt, hoping for His grace.

Maybe the king of Nineveh correctly perceived that God's forewarning was, in itself, an invitation to repentance? Maybe Jonah's own story had revealed to the king that *Yahweh* is the God of the second chance? For whatever reason, the king hoped for mercy.

David too prayed a 'Who knows?' prayer. After his adultery with Bathsheba and his arranged murder of her husband Uriah, a child is born. The child, the fruit of this adulterous relationship, is struck by a serious illness. David fasts and spends nights lying on the ground interceding for the child[377].

After seven days the child dies. The servants, seeing the intensity of David's prayer and his concern for the child, are too afraid to break the news to him. They expect he might do something crazy. However David, realising what has happened, calmly gets up, washes, and changes his clothes. He goes to the temple and worships God, then goes back to the palace and asks for some food.

The servants cannot understand David's behaviour. Why is he so calm now that the child is dead, given that he was he so upset when the child was sick? David responds;

While the child was still alive, I fasted and wept.
I thought, 'Who knows? The Lord may be gracious to me and let the child live.'

---

[377] 2 Samuel 12

But now that he is dead, why should I fast? Can I bring him back again?
I will go to him, but he will not return to me. [378]

King David, like the king of Nineveh, prays according to the 'Who knows?' principle. In so doing, they both confess that the ways of God are mysterious to them, but they hope for mercy.

There are many other Old Testament 'Who knows?' prayers. We find them being prayed by Moses, Jeremiah, Joel, Amos and Zephaniah[379]. These prayers express humility before God and confidence and hope in His goodness and mercy. In praying these hopeful prayers we admit God's ways are beyond our comprehension;

Oh, the depth of the riches of the wisdom and knowledge of God!
How unsearchable his judgements, and his paths beyond tracing out! [380]

These kind of prayers also express the conviction that;

There is no mechanical relationship between human acts of piety or worship and
God's saving action. Repentance does not entitle one to salvation. [381]

Salvation is always an unpredictable act of pure grace.

The pagan prayers recorded in Jonah express ignorance about *Yahweh*, the true God. The pagan's know little about him. So they can only relate to Him in ignorance and in hope, whereas the Jews, the ones to whom revelation had come, had a basis of knowledge for their relationship with God. As Jesus remarked,

You Samaritans worship what you do not know;
we worship what we do know, for salvation is from the Jews. [382]

Ironically, in our story, it is the pagans who prove to have a better grasp of the essential nature of God's sovereign grace than Jonah, the Jew! And amazingly, although the theological basis for their prayer is primitive, their prayers nonetheless succeed.

---

[378] 2 Samuel 12:22f, NIV
[379] See Exodus 32:30; Lamentations 3:29; Joel 2:14; Amos 5:15; Zephaniah 2:3
[380] Romans 11:33, NIV
[381] Fretheim T.E. *ibid.*, p113.
[382] John 4:22, NIV

We have already seen the Gentile ship's captain urging prayer in distress, while the prophet Jonah sleeps; here we see a Gentile king urging prayer in distress, while the same prophet of God looks on passively!

As in the storm, the prophet is silent. He, who should have set an example in prayer, he who had the divine revelation which would have enabled him to guide the Gentiles towards *Yahweh*, is still mute and silent. It seems Jonah has not changed.

So in the absence of guidance, the pagans simply try to do their best. And, in the grace and mercy of God, it is the attitude of our hearts that is the most important thing. The quote commonly attributed to St Augustine expresses this truth well,

We come to God by love, and not by navigation

That is to say, access to God is not obtained through following a map, or a rote formula, or the execution of a set of instructions. Rather it is an attitude of heart that enables us to establish contact with God. A spiritual truth that Shakespeare knew,

My words fly up, my thoughts remain below:
Words without thoughts never to heaven go. [383]

The story of Naaman the Aramean has some interesting resonances with what we see here in Jonah. This Gentile came to Israel to request healing from his leprosy. As he humbled himself and followed the rather bizarre instructions of the prophet – to bathe seven times in the river Jordan - he was healed[384].

Naaman's speech and behaviour indicate he didn't really understand much about *Yahweh,* or how he should be worshipped. Nonetheless, God favours him on the basis of his attitude of humility and faith. It would seem that when we come to God with our prayers, humility and faith are far more important than theological knowledge.

Similarly the Ninevites' response to Jonah's message has much to commend it to God – their humble repentance seems genuine. It has already been expressed in costly acts of contrition, yet the king commands they do even more. Not only are the people and animals to fast and pray, even more significantly, they are **to change their way of living**. Here the reason for God's displeasure with them is being addressed. They are dealing with the root issue, that of their wickedness. The king instructs the people to give up their evil ways and their violence.

---

[383] Shakespeare W. Hamlet, Prince of Denmark, (Act III, Scene III), in *The Illustrated Stratford Shakespeare*, London : Chancellor Press, 1993, p817
[384] 2 Kings 5:1-27

Violence seems to be something God particularly dislikes. In the Genesis flood, violence was the reason given by God for this event[385] and elsewhere is specifically stated as something God hates[386]. Leaders are particularly condemned for violence towards the weak[387]. Here we see the Assyrians, proverbial for their violence and cruelty, responding by changing their ways, altering that aspect of their behaviour which was particularly displeasing to God.

We can compare this passage to Joel chapter 2[388]. There we see the people of God being called to walk the same path of repentance as the Ninevites. This illustrates clearly that God shows no partiality with regard to sin – Jew and Gentile are treated alike. In order to avoid the judgement of God, disobedience must be acknowledged and turned from. Repentance must be expressed in genuine acts of contrition.

The prayer of the Ninevites takes three forms – fasting, the wearing of sackcloth and calling upon God. Fasting is the body's way of praying. In discomfort, the body cries out to God, This inarticulate form of prayer is supplemented by the our calling out to God in repentance and supplication. This is completed by the communal act of wearing sackcloth – dressing as beggars before God to implore His mercy[389].

The wearing of sack-cloth and sitting in ashes was a wide-spread contemporary form of physical penance. Such religious practices are not generally prevalent in Western Christianity; they are particularly foreign to Protestantism. Even in the Catholic world such expressions of personal piety are often downplayed in modern-day church life. Such practices can be considered as excessive and even unhealthy; however, they are a very human and natural response to sorrow for sin. They are also costly and very real; as such they have significance. Since the root of sin is selfishness, so following Christ should often be expressed in actions that depose the self and prioritise God and others – and acts of penance can be such actions.

---

[385] Genesis 6:11, 13
[386] Psalm 11:5
[387] Ezekiel 45:9
[388] See Fretheim T.E. *ibid.*, p106
[389] Cary P. *ibid.*, p112

Questions for Reflection and Discussion

1 How should our prayer-life be shaped by the two facts we have discussed above – the fact that we cannot know what God will do in any given situation and the fact that we know for sure that our God is a God of mercy and grace?

2 How do you respond to the idea of expressed repentance – acts of engagement or self-denial undertaken to show the reality of our sorrow for sin? What do you think of physical acts of penitence – fasting, discomfort, pilgrimage and so on? Can you think of a situation in which such acts might have value?

36 - Divine Mercy and the Scandal of Grace (Jonah 3:10-4:1-3)

When God saw what they did and how they turned from their evil ways,
he relented and did not bring on them the destruction he had threatened. But to
Jonah this seemed very wrong, and he became angry.
He prayed to the Lord, 'Isn't this what I said, Lord, when I was still at home? That
is what I tried to forestall by fleeing to Tarshish. I knew that you are a gracious and
compassionate God, slow to anger and abounding in love,
a God who relents from sending calamity.
Now, Lord, take away my life, for it is better for me to die than to live.'
Jonah 3:10 – 4:1-3, NIV

For many reasons the book of Jonah is an epistle of hope, as well as of grace. We are forced to acknowledge that even when disaster looks unavoidable, when salvation seems impossible, nevertheless hope is the proper state of mind for a Christian. We are reminded of the description of Abraham, who as an old and childless man, still held on to the promise God had given him about becoming the father of nations.

Against all hope, Abraham in hope believed... [390]

Abraham's hope, in a hopeless situation, was actually that which made him acceptable to God[391]. In fact the word 'faith' could be considered a synonym for 'hope in a hopeless situation'. Hope and faith are very much linked and are often associated;

Now faith is being sure of what we hope for and certain of what we do not see. [392]

God's power and His wisdom are beyond our comprehension. He is able to turn around the most impossible situations, He is able to provide in the most difficult of circumstances. God's compassion, grace and mercy are boundless. So even when we seem doomed to experience God's punishment because of our sinfulness, repenting and throwing ourselves on God's mercy is always a course of action, full of hope.

From this perspective, we get a completely different understanding of Jonah's message of threatened judgement to the Ninevites,

Threats of punishment in Jonah thus function as epistemological aids designed to
help those in violation of the Creator's will remedy the situation before they meet

---

[390] Romans 4:18, NIV
[391] Romans 4:22f
[392] Hebrews 11:1, NIV

the fate that attends such behaviour (this comes to classic expression in Jer. 18:7-10, and addresses worries that God does not remain faithful to his word to punish Nineveh) rather than as celestial strong-arming that corrupts the free moral will and volitional agency of the one who repents[393]

At this point in our study of Jonah we come to one of the most striking aspects of the book - Jonah's anger at the grace of God towards the Ninevites.

God changes His prophesied course of action in response to the penitence of the Ninevites. Their actions and their changed behaviour have released God's mercy. We are specifically told in scripture that God takes no pleasure in punishment of the wicked; He would much rather people avoided it by turning from their wickedness.

> *Do I take any pleasure in the death of the wicked? declares the Sovereign Lord. Rather, am I not pleased when they turn from their ways and live?[394]*

This text shows that threatened judgement is always conditional on repeated acts of disobedience. This passage from Ezekiel goes on to reveal that, in similar fashion, prophesied blessing is conditional on continued righteousness.

This principle applies equally to individuals and to groups[395]. The Ninevites fulfil the conditions required to turn away God's wrath at their sin, by repenting and changing their ways, and so they avoid the prophesied punishment.

This divine mercy angers and outrages Jonah.

> *But to Jonah this seemed very wrong, and he became angry.*

Often it is the **fear of failure** that haunts pastors, priests and preachers. However, what Jonah has dreaded from the first is the **possibility of success** in his prophetic ministry. What was implicit in his previous behaviour is now stated explicitly.

Whilst we are not told exactly why Jonah resents the fact that the Ninevites are to receive God's grace and mercy, there are several possibilities.

The Babylonian Talmud suggests Jonah's anger is partly caused by the fact that God has not informed him about His changed will,

---

[393] Timmer D. *ibid.,* p21
[394] Ezekiel 18:23, NIV
[395] Jeremiah 18:7-10

But was not such the case with Jonah,
who was not notified that the decree was changed?
There was the prophecy:
Nineveh will be overthrown, which had two meanings, to be destroyed,
and also to be turned over from evil to righteousness,
and he did not understand the real meaning.[396]

Is Jonah angry because God has not told him that the plan has changed? Is it because he feels slighted, left in the dark, that Jonah is angry?

Certainly, we have an ironic and rather amusing picture of a prophet who is blisteringly angry that God has responded to the Ninevites' repentance with grace and mercy – a repentance in response to his own preaching!

... it is embarrassing for many of us to see that God can use a crooked stick
to draw a straight line [397]

In Jonah we are forced to recognise that God uses imperfect people to accomplish His purposes. This is problematic. It creates plenty of opportunities for people to discredit the Church. Those outside can point to the obvious sins and stupidities in those ministering and say, 'Look how messed up these so-called Christians are!' 'What moral authority can such screw-ups possibly have?!'

And they're right! Christians are messed up. Christians are failures. There are no grounds in scripture for supposing that Christians are morally superior to non-Christians. We are merely saved, forgiven, redeemed, reconciled with God – **in spite of our evident and on-going problems**. That is the glory, the mystery and the scandal of grace.

In actual fact, this is the very issue Jonah is struggling with. As we learnt at the beginning, the Assyrians were the major military power of the time. They were hungry for conquest and domination, a nation notorious for their bloodlust and cruelty in war. Jonah is a Jew. He and his people have already suffered from Assyrian attack, and they live in constant fear of another Assyrian military campaign. For the Jews of Jonah's time, the only prayers they might have prayed to God concerning the Assyrians were prayers of imprecation - that God might curse, destroy, and lay waste to them entirely.

Jonah's problem is that such people don't deserve grace. His logic is that 'people like them' should have to prove they have truly undergone a change of heart and

---

[396] Rodkinson M.L. (ed. and tr.) *The Babylonian Talmud Vol. 1-10,* Second Ed., Boston: Boston New Talmud Publishing Company 1918 [1903], p1855
[397] Kendal R.T. *'Jonah',* London: Hodder & Stoughton, 1978, p170

have transformed their behaviour before they earn the right to receive God's grace and forgiveness. He is rather like our contemporaries who look at flawed Christians and messed-up churches and shake their heads and say, 'How can God accept such people?'

Jonah's anger may also be provoked by what the continued existence of Nineveh might mean for his own people. How can God let this threat continue?

Another possible reason for Jonah's anger is that God's 'no-show' regarding the promised destruction of Nineveh has undermined his own prophetic 'credentials'. This could have led to Jonah losing face in front of the Ninevites and being ridiculed. If this is a factor, then it is clear that Jonah was more concerned about himself than about the Ninevites or even God. As R.T. Kendall observes;

> I cannot help seeing the contrast between Jonah,
> a man who loved his own vindication more than the glory of the Lord,
> and Paul, who loved the glory of the Lord more than his own vindication. [398]

Saint Paul, languishing in prison, could still give thanks for his situation[399]. He could give thanks, even though some Christian preachers were using his arrest as an opportunity to supplant his position of authority in the churches he had founded. They were even deliberately stirring up trouble to try to ensure his continued incarceration, or even execution!

How could Saint Paul give thanks for this awful situation? Because his goal was that the gospel should be preached, even if it was done by sinful people, with wrongful motives and with horribly compromised goals. The gospel was still being preached! Did it matter to Saint Paul that this preaching was only made possible by his being in jail? No, not a bit!

Jonah's attitude stands out in sharp contrast. He was embarrassed, ashamed, and angry that his own position was undermined. He would have greatly preferred that the Ninevites die, rather than he should lose face.

Maybe Jonah is also angry about the pointlessness of all that he has been through. In Jonah's mind, he has suffered so much to get to Nineveh. He has been through storms. He has been tossed into the raging sea. He has been swallowed alive by some monstrous sea creature. He has languished three days inside this beast in unimaginable terror. Finally, broken by God, he has admitted defeat and accepted his mission. He has then been vomited onto the shoreline and has trudged for weeks under the scorching desert sun to arrive at Nineveh.

---

[398] Kendall R.T. *ibid*, p232
[399] Philippians 1:12-18

He fulfils his mission, preaches a message of judgement upon this city. Then what happens? The people repent and God says 'Okay, I forgive you. Judgement is suspended'. Jonah has been through such turmoil, such mental anguish and physical suffering, and for what? In Jonah's mind it has all been a complete waste of time.

Maybe Jonah is also angry that he has been forced to radically rethink his theology? Before he began this journey, Jonah was confident that he had a pretty good understanding of God and His ways. God loved the Jewish people, He had chosen them and He had formed them. Those outside the Jewish race were therefore 'way down the line' in terms of being objects of God's love and attention. Jonah's recent experiences have radically called into question this belief.

Jonah has come face to face with the reality of a God whose interest and concern extends way beyond the borders of Israel. Jonah is forced to admit that Gentiles, and even the hated Assyrians, do not fall outside the orbit of God's grace. Jonah is furious about this. His preference would be that God's mercy would be forever restricted to the nation of Israel. Anything else means he has to re-think his theology.

We see Jonah's behaviour mirrored in that of the unforgiving servant in the parable Jesus told.[400] In this parable a servant receives great grace and mercy from the king to whom he is astronomically indebted. His debt is cancelled solely on the basis of the king's mercy and pity for his subject in this impossible situation. In his turn, however, the unforgiving servant spectacularly fails to behave in the same way towards a fellow servant who is trivially indebted to him. His attitude outrages the king, who has him thrown into jail. Jesus' application of this parable is striking - **He likens us all to the unforgiving servant**. In the light of the forgiveness and grace we have all received from God, unforgiveness towards others is something God **will not tolerate**.

Jonah is a stark example of the jarring phenomenon of the unforgiving forgiven, the merciless mercied, the graceless graced, the intolerant tolerated. Scripture warns us that this is a terrifyingly serious condition. In order to force us to face up to God's command to forgive, God's tells us that our receiving forgiveness from him is conditional upon our granting forgiveness to others.[401]

Blessed are the merciful, for they will be shown mercy.[402]

---

[400] Matthew 18:21-35
[401] Matthew 6:14f
[402] Matthew 5:7 NIV

For if you forgive men when they sin against you,
your heavenly Father will also forgive you.
But if you do not forgive men their sins,
your Father will not forgive your sins.[403]

We also need to notice the extreme nature of Jonah's anger. His anger is such that he prays to die. Jonah is angry at grace. He felt that judgement was in order, and instead God has granted mercy. Jonah — whose name means 'dove' — is behaving more like a hawk. He wants justice, not mercy; punishment, not forgiveness — at least for the Ninevites.

Jonah had forgotten that God's characteristic activity is not judgement, but blessing. Judgement is always God's 'strange work';

The Lord will rise up as he did at Mount Perazim,
he will rouse himself as in the Valley of Gibeon
- to do his work, his strange work,
and perform his task, his alien task.[404]

God's essential nature is love and His primary means of self-expression is through blessing.

The Lord is gracious and compassionate, slow to anger and rich in love.
The Lord is good to all; he has compassion on all he has made[405]

God's desire is to bless universally. Acts of judgement are forced upon Him only because of human sin.

Fortunately for Jonah, God, in His graciousness and mercy, ignores his death request. As Stuart points out,

Yahweh ignored Jonah's request to die. It was a stupid request, voiced out of
frustration and pettiness, and Yahweh did not dignify it with a response[406]

Jonah's problem is not only personal, but is rooted in his cultural identity. Jonah and his people the Jews knew themselves to be the chosen people of God; it was very difficult for them to understand that the grace of God might ever extend to Gentiles.

---

[403] Matthew 6:14-15 NIV
[404] Isaiah 28:21 NIV
[405] Psalm 145:8f NIV
[406] Stuart D. *ibid.*, p503

We see that this attitude still existed seven centuries later when Saint Peter too struggled with the idea of Gentile Christians[407]. In Acts 10 it took a thrice repeated vision, and an amazing outpouring of the Holy Spirit upon some Gentiles, in order to open Saint Peter's mind to the possibility of Gentile Christians.

For Jonah, the idea that God's grace could extend to God-fearing Gentiles was already a stretch. That it could extend beyond them to the wicked and merciless Assyrians was nothing less than an outrageous and shocking idea.

The Jews were stunningly successful at ignoring the universal scope of God's love, even though, right from the beginning of the Jewish nation, God had stated that the Gentiles were to be blessed through them;

> *... all peoples on earth will be blessed through you.* [408]

Yet the Jews had mostly tried to keep God to themselves. *Yahweh* remained, in effect, primarily a national God. However, God had other ideas! God's scope for the application of His grace and mercy was, from the beginning, universal.

The Jews' understanding of mission was as something primarily centrifugal. They were prepared to accept into the Judaic fold those Gentiles who were prepared to come to them. God's idea of mission, as revealed in the Bible, was that it should be centripetal i.e. that the people of God should take the message of grace out with the confines of their own comfort zone, to those who had never heard it.

Christians today can suffer from this same problem. We can see centripetal mission as an 'optional extra' in the life of the church; something to be attempted when surplus resources are available. This, however, is **never** God's view. Emil Brunner famously wrote that,

> *The church exists by mission, just as fire exists by burning.* [409]

That is to say, mission is the expression of the church's essence, its truest nature and its natural behaviour. Of course mission is not an end in and of itself;

> *Mission is not the ultimate goal of the Church. Worship is.*
> *Mission exist because worship doesn't.*
> *Worship is ultimate, not missions, because God is ultimate not man.* [410]

---

[407] See pp40ff
[408] Genesis 12:3, NIV
[409] Brunner H.E. *The Word and the World*, London : SCM Press, 1931, p108

Mission exists in order for man to be able to fulfil his creation destiny - to love and worship God. In so doing, man also achieves his greatest glory. What can be more significant, honourable and meaningful, than to be a worshipper of the God who spoke the universe into existence?

Questions for Reflection and Discussion

1   How should the fact that promised punishment and promised blessing are conditional, affect our spiritual lives? What are the consequences of this for how we should live out our faith?

2   How is the centrality of hope expressed in your Christian faith? Are there people who you would classify as 'beyond the grasp of grace'? Do our prayers reveal a God who is too small and too weak?

3   Are there any circumstances in which Christians can pray prayers which call upon God to destroy people?

4   Is your church's expression of mission centrifugal or centripetal?

---

[410] Piper J. 'Let The Nations Be Glad!' in Winter R.D. & Hawthorne S.C. (eds.) *Perspectives on the World Christian Movement*, Pasadena: William Carey Library, 1999 3rd ed. (1981).

37 - God's Question (Jonah 4:4)

> *But the Lord replied, 'Is it right for you to be angry?'*
>
> Jonah 4:4, NIV

God stops Jonah in mid-rant with a simple question, 'Do you have any right to be angry?' The implied answer is, of course, 'No'.

Jonah had recently experienced God's unmerited mercy when he was delivered from certain death. He had set himself in flagrant opposition to God, yet God worked to bring him back to repentance, that he might receive forgiveness and experience reconciliation. Jonah has therefore absolutely no reason to quibble with God's merciful treatment of the Ninevites. Indeed, Jonah's own theology proves that God is only acting in keeping with His nature of merciful love, something Jonah says he expected from the start.

> *I knew that you are a gracious and compassionate God,*
> *slow to anger and abounding in love,*
> *a God who relents from sending calamity.*[411]

The very thing that should have made Jonah rejoice is the one thing he resents most. The wonder of the grace and mercy of God should have fired his love and animated his gospel proclamation. Instead, it is exactly the thing which disturbs, displeases and angers him, so far is Jonah from sharing the mind of God.

There is an interesting contrast here between Jonah and the prophet Elijah. Both despaired of their mission and both asked God to let them die. But the cause of their despair is inverse;

> *Elijah was in despair over his failure to turn the hearts of the idolatrous people of Israel. Jonah was in despair over his success* [412]

Maybe Jonah is most angered by the fact that it is a Gentile city that is responding so wonderfully to God. Their response to a prophetic word shames the Jewish nation, who constantly rejected the prophets and their calls to repentance. Perhaps Jonah even fears that the Gentiles might supplant the Jews in God's affections.

Another possibility for Jonah's anger is that he has too high a regard for God's dignity. Maybe Jonah is horrified that the granting of mercy makes God look

---

[411] Jonah 4:2b, NIV
[412] Fretheim T.E. *ibid.*, p121

187

weak and foolish. Maybe some of the Ninevites were already making a fool of this God who is so easily swayed.

Scripture reveals to us a God who will stoop to amazing lengths, and take enormous risks with His own reputation, in order to save sinners; to the extreme of coming into this world as a baby and suffering a shameful death on a cross.[413]

Jonah's complaint and his attempt at self-justification also has parallels with the story of Job. In the book of Job, God allows unmerited suffering to come upon a righteous man. Job resents this, and the implication of unrighteousness it might be construed to convey. Indeed, Job's friends do interpret his situation in this way - as being that of someone being punished by God for his sin.

Smarting from the injustice of it all, Job calls out to God for an opportunity to present his case before the heavenly court; to vindicate himself, to prove his innocence.

However when God finally responds to Job, He does not respond with an explanation or a justification, but merely with a series of questions[414]. These questions are designed to remind Job of the power, wisdom and majesty of God, and to reveal to him the absurdity of imagining that God should have to answer to him for His conduct. A wiser, chastened Job responds;

I am unworthy - how can I reply to you?
I put my hand over my mouth.
I spoke once, but I have no answer - twice, but I will say no more.[415]

Like Job, Jonah is silenced by God's question. Sometimes the wisest thing a person can do is to just shut up;

Even a fool is though wise if he keeps silent,
and discerning if he holds his tongue.[416]

Do not be quick with your mouth,
do not be hasty in your heart to utter anything before God.
God is in heaven and you are on earth, so let your words be few.[417]

Jonah's anger is also like that of Cain in chapter four of Genesis.

---

[413]   Philippians 2:8
[414]   Job 38 and 39.
[415]   Job 40:4f, NIV
[416]   Proverbs 17:28 NIV
[417]   Ecclesiastes 5:2, NIV

Now Abel kept flocks, and Cain worked the soil.
In the course of time Cain brought some of the fruits of the soil
as an offering to the Lord.
But Abel also brought an offering – fat portions from some of the firstborn of his
flock. The Lord looked with favour on Abel and his offering, but on Cain and his
offering he did not look with favour.
So Cain was very angry, and his face was downcast.
Then the Lord said to Cain, 'Why are you angry? Why is your face downcast?
If you do what is right, will you not be accepted? But if you do not do what is right,
sin is crouching at your door; it desires to have you, but you must rule over it.'[418]

God's question to Jonah should have set his alarm bells ringing. It is exactly the same question that God put to Cain, *Why are you angry?*[419] In fact there are tremendous parallels between these two events.

- Both of these men had just undertaken service to God. Cain had just sacrificed an offering to God, Jonah had just preached God's message to the Ninevites.
- Both of them have done so with a bad heart attitude. This was what had made Cain's sacrifice unacceptable to God. Similarly, Jonah's response to God's grace shows he is far from sharing God's heart for the Ninevites.
- Both Cain and Jonah have seen God extending His grace to others. Abel's sacrifice had been accepted. The Ninevites have been reprieved. They both react angrily to this situation.
- Both of them have murderous intent for those to whom God has been gracious. Cain subsequently kills his brother Abel, Jonah no doubt hopes that God will yet destroy the Ninevites.

Given these similarities, God's instruction to Cain has great significance for Jonah;

... sin is crouching at your door;
it desires to have you, but you must master it [420]

It is a horrible thing that we can become murderously angry when we see God extending His grace to others. It is the ultimate evidence of the twisted-ness and corruption of human nature. It is something we need to guard our hearts against. We need, like Jonah and Cain, to learn to master this most awful of temptations. We need to learn to be able to celebrate grace **whenever** and **wherever** it appears - when other peoples' relatives and friends are saved, but

---

[418] Genesis 4:2b-7, NIV
[419] Genesis 4:6 NIV
[420] Genesis 4:7b NIV

not ours; when other peoples' house-groups grow and thrive, but ours struggles; when revival comes to the church down the road, but not to ours; when others are healed, but we remain sick.

The only thing that will help us cope with these circumstances is a Kingdom vision. We need to see ourselves as a part of the global and eternal work of God. Then we will be able to celebrate God's activity wherever it takes place.

So far we have considered two biblical characters who behave in a manner similar to Jonah. Abraham, on the other hand, behaves in the opposite way. Both Abraham[421] and Jonah were told by God that He was about to punish a wicked city, however their attitudes are strikingly different.

Abraham intercedes for the wicked city of Sodom.	Jonah desires the punishment of a repentant city of Nineveh.
Abraham repeatedly entreats God for the salvation of the city.	Jonah sits outside hoping that destruction will come.
Abraham involves himself with a city that is not his own.	Jonah distances himself from a foreign city.
Abraham cannot bear the thought of sinful men being destroyed.	Jonah cannot bear the thought of penitents being saved.

Table 4- Contrasts between Abraham and Jonah

It should be clear which of these two men should be our model.

Questions for Reflection and Discussion

1   Have you ever been tempted to react negatively to God's grace reaching out to others? What attitudes or practices can you embrace that might guard against this possibility?

2   How can we be more like Abraham and less like Jonah in the face of evident wickedness?

3   How do you respond to the idea of the 'wisdom of silence before God'?

---

[421] Genesis 18:16-33

38 - Watching and Waiting (Jonah 4:5-6)

Jonah had gone out and sat down at a place east of the city.
There he made himself a shelter,
sat in its shade and waited to see what would happen to the city.
Then the Lord God provided a leafy plant and made it grow up over Jonah to give
shade for his head to ease his discomfort,
and Jonah was very happy about the plant.

Jonah 4:5-6, NIV

It is hard for us not to feel some sympathy for Jonah. He has been through the most traumatic storm at sea. He has had the most terrifying, horrifying experience of being swallowed by a great fish. He has languished close to death for three days, expecting that at any moment his life would be snuffed out. Then, against all hope, he has been delivered from this experience. More dead than alive he has trudged the 600 miles to Nineveh. He has preached the message that God gave him; that divine wrath and judgement was about to fall upon this violent, sadistic, idolatrous city. But the Ninevites' repentance has provoked God's mercy and God has relented. So Jonah has been made to look a fool; his prophetic credentials lie in tatters at his feet.

Why does Jonah build himself a little shack outside Nineveh? Does Jonah still expect – or perhaps even hope - that some disaster might yet be visited upon the city? Was Jonah no longer welcome there? Was he so emotionally disturbed that he just wanted to be alone? Does he separate himself from these idolatrous people to show his sense of self-righteousness in contrast to their sinfulness? Or is Jonah simply defying God?

God had better take another look at the situation and the city. [422]

Poor Jonah! His whole belief system has been turned upside down – God is extending His grace to Gentiles! Ashamed at his loss of face, confused about God's actions, Jonah doesn't want to go back to Israel, but neither does he want to live amongst the unclean Gentiles in Nineveh. So he builds a little shelter outside the city and he just prays that he might die. He withdraws from Nineveh. His preaching stops. He just builds himself a little shelter and settles down to wait and see what will happen.

Interestingly, the word used for 'shelter' is the same word used to refer to the booths lived in by the Jews during the Feast of Tabernacles[423]. This seven-day festival was to commemorate the journey from Egypt to Canaan and to give

---

[422] Fretheim T.E. *ibid.*, p123
[423] Leviticus 23:33-43

thanks to God for the fruitfulness of the Promised Land. It was a celebration of His goodness to the people of Israel. Significantly for our story, this was to be a time of particular hospitality towards foreigners.

> Be joyful at your Feast – you, your sons and daughters,
> your menservants and maidservants,
> and the Levites, the aliens, the fatherless
> and the widows who live in your towns[424]

So we have the picture of a Jew living in a booth which recalls God's grace and mercy to Israel and which is a reminder of the duty to care for foreigners, yet here he is fuming at God's grace and mercy to the Ninevites![425]

There is, however, some wisdom in Jonah's chosen course of action. When we don't know what God is doing around us, when we have no clear sense of where our paths should go it is often wise just to sit tight and wait. Jonah has followed God's instructions; these instructions have brought him to Nineveh. He has faithfully accomplished his task. This done, he has no further instructions; therefore he waits.

We are often a lot more impatient than God. We want to dash about 'making things happen', moving from one project to the next. God seems to operate at a much more relaxed pace. I once heard someone say that God takes a long time to act suddenly. Moses spent 40 'wasted' years being a shepherd before God's call comes to him. Joseph 'wasted' 15 years as a slave and a prisoner in Egypt before God brought him to national leadership. Jesus 'wasted' 30 years before beginning to minister. Paul 'wasted' 10 to 15 years between the time of his conversion and call and his first missionary journey.

Obviously these periods of time were not 'wasted'. Rather they were essential preparation. God was preparing the individual he would use, or preparing the people or the circumstances into which they would be sent to minister. Thinking back to Jonah, we see that if he had arrived earlier at Nineveh, they would not yet have been destabilised by adversity, celestial portents and the long-term failure of their own religion to resolve their problems. They would therefore have been much less likely to respond to his message. Similarly, had he not been through the whole experience of the shipwreck and the great fish, he would not have had such an impact upon them.

Waiting, therefore, is not wasted time but rather essential preparation. And so the lesson is - Learn to like waiting!

---

[424] Deuteronomy 16:14, NIV
[425] Glardon T. *ibid.*, p38

Jonah had thought himself finished with God when he fled to Tarshish. God, however, had other ideas, and used some amazing events to bring Jonah back into a functioning relationship with Himself. Yet Jonah's subsequent behaviour has shown this reconciliation was not yet 'the real deal'. Jonah still has 'issues' to resolve. His attitudes and his thinking have not yet been transformed. And so God begins another process of theological re-education - but this time, He starts with a blessing.

Jonah is suffering from the burning sun. Remember that it is likely that he has acid-damaged skin. He is probably in a lot of pain and discomfort, which the stinging sun will only make worse. So God causes a gourd plant to grow supernaturally quickly. This leafy plant provides cooling shade for Jonah and he greatly appreciates it. The plant was identified by the ancients as the *Ricinus*, or the Castor Oil plant. This plant is noted for its extraordinarily rapid growth and is often cultivated in the Near East in order to give shade.

Figure 11 Castor Oil Plant[426]

*It forms a shade that is absolutely impenetrable to the sun's rays,
even at noon-day. It flourishes best in the very hottest part of summer;
and, lastly, when injured or cut it withers away with equal rapidity* [427].

These natural characteristics seem to fit with the description of the plant in this story. Somehow Jonah recognizes God at work in this plant. Maybe the plant's natural capacity for rapid growth was further augmented by God and Jonah noticed this? Maybe it also withered so very quickly that Jonah knew this was not a natural occurrence?

What this episode does show is that God is sensitive to our human weakness. Jonah is wrong to feel as he does, but God doesn't batter him, He blesses him. This might well have been wrongly interpreted by Jonah. He could have seen it as a vindication from God that his feelings and attitudes were correct; they weren't, as subsequent events will show. But God won't kick a man when he is down. Gentleness is one of God's key attributes;

> A bruised reed he will not break, and a smouldering wick he will not snuff out.
> In faithfulness he will bring forth justice. [428]

God does not break people. He sometimes has to break wrong things in people - such as pride. But He does not break people.

> ...God is faithful; he will not let you be tempted beyond what you can bear.
> But when you are tempted, he will also provide a way out so that you can stand up under it. [429]

I vividly remember one of the key moments in my own spiritual pilgrimage. After finishing Bible college, my wife and I felt God calling us to live by faith and to continue to serve our local church in a voluntary capacity. This meant not taking on paid work, but trusting God to supply our financial and material needs - a hard step to take when you have a family to look after. However, we took this step and God did provide for us. But the level of God's provision was not sufficient to prevent us from regularly falling into debt. Every now and again God would provide a large financial gift and we would see our bank account balanced. But in a few weeks we would be back firmly in the red.

This went on for two years. Eventually we reached our overdraft limit and one fateful day, as we tried to pay for our shopping at the local supermarket, our bank card was refused. This was a breaking point for my wife and I. We were ashamed, confused and angry. We came home and wept before God. Why was He doing this to us? Why was His provision never quite sufficient to meet our modest needs? Why was He seemingly punishing us for our faith and obedience?

---

[427] Thomson W.M. *The Land and the Book – Volume 1*, New York : Harper and Brothers, 1880, p13
[428] Isaiah 42v3 NIV. See also Matthew 12v20
[429] 1 Corinthians 10v13, NIV

That morning as we cried together before God, my wife and I were broken people. We had to make a decision. Would we continue to trust God, even though we didn't understand what He was doing or why? Or, would give it all up as a bad idea, and take back control of our lives?

We decided, like Job;

> Though he slay me, yet will I hope in him. [430]

We re-committed ourselves unreservedly to God. We swore to follow Him whatever might happen - death or disaster, shame or dishonour, whatever. We gave Him the right to do whatever He wanted in our lives.

From that point on our financial circumstances turned around. We were never overdrawn after that point. God had done what needed to be done in our lives at that time and He had used financial pressure to do it. We know of others who have had the same kind of experience. Sometimes God has used illness, relationship difficulties, or a serious failure in ministry, as His means to get other people to the point that we reached on that fateful day – a point of total commitment. The fundamental principle is this - God brings pressure into our lives to teach us lessons. But He will never push us beyond what we can bear.

Here, Jonah is at the end of his tether. He has had absolutely all the pressure he can stand. Therefore God graciously grants him a moment of relief. The lessons are not finished; the process of transformation has neither been completed, nor cancelled. But Jonah cannot take any more for the present, so God lets him have some time to rest.

We see a similar event in the life of Elijah. After a crisis in his life and ministry he is emotionally, spiritually and mentally exhausted and he too, like Jonah, prays to die;

> He came to a broom tree, sat down under it and prayed that he might die.
> "I have had enough, LORD," he said.
> "Take my life; I am no better than my ancestors."
> Then he lay down under the tree and fell asleep.
> All at once an angel touched him and said, "Get up and eat." He looked around,
> and there by his head was a cake of bread baked over hot coals, and a jar of water.
> He ate and drank and then lay down again. [431]

---

[430] Job 13:15, NIV
[431] 1 Kings 19:4-6 NIV

Note that God doesn't scold or reprimand Elijah. Instead God sends an angel to minister to him. God meets Elijah's physical needs. God allows him time to recover his physical strength; his spiritual and emotional balance.

In our own spiritual ups and downs sometimes we need a 'kick in the pants', but sometimes we need a 'pat on the head'. God is the master in terms of spiritual direction. He knows exactly where we are physically, spiritually and emotionally at every moment. God knows us better than we know ourselves. His activity in our lives is always superbly suited to our circumstances. Sometimes we might feel that things are too rough, that the way is too hard and that our circumstances are too difficult. But God promises He will not push us harder than we are able to bear.

No temptation has overtaken you except what is common to mankind.
And God is faithful; he will not let you be tempted beyond what you can bear.
But when you are tempted,
he will also provide a way out so that you can endure it.[432]

Note too that God replaces Jonah's attempt at self-sufficiency with divine provision. God re-expresses His duty of care for His servant Jonah. Where Jonah had only his own handiwork to meet his physical needs, now he has a miraculous expression of God's love and care for him.

In reflecting upon this event in Jonah's life, the Early Church Fathers, with their genius for seeing Christian symbolism in Old Testament stories, interpreted the story in the following manner.

-   The shelter that Jonah built as representing the Jewish religion. Something which was of the nature of a temporary and provisional dwelling and which would ultimately be replaced by the eternal Church of Christ.
-   The plant that God caused to grow up over this shelter was understood as representing the promises of the Old Testament; promises that gave the Jews hope and allowed them to stand firm under the 'burning heat' of persecutions and calamities. The 'shelter' these promises provided was what Saint Paul would term, 'shadows of the things to come'[433].
-   Somewhat shockingly, Jesus is seen in the symbol of the worm. Jesus, in preaching the Kingdom of God and in calling all nations – Jew and Gentile - to it, 'bites' the hopes and dreams of earthly glory which had comforted the Jews. He 'dried them up' and brought to an end this temporary consolation; for this lesser glory was to be replaced by the

---

[432] 1 Corinthians 10:13, NIV
[433] Colossians 2:17, NIV

greater glory of the One New Man – Jew and Gentile united in the glorious, everlasting Kingdom of God.

Interestingly, we see biblical support for this striking imagery in the psalm quoted by Jesus at the moment of his death on the cross. Psalm 22 begins with the words, 'My God, my God why have you forsaken me?' and ends with the phrase, 'he has done it' – otherwise rendered, 'it is finished'. In so citing the beginning and the end of this psalm at this crucial moment, Jesus seems thereby to infer that this psalm has a particular reference to Himself. This said, it is noteworthy that we find within this psalm the phrase,

> *But I am a worm and not a man,*
> *scorned by men and despised by the people.*[434]

Dom Jean de Monléon makes spiritual application of this symbolism to the Christian life by reminding us that Jesus, 'the divine worm', comes to bite and to dry up all that is in us that is earthly, fleshly; all that attaches us to the world below; all that would hold us back from the greater, eternal glory of participation in God's everlasting Kingdom[435].

Questions for Reflection and Discussion

1   Have you experienced times of waiting in your own Christian life? How did you respond to these times? Were they ultimately a positive or a negative experience?

2   We see God's gentleness in providing Jonah with shelter, in giving Elijah rest and food, **before** He starts to address the issues in their lives. What does this reveal to us about God? How do you respond to the promise in 1 Corinthians 10:13, that God will not allow us to be tempted / tested beyond what we are capable of bearing?

---

[434] Psalm 22:6, NIV
[435] de Monléon Dom J. *ibid.*, p114

Jonah – The Scar

And day by day I watched God bless
A pagan people by His grace.
And every day I touched my face,
And ran my finger on this scar
And felt with shameful fire: how far
I'd fallen from the mercy that
It meant.[436]

---

[436] Piper J. Jonah – Part 3

Ionah : the fourth part - Fig Tree Bloom

It was just a fig tree touched by creation's grace
To shade and hide another's face
Keeping the scorching, drying heat
From scorching his tired and weary place.

A worm it stirred beneath the soil
Growing on roots like an oozing boil
Taking the life sap of the tree
Destroying the fruit as it grew and blossomed.

Did this worm from a sea serpent come?
Hidden inside his tattered clothes
Biding its time for a moment precise
Killing the bloom from the inside.

A.P. McIntyre   2012.

39 - A Worm and a Wind (Jonah 4:7-9)

> *But at dawn the next day God provided a worm,*
> *which chewed the plant so that it withered.*
> *When the sun rose, God provided a scorching east wind, and the sun blazed on*
> *Jonah's head so that he grew faint. He wanted to die, and said,*
> *'It would be better for me to die than to live.'*
> *But God said to Jonah, 'Is it right for you to be angry about the plant?'*
> *'It is,' he said. 'And I'm so angry I wish I were dead.'*
>
> Jonah 4:7-9, NIV

God doesn't grant Jonah much respite - just one day. The next day, at dawn, a worm attacks the vine. The vine shrivels and Jonah is left exposed to the blazing sun and burning desert sirocco. Jonah starts to feel faint and he is so uncomfortable that, once again, he just wants to die.

In some senses Jonah is similar to the pagan prophet Balaam. Balaam, a renowned Babylonian magician, was hired to put a curse on the people of Israel. He tries repeatedly to do this, but every time God intervenes and overrules. Instead of pronouncing curses, Balaam finds himself pronouncing blessings[437].

Jonah too has come to Nineveh hoping to see a divine curse fall. He finds, however, that he has only brought them blessing. This experience so upsets and confuses him that he is at his wits' end.

Now, deprived of shelter, he has to endure the unblinking desert sun. Then, to make matters worse, a sirocco wind gets up. The effect of this should not be underestimated. The desert sirocco is,

> *...so full of positive ions that it affects the levels of serotonin and other brain*
> *neurotransmitters, causing exhaustion, depression, feelings of unreality, and*
> *occasionally, bizarre behaviour. In some Moslem countries, the punishment for a*
> *crime committed while the sirocco is blowing may be reduced at judicial discretion,*
> *so strongly does the prolonged hot wind affect the thinking and actions.* [438]

Poor Jonah is really suffering. Added to his spiritual trauma are the physical and psychological effects of the heat and the sirocco.

This leads to a real spiritual reversal for Jonah. He had been taking delight in God's miraculous provision. Now, as it disappears, he has to ask himself, 'Was I deceived?', 'Was the vine really a blessing from God?' Such reversals are a major

---

[437] Numbers 23
[438] Stuart D. *ibid.,* p505f

problem for those who place their faith in the subjective evidence of God's grace. Can God still be good when life gets bad?

This situation highlights a fundamental necessity for healthy Christian faith. Our faith must be based, not on our subjective experience, but on our objective knowledge of God. We must worship God because of who He is, not just because of what He does. We worship him because He is the God who created the universe and who holds it in existence by His word of power. We worship Him because He reveals His goodness, majesty, wonder and love through everything that He has made and through His self-revelation to man.

We do this because it is the way things should be – it is simply the right thing to do. I vaguely remember reading a statement (I think it was C.S. Lewis who wrote it), which said that when we are worshipping God, it is one of the few times in our lives when we **absolutely** know that we are doing the right thing. Worship is **always** right.

In the context of blessing, worship flows naturally, something Lewis pointed out in his brilliant book on the Psalms. He noted that,

> *...all enjoyment spontaneously outflows into praise* [439].

Lewis also reminds us that a great part of the pleasure involved in any glorious new discovery - be it in music, art, literature, love - is that which we experience when we **share it with others;** when we make it known **through our praises**. To exclude our experience of God from this process would be to make Him a case apart from every other aspect of our lives. So when life is good and things go well, worship should be a natural response.

We are puny creatures inexplicably loved by the awesome God. We have no other eternal significance or purpose outside of that which comes from our loving, serving and worshipping God. Such worship is therefore our greatest honour and privilege, and, as such, it should be our top priority.

However, when things are not going well for us, when life is difficult, when there is no **experience** of blessing, what then?

If our worship is based upon an understanding of the **character** of God, then **no matter the circumstances** we can still love Him, worship Him and praise Him.

---

[439] Lewis C.S. *Reflections on the Psalms*, Glasgow: Fontana Books, 1958, p80

Though the fig-tree does not bud and there are no grapes on the vines, though the olive crop fails and the fields produce no food, though there are no sheep in the pen and no cattle in the stalls, yet I will rejoice in the LORD, I will be joyful in God my Saviour. The Sovereign LORD is my strength;
he makes my feet like the feet of a deer, he enables me to go on the heights [440]

Habakkuk's praise is based upon God's character, not upon his circumstances. This objective faith enables him to ascend to the heights - to see events from God's perspective, not to have his horizons filled with his own passing tribulations. In the wonderful 'Experiencing God – Knowing and Doing the Will of God' discipleship course, Henry Blackaby states that,

> *You cannot know the truth of your circumstances*
> *until you have heard from God* [441].

Henry's own practice in tough times was not to look at God through his circumstances, but rather to try to look at his circumstances in the light of God's love. This love finds its highest expression in Jesus' death on the cross. Starting from this perspective of Calvary, Henry was then in a position to seek God for an understanding of what was currently happening in his life. Keeping his eyes on the cross prevented Henry from ever doubting God's love and goodness towards him, **regardless of his circumstances**.

Similar faith is implicit in the 'other half' of Hebrews chapter eleven[442]. In the first half of the chapter we have a list of the many men and women who experienced God's miraculous intervention in their circumstances. These individuals are honoured and praised as 'heroes of faith'. However, the second half of the list contains the nameless ones, those who didn't see any miraculous intervention. They just suffered, or were tortured, and many died. Is this because theirs' was a lesser faith?

The writer to the Hebrews answers with a dogmatic 'No'. God commends **all** of them for their faith[443]. Why God took some of them **out** of their difficulties and required others to go **through** their difficulties is a mystery. We need, therefore, to be very wary of any gospel which excludes suffering and negative outcomes; they seem to be an intrinsic part of following Christ.

---

[440] Habakkuk 3:17-19 NIV
[441] Blackaby H. & King C. *ibid.*, p98
[442] Hebrews 11:35b-38
[443] Hebrews 11v39

Poor Jonah is struggling with this very issue – what is God doing? Why is bad stuff happening to him? In the midst of this spiritual turmoil, God asks him a second question,

Do you have any reason to be angry about the vine?

Jonah had been angry about the non-destruction of the city, now he is angry about the destruction of the vine. The basis of this different emotional attitude is because Jonah didn't care about Nineveh, but he did care about the vine. Most likely he despised Nineveh as a city of 'unclean' Gentiles; the home of the oppressors of his people. But he delighted in the vine as a divine blessing and a source of personal comfort. Jonah valued things solely based on his own personal experience and understanding. Suddenly the reason for the seeming cruelty of God becomes clear – God is trying to teach Jonah something, to help him have a correct perspective on recent events.

In asking Jonah this question, God is forcing Jonah to acknowledge the truth of the situation. If Jonah answers 'Yes' to God's question, and claims the right to be concerned about the vine, then he is forced to recognise God's greater right to be concerned for Nineveh. If Jonah answers 'No', then he admits that the vine, which God made grow and then caused to die, is none of his business; in which case Jonah has no right to be angry about what God does with the city of Nineveh.

Jonah's problem is summed up by;

A lack of confidence in God's wisdom.
A lack of submission to God's will[444].

These are opposite sides of the same coin. Jonah thought God was making a mistake in sending him to the Ninevites, and also in subsequently showing grace and mercy towards them. Jonah, consequently, had great difficulty in being obedient to God's will. Both Jonah's initial flight and his angry reaction to God's merciful sparing of the Ninevites, are rooted in the same spiritual problem.

Jonah didn't value things in the same way that God did. Jonah's value system was upside down. This is evidenced throughout the story;

- In his decision-making he prioritises his own wisdom and understanding over God's clear instruction.
- He cares for his own people (the Jews), but very little for the Gentiles.
- He cares more about his own reputation than for a city's survival.

---

[444] Catron J.L.R. *The Minor Prophets*, Dubuque: Emmaus Bible College, 1991, p29.

206

- He cares more for a plant than for people.

God has worked in Jonah's life to expose these errors in his value system.

Questions for Reflection and Discussion

1	How do you respond to the challenge to not look at God through our circumstances, but rather to look at our circumstances in the light of God's love; a love that is expressed most completely by Jesus' death on the cross? How does this change things?

2	Have you had an experience where God has worked to help you see His perspective on events in your life? How did God do that, what did He use?

Jonah – The Worm and the Wind

There are no giant fish outside
Of Nineveh to eat the pride
Of prophets in their ease, but there
Are worms and wind, and when and where
He please, God orders them and makes
Them do his bidding. If he takes
No pleasure in my callous mind
And heart, then there will be assigned
A worm, and so there was, to slay
The leafy plant and take away
My shade. And then he blasted me
With sultry wind until with three
Small words I cursed the brazen sky:
And spoke to heaven, 'Let me die!'[445]

---

[445] Piper J. Jonah – Part 3

40 - Should I Be Like You? (Jonah 4:10-11)

But the Lord said, 'You have been concerned about this plant, though you did not tend it or make it grow. It sprang up overnight and died overnight.
And should I not have concern for the great city of Nineveh, in which there are more than a hundred and twenty thousand people who cannot tell their right hand from their left – and also many animals?'

Jonah 4:10-11, NIV

Here we are at our last day's study! All of our previous days have brought us up to this final resounding question. In posing Jonah this question, God brings him smack up against the outrage of his wrong ideas. He shows him the horrific result of his skewed values, which lead him to be more caring of a wild plant than a populous city.

God describes Jonah's relationship with the vine. He said; *'You did not plant it'*, *'You took no care of it'*. Jonah has made no investment in the vine. It was a pure gift, involving no input on his part. Interestingly, this may be interpreted to infer that God **had** cared for, and made grow, the city of Nineveh. This, for a Jew of Jonah's time, would have been a revolutionary and shocking idea, that *Yahweh*, should be intimately involved in the fate of a Gentile city![446]

God's description of the vine also communicates the idea of impermanence, *'It sprang up overnight'*, *'It died overnight'*. It is a transitory thing and of no lasting consequence.

In stark contrast God describes the city of Nineveh as having,

'...more than 120,000 innocent children',
'There are many livestock within it', *'It is an important city'.*

As we have noted previously, the Bible presents clearly a sense of the solidarity and common destiny of man and animals. Here we note that God's compassion is not motivated solely by His concern for the innocent children, but also for the innocent animals.

...several midrashim even suggest that sometimes the Lord saves human beings only because of the animals who are blameless. [447]

God's merciful concern for His creation – mankind and animal-kind – is now summed up in a final question that God poses to Jonah,

---

[446] Caiger S.L. *Lives of the Prophets*, London : SPCK, 1936, p258
[447] Shemesh Y. *ibid.*, p23

'Should I not be concerned about that great city?'

Again Jonah gives no answer. Of course the correct answer, implied in the question, is 'Yes'. However, at this time Jonah still cannot bring himself to agree with God.

Ending with this unanswered question ringing out, calling for a response, we are drawn into the story. Each of us has to give our own response;

Here, on the open page in front of us - in the utter silence after the question - we are being offered the surprising freedom and opportunity to write out for ourselves, as it were, the final paragraph of the Book of Jonah. [448]

What will our response be to the shocking extent of God's mercy? How will we react to the news that God loves those that hate us, and that we hate in return? How do we feel about God using a sinful, twisted, melancholy, petulant, rebellious prophet as His messenger of grace?

And so the book of Jonah ends. In the absence of any response from Jonah, some have gone so far as to say that,

Jonah leaves the stage of history shaking his fist at God [449]

However, whilst there is no information given regarding Jonah's final response to God's question, there is much to imply that Jonah's final answer to God was 'Yes'. There is a strong indication that Jonah did indeed change his attitudes and embrace a new understanding of God; as being loving and merciful to all mankind, not just to the Jews, not just to the deserving.

A Jewish midrashim makes the suggestion that,

...in that hour Jonah fell on his face and said,
"Govern your world according to the measure of your mercy, as it is said,
'To the Lord our God belong mercy and forgiveness (Daniel 9:9) [450]

Indeed, the very fact that we have the book of Jonah can be interpreted as evidence that Jonah's final answer to God was 'Yes'. Only someone who was humbled and broken could have shared such an honest account of his own sinfulness and failings. In this account Jonah's rebellion and anger with God are fully documented, without a trace of any attempt to mitigate or to justify; the

---

[448] Murray P. *ibid.*, p57.
[449] Keddie G.J. *Preacher on the Run*, Welwyn: EP Books, 1993, p104 cited in Dray S. *ibid.*, p69
[450] Ellison H.L. *ibid.*, p390

book hides nothing. Jonah's horror concerning the idea of grace for the Assyrians is held up for all to see. Jonah's very personal struggle with God is laid bare. Indeed, Jonah is the anti-hero rather than the hero,

> *The animals in the story perform God's behest,*
> *the humans characters try to do His will,*
> *and only Jonah flees from his mission.*[451]

Only someone who had really made a dramatic turn-around, and who had finally come to see things from God's perspective, could have shared such an honest account of his experiences.

Jonah's story has an important place in the unfolding process of divine revelation. In this book we see, for the first time in Scripture, an explicit presentation of God's concern for the Gentiles. Jonah's prophecy prepares the way for the prophecies of Isaiah and Jeremiah. These later prophecies will develop even more clearly the fact that the Gentiles are to be included in the future blessings of Israel.

In terms of his ministry, by any measure, Jonah was successful during his lifetime. Prior to his adventures in this book, he was already an attested prophet in Israel with close links to the royal court. His rebellion rectified, his missionary endeavour saw a massive Gentile city turn around to the worship of the true God. However **neither** of these incredible successes are Jonah's most important ministry.

Jonah's most significant ministry is to the millions of Jews, Christians and Muslims who, down through 2,500 years, have valued his story as divine revelation; who, in studying it, have found deep spiritual sustenance and encouragement and have therefore included it within their Scriptures.

Perhaps it is the complexity, and the paradoxical nature of Jonah, that makes it so rewarding to meditation. For Jonah is not an easy book, nor does it contain a wholly joyful message.

Indeed, one of the key lessons Jonah teaches, is how we should respond to the harsh reality of oppressive regimes. The book reminds us of our duty to witness to such powers, and gives us hope that they may even respond. Yet the book also shows us that this kind of action is costly and creates a complex and dangerous interplay. Even if, through our prayers and our witness, these

---

[451] Shemesh Y. *ibid.*, p15

oppressive regimes experience God's grace, there is no guarantee that they will not return to their old ways.

> *Mercy in Yahweh may lead, paradoxically,*
> *to the merciless actions of those who receive grace.*
> *Such can create a real angst in those who are seeking to live out their faith,*
> *to hold firm in their beliefs, amid such excruciatingly existential circumstances.*[452]

Jonah is therefore a 'grown-up' book. It presents the costly reality of God's mysterious, wild and unpredictable grace. God's people are charged to be messengers of His grace, yet they may themselves become the future victims of those who benefit from that grace – as indeed Jonah's people in the Northern Kingdom would be. Grace abounds, yet grace costs. God Himself and His people are the ones who pay the price.

As we seek to sum up the message of Jonah it is important to make the connection with the book of Nahum. These two books form mirror-images of each other.

- They are both concerned with Nineveh.
- They are both about the same size – Jonah has 47 verses, Nahum has 48.
- The book of Jonah shows God offering grace and mercy to a wicked people; a people who respond and repent and so avoid judgement. The book of Nahum is the prophecy of God's final judgement on a later generation of Ninevites. A prophecy of destruction that was fulfilled in 612 B.C.

Jonah shows us that God offers His grace and mercy even to those who seem the least deserving. Nahum shows us that this willingness to forgive has limits[453].

However, it is important to remember that Jesus identified himself with the prophet Jonah and not with the prophet Nahum – a sign that grace and mercy are ever the truest qualities of God.

> *Here is the true sign of Jonah –*
> *to be able to give up to sacrifice that which is fair and just for oneself*
> *in order to extend God's mercy to those who clearly do not deserve it*[454]

---

[452] Dray S. *ibid.*, p82

[453] Wörhle J. A Prophetic Reflection on Divine Forgiveness: The Integration of the Book of Jonah into the Book of the Twelve, Journal of Hebrew Scriptures, Vol. 9, Art. 7, 2009, p14

[454] Burrows D.P. *ibid.*, p152

In the deafening silence of this final unanswered question, we have much to respond to.

Questions for Reflection and Discussion

1   Now we have arrived at the end of our studies in Jonah, how do you respond to the message of the book? What aspects of this study have impacted you the most? How will your life and your understanding of God be different for having spent this time thinking about Jonah and his story?

2   What final response do you think Jonah made to God? What answer do you think he finally gave to God's question?

Jonah – The Dove and the Snake

...The bowl
Of wrath I would have poured on that
Great city, God did make a vat
Of boiling mercy for my sin,
And cast me into it. And in
That fierce and cleansing clemency,
At last, did make me feel and see
His ways, which are as high above
My own as is the flying dove
Above the crawling snake.[455]

---

[455] Piper J. Jonah – Part 3

Afterword

Our study of the book of Jonah is now complete so what do we take away as the fruit of our involvement with this sacred text?

As we have seen throughout this study, the book of Jonah touches on almost every theme in salvation history; and all this in a book of only 689 words!

We have seen the radical nature of God's grace which is offered to all; the universal possibility of salvation. We have seen a picture of the Church that results from that work of salvation and which takes her place in the mission of God to the world. We have also seen the shadow side of that reality; the cycles of backsliding, rebellions, the remedial action of God, confession, repentance, reconciliation and re-commissioning.

It is important to note that the repentance of Jonah has to be expressed both in personal acts of worship and re-dedication (Jonah's psalm) and also the commitment to re-engage in the worshipping life of God's people (the Temple). It is only after this happens that God re-commissions Jonah for mission.

The book of Jonah also reveals the amazing wisdom and power of God. We find that when the prophet arrives in Nineveh and begins his work of proclamation, not only has his sinful rebellion not diminished his usefulness to God, but actually it has prepared him for the task. Indeed, Jonah's success is almost entirely based upon his experiences caused by his rebellion! Such is the amazing power of God to draw straight lines with crooked sticks!

Yet at the end of Jonah's amazing story and experience of successful ministry, we find him still struggling, still broken.

Indeed, it is this very human reality in the book of Jonah that explains the important place that the story has found in popular piety.

We know that we are Jonah.

- Like Jonah we are imperfect, broken people. We are committed to God but we also struggle to live with God.
- Like Jonah we find that God often seems to stretch us almost to breaking point and we often fall.
- Like Jonah we might sometimes experience great things in God, yet we also know that we remain spiritually fragile beings. The light is at work in us but the dark is never far away.

For me, the key truth that Jonah teaches us is this;

Never underestimate the grace of God.

We should never think we can put limits on the extent of God's grace, the reach of God's grace, or the power of God's grace. Jonah discovers grace in Joppa, at sea, under the sea, in a pagan city, in the burning desert; in fact everywhere he goes he finds himself - much to his own shock and even horror - confronted by the glory of God's grace. That, I believe, is the key truth that Jonah communicates to us. God's grace is wild!

You can't put limits on it.
You can't put a lid on it.
You can't box it in.
You can't fence it off.
You can't domesticate it.
You can't tame it.
You can't control it.
You can't direct it.
You can't understand it.
You can't predict it.
It burst out in a Jewish port.
It bursts out on a pagan boat.
It bursts out in a fish's belly.
It bursts out in a wicked city.
It finally bursts out in the burning desert,
even in the heart of a reluctant prophet.
God's grace is wild!

Jonah had a hard time living with the wildness of grace. He appreciated God's grace when it came to him. But he had a difficult time celebrating that same grace when it came to others he didn't think deserved it. He had to learn that God's grace *always comes to people who don't deserve it* - that's why it is called grace! It even comes to people who don't know about it, who don't know that they need it, or who may even not want it! Jonah tried his hardest to refuse God's grace before eventually capitulating before it.

God took Jonah through a long process in order to reveal to him the truth that;

God's grace is God's business.

God doesn't have to answer to us or to ask for our advice about how He should pour out His grace. Our place is merely to celebrate that grace, to welcome it, to glory in it. Every time we see God's grace in action our reaction should be to jump up and down and say 'Look, God's done it again! Grace has broken out! Praise the Lord!'

I remember reading about an English evangelist called Billy Bray. He ministered in Cornwall, England in the early 1800's. Whenever anyone got saved in one of his meetings he would physically pick them up and run around the church with them in celebration. This wiry, former tin miner, would carry these new converts in triumph around the church, singing and dancing and praying at the same time! 'Look, God's done it again! Grace has broken out! Praise the Lord!'

Grace. It is our only hope. It is all that stands between us and sin and death and Hell. We need to celebrate it. To glory in it. To wonder at it. To proclaim it.

The hope of grace is all that we have to offer the World. The hope of grace is the only 'product' that the Church has. Why should people come to us? Grace! We exist as a distribution network for grace.

Brothers and sisters, Grace is wild!

This is the wonderful, glorious and encouraging message that Jonah teaches us. However the message of the book of Jonah also reveals to us a sobering truth about the human response to grace. In this story the wonderful, omnipresent, boundless grace of God is **only** ever appropriated by people *in extremis*.

- The sailors had to be on the verge of sinking before they cried out for grace.
- Jonah had to be swallowed by a sea monster and at the bottom of the ocean before he turned from his rebellion and sought grace.
- The Ninevites had to be certain of their imminent destruction before they would cry out for God's grace.

This is the shadow-side of the message of Jonah. We learn through Jonah that although God is gracious beyond our imagining and that He reaches out to all with His grace, yet it seems that human beings are only motivated to receive this divine grace **when it is all that stands between them and disaster**.

This is the complex and serious message of the book of Jonah, a message that is both full of hope and sobering. Jonah shows us the remarkable truth that the earth is bathed in God's generous grace, a grace which is accessible to all; however it also shows us the sad reality that it is often only in situations of dire need that human beings realise their need of grace and reach out towards it; but when they do so they discover that God's grace **never** fails.

221

May the Lord bless you as you seek to live in the light of this wonderful and glorious grace.

The following final pages will look at how this story has inspired, instructed and challenged people of faith over the past 2,500 years. We will look at the way in which the story of Jonah has influenced Jewish, Christian and Muslim piety, and we will round off our study with a look at the different legends regarding Jonah's later life.

Jonah in Judaism

As Blumenthal remarks concerning the book of Jonah,

The inclusion of this book in the Hebrew Bible and the many references to it in the Talmud and Midrash show that the sages of the Talmudic era saw in its text ideas or lessons valuable for all times.[456]

The text of Jonah has found a privileged place in the liturgy of Judaism. The Babylonian Talmud also refers to Jonah in some of its prayers,

May He who answered Jonah in the bowels of the fish answer you, and listen unto your cry this day. Blessed art thou, O Lord, who answerest in the time of distress![457]

It is, however, in the liturgy for *Yom Kippur* – the Day of Atonement – that the texts of Jonah have found their most significant role in Jewish usage. From at least the second century A.D. the text of Jonah has formed part of the Jewish liturgical services for this celebration[458].

An anonymous Midrash on Jonah for the festival of *Yom Kippur* powerfully sums up the closing message of Jonah,

And then, at the end of the story,
God said to me, in God's great and wise chutzpah:
"Jonah son of Amittai: What do you want from me? You mourn for the tree that
you did not plant, nor did you make it grow; which came up in a night, and perished
in a night. Should we not work together to heal the people of Nineveh, and the
people of the world? In spite of our doubt and uncertainty? Even in the face of long
odds and long experience? I know that life sometimes seems to you, easy come,
easy go. But will you love it while it lasts? Will you strive to make it better? The
reason death exists is to give meaning to life. Only things that are limited have
meaning. Or would you prefer that the people of Nineveh and the people of the
world simply give up and go to their Eternal home? Jonah: What will it be?"
And when God finished, it was I who was silent.[459]

In the liturgy of *Yom Kippur*, citations from Jonah are used in order to remind the Jewish faithful that it was not the fasting of the Ninevites that turned away the anger of God, but rather,

---

[456] Blumenthal F. *Jonah the Reluctant Prophet : Prophecy and Allegory*, Jewish Bible Quarterly, Vol. 35, No. 2, 2007, p103
[457] Rodkinson M.L.(ed. and tr.) The Babylonian Talmud Vol. 1-10, 1918, Second Ed., Boston: Boston New Talmud Publishing Company 1918 [1903], p2171
[458] Dray S. *ibid.*, p72
[459] Anonymous *A Midrash on Jonah Yom Kippur 5772*

*When God saw what they **did** and how they **turned** from their evil ways, he
relented and did not bring on them the destruction he had threatened.*[460]

This forms a stark contrast with the later history of Israel. For, whilst the
Ninevites responded to God's message and repented, God's own people will
refuse to repent; and so will experience the conquest of the Assyrians and exile
to Babylon. The usage of Jonah on the fast day of *Yom Kippur* is a powerful
reminder that the religious act of fasting, in and of itself, is of little import.

*...the book of Jonah has a subversive function, that of challenging the popular
presuppositions about the Day of Atonement itself. The theological implications of
Yom Kippur may be rather hazy to the average Jew at his once-a-year attendance
in synagogue, but at least the fast, whether observed or self-consciously ignored, is
remembered. And Isaiah and Jonah forcibly remind us that fasting alone is not the
essence of the day.*[461]

What God seeks is true repentance, as expressed in changed lives. Indeed, this
focus on the power of repentance is the key lesson that Rabbi Eliezer the Great,
a first-century figure, draws from the story of Jonah[462]. Wünsche presents the
Midrash Jonah where the truths learned by Ninevites are drawn out,

*Our brothers! (from the people of Nineveh we have learned) that sackcloth and
fasting do not bring about (forgiveness), but repentance and good works, as it says:
'When God saw what they did, how they turned from their evil ways...'*[463]

In the liturgy of *Yom Kippur* the Jonah texts also foster a reflection on Nineveh.
The city is seen as representing all the world powers, down through history,
which have threatened the Jews. The Jewish attitude towards those oppressive
powers is radically defined.

*Nineveh is the Rome that destroyed the second temple, the European countries
that ignored the massacres of the Crusaders, the Spanish cities of the Inquisition,
the East European centres of pogroms, Berlin of the Third Reich.*
*To all these Ninevehs, Jonah is sent to discover behind "the violence in their hands"
human beings on the verge of repentance awaiting only the word ...*
*But Nineveh need not be so dramatic. It is whatever place Jonah does not want to
go because his experience of God is too narrow, his compassion too grudging, his
piety too comfortable and convenient.*

---

[460] Jonah 3:10, NIV

[461] Magonet J. *ibid.*, p5

[462] Friedlander G. *ibid.*, pp342-343

[463] Wünsche A. *Aus Israels Lehrhallen*, Vol.2, Hidelsheim : Georg Olms, p49, cited in Limburg J. *ibid.*,
p112

*As the day draws to its end ... Jonah forces us to look at this world to which,
purified, we must return, with all the myriad tasks that await us there.* [464]

Perhaps the best way to sum up how Jonah has inspired Jewish reflection and
piety is to cite a Jewish prayer, also linked to *Yom Kippur*, the Day of Atonement;

*'Lord, you are revealed in the story of Jonah, and we relate its meaning to
ourselves; for Nineveh is the repentant world, and we are Israel, its unwilling
prophet. You have chosen us to know You and to love You, and this knowledge is
our glory, and this love is our burden ... such knowledge is too wonderful for us. By
it you reveal our kinship to friend and foe, our duty to those who love us, and to
those who hate us; our task in a world where everything and everyone is Your
work. If we are not for others, we are not for Israel. It is for us to bring the prisoner
freedom, to give the homeless refuge, and the starving food. It is for us to sow the
seed of friendship on unfriendly soil, to reconcile enemies, and bring redemption to
our oppressors ... Your command is beyond all calculation.'* [465]

---

[464] Magonet J. *ibid.*, p6-7
[465] Assembly of Rabbis of Reform Synagogues of Great Britain, *Forms of Prayer for Jewish Worship Vol
3 Prayers for the High Holydays*, London: Reform Synagogues of Great Britain, 1985, p551,quoted in
Murray P. *ibid.*, p56.

Jonah in the Christian Church

What has the Christian Church made of the book of Jonah? As we saw at the start, there is much debate over the main message of this book. Some see the book as a critique of the insularity and the 'missions failure' of Judaism. However, as Ellison remarks,

Quite simply, the book contains no call to action.
It is rather, a revelation of God's character and attitude towards His creation given to Jonah and through Jonah to Israel and to us.[466]

Others have seen the book as an apologetic for a new way to understand the glorification of Israel - one which would include the Gentiles within the orbit of God's grace[467].

Others would simply reduce the message of the book to a simple warning,

Don't be like Jonah! [468]

Certainly it seems clear that the key to understanding the message of the book is in its final climax. It is in the final conversation between God and Jonah that we find the key truth the story is designed to present to us.

In this final exchange we are confronted with the stark reality of God's grace - a grace that breaks out gloriously, in the most unlikely of situations and touches the most unlikely of persons. Yet it is a grace that is often confusing, and which leaves its agents at a loss to comprehend it. It is often-times a risky and a costly grace for those who are the closest to God.

In trying to resume the purpose of the book of Jonah, Von Orelli states,

What runs like a red thread through the whole, and at last becomes a knot, whose unloosing in 4:10 forms the glorious finale, is the conduct of God to the heathen world, which is here revealed as full of goodwill and love, in opposition to the limited, narrow-hearted notion current in Israel, and not impossible even to a prophet like Jonah ; while the conduct of the heathen to God, both that of the seamen and the Ninevites, must put the Jews to shame by their reverence for the Deity and their ready repentance. The national limits of the Old Covenant are here wondrously broken through ; the entire heathen world opens as a mission-field to the messengers of Yahveh.[469]

---

[466] Ellison H.L. *ibid.,* p390
[467] Isaiah 49:6, Zechariah 8:20-23.
[468] Stuart D. *ibid.,* p434
[469] Von Orelli C. *ibid.,* p170

Understood in this way, Jonah's story is Israel's story, in fact Jonah **is** Israel. The book acts as a mirror which held up to the Israelite nation,

> *...a mirror in which it may see with shame its own incapacity to understand God's great dealings, and to take part in His world-embracing love*[470]

> *The 'sign of Jonah' is a sign of God's desire to save the Gentiles,*
> *that is, humankind awash in the terror of a world which sin is destroying.*[471]

However, the story is also about the sovereignty of God – that He is free to do as He wills. Our ability to understand His will is completely irrelevant. We remember that we have seen in Jonah's story a God who is constantly working 'behind the scenes', controlling His creation and the history of mankind, in order to achieve His purposes. We are made aware of the fact that this preparation is mostly hidden, not only from the objects of God's grace, but also from the agents of God's grace – and so God's grace always has a strong element of surprise.

We also see that the grace of God is often transmitted by those least suited to the job - God uses a jingoistic, broken and confused prophet as his agent of grace to Nineveh. God chooses Jonah for this assignment not because he is suited to it, but because he needs it. Through this experience God will teach His prophet about Himself and about His ways.

Perhaps one of the most powerful lessons in the book of Jonah is the observation that,

> *Those whom God refuses to regard as His enemies*
> *the Christian cannot regard as enemies.*[472]

Another key message in the book of Jonah is well summarised by Tchividjian, when he writes,

> *Except for God, everyone in the story – Jonah, each sailor, each Ninevite – is messed up. Jonah has his stubborn, prideful rebelliousness. The sailors have their worship of false gods, and the people of Nineveh have their 'exceeding wickedness'. They're all dysfunctional*[473]

---

[470] ibid., p171
[471] Burrows D.P. *ibid.*, p41
[472] ibid.
[473] Tchividjian T. *Surprised by Grace*, Wheaton: Crossway, 2010, p145

At its heart, Jonah's story is a hymn to God's remarkable grace that reaches out to messed-up people everywhere.

> *The whole story of Jonah is God's going after depraved, fallen fugitives ...*
> *There's no place you might be now, or where you might have been in the past,*
> *or where you might be in the future*
> *that will ever be beyond the reach of God's grace – nowhere.*[474]

The book of Jonah has helped Christians recognize this amazing reality and they have been inspired, encouraged and strengthened by it for over 2,000 years.

But Jonah also reveals to us another important aspect of God's grace – that it is God and God alone who decides how and where it is to be poured out.

> *If we are to succeed in living by grace, we must come to terms with the fact that*
> *God is sovereign in dispensing His gracious favours, and He owes us no explanation*
> *when His actions do not correspond with our system of merits.*[475]

Perhaps the greatest challenge Jonah places before us is therefore that of learning to love, and to live with, a grace we cannot comprehend.

Jonah teaches us one more thing about grace – it is costly. We see two groups of people who experience grace in the book – the sailors and the Ninevites.

For the sailors, their grace was obtained through Jonah's self-sacrifice; it was this act that released the grace they received.

For the Ninevites, the grace they received cost Jonah the disgrace of being considered a false prophet. Furthermore it would ultimately cost the existence of the ten Northern tribes of Israel; destroyed by a resurgent, and no longer penitent Nineveh (Assyria), some 40 years after Jonah's visit. In 722/1 B.C. the Assyrians conquered Northern Israel and carried its people off into exile in Babylonia – an exile from which the ten Northern tribes never returned[476].

Jonah became one of the most well-known biblical characters in Christian spirituality due to his adoption as a symbol of Christ. At the very beginning of Christian art, when overt representations of Christ were still dangerous, the symbol of Jonah became the most popular symbol used to represent Christ. Jonah was often shown being vomited out of the sea-monster as a symbol of Christ's resurrection from the dead. Indeed, Saint Paul's reference to Christ's

---

[474] *ibid.*, p148/9
[475] Bridges J. *Transforming Grace*, Colorado Springs: Navpress, 1991, p70
[476] Cary P. *ibid.*, p35

resurrection on the third day having been 'according to the Scriptures'[477] can only have two possible Old Testament references – Jonah's experience with the sea-monster or a citation from Hosea,

> *After two days he will revive us; on the third day he will restore us,*
> *that we may live in his presence*[478]

From the fact of Jonah's adoption as the earliest and most popular symbol of the resurrection, it seems most likely that the Old Testament reference that Saint Paul had in mind must have been Jonah.

In fact the series of parallels between Jonah and Jesus are quite striking.

- They both come from the same region.
- They both offer their lives to save others.
- They both announce coming judgement and call for repentance.
- They are both are delivered from death by God's miraculous action and are they are thereby both vindicated as God's messengers[479].

With regard to the use of Jonah as a symbol in early Christian art, it is interesting to note that in artistic usage Jonah's mission to Nineveh and the repentance of Ninevites are largely ignored. The major focus is the 'big fish' episode and its resurrection symbolism. It was Christ's words in Matthew 12 which gave impetus to this use of Jonah[480];

> *He answered, 'A wicked and adulterous generation asks for a sign! But none will be given it except the sign of the prophet Jonah. For as Jonah was three days and three nights in the belly of a huge fish, so the Son of Man will be three days and three nights in the heart of the earth. The men of Nineveh will stand up at the judgment with this generation and condemn it; for they repented at the preaching of Jonah, and now something greater than Jonah is here.*[481]

It seems that Jonah was considered as a 'type' of Christ, a forerunner whose life in some way points towards that of Jesus. The Old Testament types of Christ were something that could only be seen in retrospect. It was not the Jews who would identify them, and through them anticipate the Messiah. Rather it was the Church, comprised of both Jew and Gentile, now united in the 'one new man',

---

[477] 1 Corinthians 15:4

[478] Hosea 6:2

[479] Edwards R.A. The Sign of Jonah in the Theology of the Evangelists and Q, London: SCM Press, 1971, p86

[480] Barclay-Lloid J.E. *The Prophet Jonah in Early Christian Art*, Service International de Documentation Judeo-Chrétienne (SIDIC), XVIII, 1985/1, p18

[481] Matthew 12:39-41, NIV

who would look back at the Old Testament and recognise these types, and see in them the reality of Christ's fulfilment of the Old Testament and the Jewish Messianic hope.

Whilst the other Old Testament prophets point to Jesus Christ primarily by their words, Jonah points to Jesus primarily by his actions and the experiences he undergoes[482]. As such, Jonah is a powerful symbol of Christ. Interestingly, Jonah was also used as a symbol of the archetypal Christian.

...a forerunner or example of the individual Christian in his relationship to the Almighty and in his hope of salvation, resurrection and eternal happiness ... The story of the prophet, ranging through disobedience, repentance, prayer, redemption, obedience, rest and a final understanding of God's mercy and love for all of His creation provided a fine example for a member of the Early Church.[483]

The story of Jonah was therefore seen as an encouragement for early Christians,

He (God), who after three days dragged Jonah alive and intact from the belly of the sea-monster ... will not lack strength to tear us, too, away from death[484]

Jonah's influence on the Early Church is not, however, solely limited to his use as a symbol in art. His story also inspired an act of piety that has taken permanent root in the spirituality of the Eastern Church. The Assyrian church is one of the oldest branches of Christendom, traces its origin to the year 33 A.D.; when Saint Thomas is said to have brought the gospel message to Assyria only 4 months after Christ's crucifixion. Not unsurprisingly these Assyrian Christians felt a strong bond with Jonah – the first missionary to Assyria.

In the 6th century A.D. a great plague hit this region and the Assyrian Christians, remembering the story of Jonah and the power of repentance, proclaimed a fast. Following this fast, the plague subsided. This event gave rise to an annual 'Jonah's Fast'. Otherwise known as 'The Rogation of the Ninevites', this 3 day fast is held between 14th and 16th February and is still observed by all Assyrian Christian denominations and by most of the Eastern churches[485].

---

[482] Calmet Dom *ibid.,* p341
[483] Barclay-Lloid, *ibid.,* p19
[484] *ibid.,* quoting Migne PG 5, 7, 843
[485] Shirsha A. Jonah, the Whale, the Assyrians, Christianity and Islam – Guest Editorial, Assyrian International News Agency 11-29-2010.

In the story of Jonah, the Early Church saw many resonances with other biblical figures. Jonah' story is quite like that of Samson[486], another tragic hero. Biblical tragedy is a specific genre in which the following elements are always present,

...a privileged protagonist falls from a position of honour and respect,
to one of rebuke and death[487]

Indeed this combination of saint and sinner, of hero and villain, is the central Hebrew understanding of humankind.

The Hebraic answer to the question of existence was never unambiguous or
utopian; the double vision of tragedy – the snake in the garden, the paradox of
man born in the image of God and yet recalcitrant, tending to go wrong –
permeates the scriptures.[488]

Jonah and Samson, both show the complex reality of human/divine relationships.

There is also a strong parallel in the story of Jonah and that of Joseph. Both Joseph and Jonah are sent against their will to pagan lands – to nations which often posed a threat to Israel. Both Joseph and Jonah are a means of God's blessing the pagan nation to whom they are sent. In both stories the people of God will ultimately suffer at the hands of these same pagan people.

For Jonah, the fact that God's own people should have to bear the price of God's grace to pagans was an impossible conundrum. For us, living in the light of Calvary, it is less so. We have seen first-hand how much grace cost God Himself; we can be less shocked when some of that cost is also experienced by His people. Saint Paul expresses this truth,

Now I rejoice in what I am suffering for you,
and I fill up in my flesh what is still lacking in regard to Christ's afflictions,
for the sake of his body, which is the church.[489]

As a consequence of the mystical union between Christ and His Church, we share in Christ's ministry here on earth. One consequence of this is the activity of sharing in His sufferings;

Being one with Christ also means that we will suffer.

---

[486] Judges 13-16

[487] Woodward B.L. *Death in Life: The Book of Jonah and Biblical Tragedy*, Grace Theological Journal, 11.1, 1991, p12

[488] Sewall R. *The Vision of Tragedy*, New Haven: Yale, 1959, p9-10 cited in Woodward B.L. *ibid.*, p15

[489] Colossians 1:24, NIV

The disciples were told that they would drink the cup that Jesus drank,
and be baptized with the same baptism (Mark 10:39).
If tradition serves us correctly, most of them suffered a martyr's death.[490]

In some mysterious way, our sufferings can become – in union with the sufferings of Christ – redemptive acts.

For just as we share abundantly in the sufferings of Christ,
so also our comfort abounds through Christ.
If we are distressed, it is for your comfort and salvation;
if we are comforted, it is for your comfort,
which produces in you patient endurance of the same sufferings we suffer.[491]

For Saint Paul, this aspect of his union with Christ was key,

I want to know Christ – yes, to know the power of his resurrection and participation
in his sufferings, becoming like him in his death,
and so, somehow, attaining to the resurrection from the dead.[492]

As C.S. Lewis put it,

The people who are selected (chosen by God) are, in a sense, unfairly selected for a
supreme honour; but it is also a supreme burden. The People of Israel come to
realize that it is their woes which are saving the world[493]

God's intentions are very clear: he wants his world back, a world alienated from
him by sin; his chosen people are commissioned to get the world back for him –
whatever the cost to themselves.[494]

In conclusion, we can state that the book of Jonah is wholly about mercy,

...the first time in world's history when mercy is entirely the subject is in Jonah ...
Jonah is told to go and prophesy against the city –
and he knows that God will let him down. He can't trust God to be unmerciful.
You can trust God to be anything but unmerciful[495]

---

[490] Erickson M.J. *Christian Theology*, Grand Rapids : Baker Book House, 1994 (1983), p954
[491] 2 Corinthians 1:5-6, NIV
[492] Philippians 3:10-11, NIV
[493] Lewis C.S. (Hooper W. ed.) *The Business of Heaven*, Glasgow : Collins, 1984, p20
[494] Burrows D.P. *ibid.*, p144
[495] Dick K. (ed.) 'Robert Frost' in Writers at Work: The Paris Review Interviews, quoted in Murray P. *ibid.*, p54

And yet God undertakes His vital business of pouring out His grace and mercy through the use of rather comic figures. Poor Jonah,

> *...he does everything wrong, almost,*
> *yet through him the Lord God of Israel does everything right*[496]

And it is perhaps here that we see the enduring appeal of Jonah – he is flawed, he is like us. He loves God truly, but he still struggles to live with God, to obey God and to understand God. Jonah mirrors our own spiritual life and struggles and his story gives us hope that God will not abandon us in our folly and our confusion. We can have confidence that God will refuse to allow our sin and failure to be the last word in terms of our relationship with Him. Neither will they in any way undermine God's ability to achieve His purposes to His glory and our salvation.

---

[496] Cary P. *ibid.*, p17

Jonah in Islam

To complete this look at how Jonah's story has inspired piety down through the millennia, we will now look briefly at the place Jonah has in the Muslim faith. Of all the major and minor biblical prophets, Jonah is the only one whose story has found inclusion in the Qur'an[497]. This tells us clearly that something in the story of Jonah speaks to the Muslim soul[498]. Jonah is honoured in having not one but two titles in the Qur'an, *Dhun-Nun* – Lord of the Fish (11:87) and *Sahibil-Hot* – Companion of the Fish (68:48).

While the Qur'an contains only an abbreviated version of the story of Jonah, this is often felt to be so because the story was already so well-known in Arab culture that the details were not necessary. The Muslim faith sees two key lessons in the story of Jonah. The first is that repentance is powerful and can bring life where only death is in view. The second is that Nineveh's repentance is a challenge and a powerful critique of the disobedience which often characterises the lives of those who would call themselves followers of God.

In Muslim piety the prayer of Jonah is recorded in the Qur'an,

> *There is no god save Thee. Be Thou glorified!*
> *Lo! I have been an evil doer (21:87)*

This prayer is believed to be particularly efficacious and is often prayed by Muslim believers in times of distress [499].

The story of Jonah in Muslim piety is primarily understood as giving a perfect example of repentance. The Ninevites are held up as an example of how one should respond to the convicting message of sinfulness;

> *If only there had been a community of people who believed and profited by their belief as did the people of Jonah!*
> *When they believed, We refrained from (delivering) the severe punishment (intended for them) in this life and gave them comfort for a time. (10:99)[500]*

The Mosque Nabi Yûnis (Mosque of the Prophet Jonah) situated outside the remains of Nineveh, near Mosul, has been an important Muslim pilgrimage site since at least the tenth century. This is evidenced,

---

[497] Limburg J. *ibid.*, p113
[498] Schwartz J. *ibid.*, p1
[499] Mermer A. & Yazicioglu U. *ibid.* p4
[500] Cited in Michel T. *The Prophet Jonah in the Qur'an*, Service International de Documentation Judeo-Chrétienne (SIDIC), XVIII, 1985/1, p20

...by the saying recorded by Mukaddasi that seven pilgrimages to Nineveh were as valuable as the great pilgrimage to Mecca[501]

In addition to the tomb of Jonah, the medieval sources also note a holy well *Ain Yûnis* (The Well of Jonah). This well is believed to have healing powers. It is said to have been where the prophet directed the Ninevites to go, to purify themselves before coming to the hill on which the mosque now stands, in order to pray to God. Streck comments that the sulphurous spring that feeds this well was still extant in the 1930s, although he noted that it was named *Damlamadja* from the Turkish verb 'to drip' because of its slow rate. However it was still an important religious site where votive offerings were still being made - clear evidence that even in modern times the prophet Jonah is an important religious figure in Muslim piety.

---

[501] Streck M. 'Ninawa' in Houtsma M. (ed.) E.J. Brill's First Encyclopaedia of Islam 1913-1936 Supplement Vol. 9, Leiden : Brill, 1987, p168

Jonah after Jonah

The book of Jonah ends abruptly. There is no 'tag-line', no concluding paragraph that nicely brings us to a satisfying conclusion; no information about what Jonah did subsequently.

In the absence of any biblical data, we can only turn to the many Jewish and Muslim traditions that have sprung up surrounding Jonah's later life. We will examine these possible 'afterwords' to the biblical book of Jonah by considering the many sites that are anciently reputed to have a connection with him.

Perhaps the oldest legend concerning Jonah after his mission to Nineveh, is found in the writings of *Epiphanius,* a fourth century Bishop of Constantia. His 'Lives of the Prophets' was a translation of a text believed to have been written in the first century. He wrote of Jonah that, after God's change of heart in response to the Ninevites repentance, Jonah left Nineveh but did not return to his homeland. Instead he went to live in the territory of *Sour* (possibly to be identified with *Tyr*), a place where foreigners (i.e. Gentiles) lived. Jonah's motivation for this is stated as being,

> *So shall I remove my reproach,*
> *for I spoke falsely in prophesying against the great city of Nineveh.*[502]

We are further told that Jonah moved on to the land of *Saraar* (probably *Seir*), where he died and was buried. His body was put in the cave of *Kenaz* the judge (Judges 3:9).

This information corresponds with the site of *Halhoul (Halhûl)* for the prophet's burial. Ali of Herat, a medieval Muslim pilgrim, whose travel diary of his journey to the Holy Land is included in *'Peregrinatores Medii Aevi Quatuor'* (Four Medieval Tourists) which dates from 1173. Quoting from this work, Le Strange notes,

> Halhûl.—'A village', writes 'Ali of Herat, 'in which is the tomb of Yûnis ibn Mattâ
> *(Jonah, son of Amittai)'. (A.H., Oxf MS., folio 42.)*
> *This is the Halhûl of Josh. xv. 58...*[503]

Le Strange also cites another Muslim source, *Mujîr ad Dîn*, who wrote in 1496,

---

[502] Hare D.R.A. 'The Lives of the Prophets : A New Translation and Introduction', in Charlesworth J.H. *The Old Testament Pseudepigraphe – Volume 2*, Massachusetts : Hendrickson, 1983, p393
[503] Le Strange G. *Palestine Under the Moslems*, London : Alexander P. Watt, 1890, p447f

Halhûl, not far from Hebron, and on the road to Jerusalem,
is the burial-place of Yûnis (Jonah).
The mosque and minaret seen here were built in 623 (1226 A.D.).
Mattâ, the father of Yûnis, is buried not far off at the village of Bait Amur. [504]

Another site with links to Jonah is the village of *Mash'had*, meaning 'the grave of the holy man' in Arabic. This site is 5 km (3.1 miles) north-east of *Nazareth*. Known as *Gath Hefer* in biblical times[505], this was also the birthplace of Jonah.

In 395 A.D. Jerome mentions passing by the tomb of Jonah at this site 3km (2 miles) from *Sipphoris (Tsippori)*[506]. The sixth century 'Midrash Genesis Rabba' also identifies the tomb of Jonah at this site[507]. A Spanish Rabbi pilgrim from the twelfth century, Rabbi Benjamin of Tudela, also mentions *Tsippori* as the site of Jonah's tomb,

...Sufurieh, the Tsippori of antiquity. The sepulchres of Rabenu Hakkadosh, of R.
Chija, who came back from Babylon, and of Jonah ben Amittai the prophet are
shown here; they are buried in the mountain,
which also contains numerous other sepulchres. [508]

A rival site for Jonah's tomb is on a nearby hill close to *Tsippori,* at a place called *Kafar Kannah* (one of the possible sites for the biblical locations of Cana of Galilee John 2:1-11). The Muslim pilgrim *Nâsir-i-Khusrau* visited this village in 1047. He writes in his diary,

I proceeded on to a village that is called Kafar Kannah.
To the southward of this village is a hill,
on the top of which they have built a fine monastery.
It has a strong gate, and the tomb of the Prophet Yûnis (Jonah) - peace be upon
him!—is shown within. [509]

Ali of Herat, who we have earlier noted tells us that Jonah's tomb is in *Halhûl*, also affirms the site of *Kafar Kannah* as a location having connections to Jonah,

[504] *ibid.*

[505] 2 Kings 14:25

[506] Abel F-M. 'Le Culte de Jonas en Palestine' in Danby H. (ed.) *Journal of the Palestine Oriental Society Vol. II*, Jerusalem : Palestine Oriental Society, 1922, pp176

[507] ibid.

[508] Tudela B. (tr. Asher A.) *The Itinerary of Benjamin of Tudela Vol . 1*, New York : Hakesheth Publishing Co., 1841, p80

[509] Khusrau N-I. (tr. Le Strange G.) 'Diary of a Journey Through Syria and Palestine' in Anonymous *The Palestine Pilgrims' Text Society Vol. IV*, London : Palestine Pilgrims ' Text Society, 1888, p19

'Kafar Kannah', says *'Ali of Herat, 'is where may be seen the Station of Jonah (Makam Yûnis), also the tomb of his son.'*[510]

Yet another Jonah site is *Khan en-Nebi Yûnis* at the village of *Gyeh (el-Djiyeh)* between Sidon and Beirut in the Lebanon. This site is noted in the travels of the French knight *Laurent d'Arvieux* (1635-1702) from Marseille who visited the Holy Land in 1660. Abel quotes from his *'Memoires du Chevalier d'Arvieux'*,

...arriving in the village of Gyeh (el-Djiyeh) where a small, white mosque marks the spot where Jonah was spewed out by the whale. (my translation)[511]

D'Arvieux also notes the respect shown by the locals towards Jonah. They would respectfully bow towards the site and request the prophet's permission to pass in front of his dwelling.

This location is also supported by the mosaic map in the church of Madaba. This mosaic is the earliest map that exists of the Holy Land and was made as a decoration of the church in Madaba. It dates from between the sixth and seventh centuries.

Figure 12 - Mosaic Map of Madaba[512]

---

[510] Le Strange G. *ibid.*, p469
[511] Abel F-M. *ibid.*, p179f
[512] Image source 198.62.75.1/www1.ofm/mad/sections/section7.html

The section of the map illustrated includes, in the bottom left section, the Southern coastline of the Holy Land. The lowest place name on the left hand side is given in Greek as,

ΤΟ ΤΟΥ ΑΓΙΟΥ ΙΩΝΑ

This translates to, 'The (Temple/Place) of Saint Jonah'[513]. The location indicated ties in well with *Khan en-Nebi Yûnis*.

This site for Jonah's landfall after his being swallowed by the monstrous fish is in contradiction to a story recounted by *Al-Hassan Ibn-Mohammed Al-Wezaz Al-Fasi*, baptised with the Christian name *Giovanni Leone* (John Leo) but better known as *Leo Africanus* (1465-1550). This man was a Moorish traveller who wrote a three volume work about the history of Africa and of his travels.

He tells of visiting the three villages of *Messa* in the region of *Sus* (modern Morocco) and of seeing there a temple constructed from whalebones which was held to be the site where Jonah was ejected from the monstrous fish,

> *Not farre from the sea side they haue a temple, which they greatly esteeme and honour. Out of which, Historiographers say, that the same prophet, of whom their great Mahumet foretold, shoulde proceed. Yea, some there are which sticke not to affirme, that the prophet Ionas was cast foorth by the whale vpon the shoare of Messa, when as he was sent to preach vnto the Niniuites. The rafters and beames of the saide temple are of whales bone.*[514]

Of course the most impressive monument to Jonah is just outside the ruins of ancient Nineveh, the *Nabi Yûnis* Mosque (Mosque of the Prophet Jonah). The Muslim tradition holds that Jonah did not go back to Palestine, but that he stayed at Nineveh and spent his life teaching the repentant Ninevites about the true God. The mosque is said to contain his tomb.

---

[513] Able F-M. *ibid.*, p180

[514] Africanus L. (tr. Pory J.) *The History and Description of Africa*, Vol. II, London : The Hakluyt Society, 1896 (1600), p248

Figure 13 - Nabi Yunis Mosque[515]

However, this would seem unlikely, as this Muslim shrine seems to have originally been the site of a Christian church and monastery (*Mar Yonnan* – St Jonah's Church). Indeed, visiting the mosque in 1842-4, the Rev George Percy Badger noted that the layout of the mosque gave evidence of its Christian origins,

> *The Christians say that this building was once a church.*
> *The order of the interior as above described, so foreign to the plan general in mosques, seems to favour the common tradition.*[516]

An opinion that Streck confirms after making two visits to the site in 1927/8[517]. So it seems that the Muslims took over this site, which was formerly a Christian monastery and convent, in around the twelfth century. However it is clear that the site had become an important Muslim pilgrim site from the tenth century on[518].

---

[515] Nabi Yunis Mosque on Al-Tawba Mountain in Mosul City, 2006 image in the public domain, sourced from http://commons.wikimedia.org/wiki/File:Nabi_Yunis_Mosque_in_Mosul.JPG
[516] Badger G.P. *The Nestorians and Their Rituals Vol I*, London : Joseph Masters, 1852, p85
[517] Streck M. 'Ninawa' in Houtsma M. (ed.) *E.J. Brill's First Encyclopaedia of Islam 1913-1936 Supplement Vol. 9*, Leiden : Brill, 1987, p169
[518] ibid., p168

Badger quotes from the writings of *Bar Saliba* (*Ibn Sleewa*), a Christian monk-priest who died around 1340,

> *Writing of the Patriarch Hnan-Yeshua,*
> *who was raised to that dignity... cir. A.D. 686, he says:*
> *'Hnan-Yeshua resided in the convent of the prophet Jonah, which is situated on the western side of the wall of Nineveh facing the eastern gates of Mosul, and the river Tigris separates the two cities. When he died, he was buried here, in a coffin made of ebony. Six hundred and fifty years afterwards, the tomb containing the coffin was opened, and the body was discovered whole, and looked as if sleeping. Most of the inhabitants of Mosul went out to see this sight, and we also went and saw it with our eyes. And, even now, whoever desires to behold it, and to receive a blessing therefrom, is at liberty to do so;*
> *and if any disbelieve, let them go, and see and believe.'*
> *Bar Saliba, or Ibn Sleewa, lived in the fourteenth century, and as he introduces himself as an eye-witness of the above fact, it is clear that the convent was not converted into a mosque till a later period.*
> *Perhaps a peep beneath the sumptuous covering of the so-called tomb of Jonah might detect the ebony coffin of the Nestorian saint.*[519]

It seems therefore likely that the tomb currently being venerated by Muslim pilgrims in the Mosque *Nabi Yûnis* is therefore not that of the prophet Jonah but rather that of the Christian Patriarch *Hnan-Yeshua*.

In conclusion we can say that Jonah's life after the biblical account remains a mystery. However, the presence of many places and traditions connected with him indicates his continuing importance in the faith of Jews, Christians and Muslims.

---

[519] Badger G.P. *ibid.*, p401 (DD)

Nineveh's Subsequent History

In our study we noted that after Jonah's story ends a resurgent Assyria conquered Israel and took her into captivity. This event took place in the following manner.

Under King Tiglath-Pileser III (745 - 727 B.C.) the Assyrian empire recovered its strength. Concurrently, the Northern Israelite kingdom was in decline.

Around 733 B.C. King Ahaz of Judah (the Southern kingdom) was pressurised to join with the Kings of Aram and Israel in order to resist the Assyrians. Instead of adopting this tactic, King Ahaz sought an alliance with the King of Assyria, Tiglath-Pileser III.

In support of Judah (the Southern kingdom), Assyria fought against Israel (the Northern kingdom) and conquered her. Then, treaty forgotten, the Assyrians headed towards Jerusalem, the capital of Judah. Sennacherib, Tiglath-Pileser III's successor, laid siege to Jerusalem. In Isaiah chapters 36 - 37 we have an account of this siege and of God's dramatic intervention. Although Judah survived, the Northern kingdom never recovered. Her peoples were carried off into exile and these ten Northern tribes never returned.

Sometime between 663 and 612 B.C. the prophet Nahum prophesies the destruction of Nineveh. Although they had repented of their violence and wickedness under the preaching of Jonah, this repentance was short-lived. *Rabbi Eliezer* cites a rabbinic tradition that states,

> *For forty years was the Holy One, blessed be He, slow to anger with them, corresponding to the forty days during which He had sent Jonah.' After forty years they returned to their many evil deeds, more so than their former ones, and they were swallowed up like the dead, in the lowest Sheol.*[520]

The following items were prophesied by Nahum about the destruction of Nineveh:

> *An "overwhelming flood" will "make an end of Nineveh". (Nah. 1:8)*
> *Fire would destroy the city gates and leave her unprotected. (Nah. 3:13)*
> *The destruction of the city would be total and permanent. (Nah. 3:19)*
> *The city's downfall would be remarkably easy for the invaders. (Nah. 3:12)*

Although no account of the fall of Nineveh has been left to us, its destruction was nonetheless total.

---

[520] Ben Hyrcanus E., *ibid.*, p343

We do not know, unfortunately, the story of that memorable siege.
A people civilized for centuries was walled in by the forces of a new people fresh,
strong, invincible. Then, as often in later days, civilization went down before
barbarism. Nineveh fell into the hands of the Scythians.
Later times preserved a memory that Sin-shar-ishkun perished in the flames of his
palace, to which he had committed himself when he foresaw the end.
The city was plundered of everything of value which it contained, and then given to
the torch. The houses of the poor, built probably of unburnt bricks, would soon be a
ruin. The great palaces, when the cedar beams which supported the upper stories
had been burnt off, fell in heaps. Their great, thick walls, built of unburnt bricks
with the outer covering of beautiful burnt bricks, cracked open, and when the rains
descended the unburnt bricks soon dissolved away into the clay of which they had
been made. The inhabitants had fled to the four winds of heaven and returned no
more to inhabit the ruins. [521]

Whilst other razed capitals of antiquity left some remnant to indicate their former location and significance, Nineveh disappeared so completely that Xenophon, the Greek historian, passing close by in 401 B.C. saw absolutely nothing[522].

---

[521] Rogers R.W. ibid., p73
[522] ibid.

Bibliography

Abel F-M. 'Le Culte de Jonas en Palestine' in Danby H. (ed.) *Journal of the Palestine Oriental Society* Vol. II, Jerusalem : Palestine Oriental Society, 1922

Africanus L. (tr. Pory J.) *The History and Description of Africa*, Vol. II, London : The Hakluyt Society, 1896 (1600)

Alders G.C. *The Problem of the Book of Jonah*, London: Tyndale Press, 1948

Anonymous *The Buried City of the East – Nineveh*, London : National Illustrated Library, 1851

Anonymous *A Midrash on Jonah Yom Kippur 5772*, 10/07/11 accessed online at http://bethhaverim.org/wp-content/uploads/2012/02/A-Midrash-on-Jonah-5772.pdf on 30/01/13

Anonymous Proceedings of the Society of Biblical Archaeology Vol. XX, Twenty-eighth session, January-December 1898, London : Society of Biblical Archaeology, 1898

Anonymous *The Palestine Pilgrims' Text Society Vol. IV*, London : Palestine Pilgrims' Text Society, 1888

Assisi F. *Regula non bullata or Earlier Rule (1221),* accessed online at http://www.francis-bible.org/writings/witings_francis_earlier_rule_1.html#regula_non_bullata on 15/01/13

Badger G.P. *The Nestorians and Their Rituals Vol I*, London : Joseph Masters, 1852

Bailey K. E. *Poet and Peasant and Through Peasant Eyes* (Combined Edition), Michigan: W.B. Eerdmans, 1983 (1976, 1980)

Balcombe J. *Pleasurable Kingdom*, Hampshire: MacMillan, 2006

Balcombe J. *Second Nature*, New York: Palgrave MacMillan, , 2010

Barclay-Lloid J.E. *The Prophet Jonah in Early Christian Art*, Service International de Documentation Judeo-Chrétienne (SIDIC), XVIII, 1985/1, pp17-19

Black, J.A., Cunningham, G., Fluckiger-Hawker, E, Robson, E., and Zólyomi, G., *Inana's descent to the nether world: translation,* The Electronic Text Corpus of Sumerian Literature, Oxford 1998, accessed online at http://etcsl.orinst.ox.ac.uk/section1/tr141.htm on 01/03/13

Blackaby H. & King C. Experiencing God – Knowing and Doing the Will of God, Tenessee: Lifeway Press, 1990

Blaiklock E.M. 'Tarshish' in *The Illustrated Bible Dictionary – vol.3*, Leicester: IVP, 1980

Blumenthal F. *Jonah the reluctant prophet – Prophecy and Allegory*, Jewish Bible Quarterly, vol.35 no.2, 2007, pp103-108

Bolin T.M. Eternal delight and deliciousness : The book of Jonah after ten years, The Journal of Hebrew Scriptures, vol.9 no.4, 2009

Bradley I. *God is Green*, London: Darton, Longman and Todd, 1990

Bridges J. *Transforming Grace*, Colarodo Springs: Navpress, 1991

Brunner H.E. *The Word and the World*, London : SCM Press, 1931

Budge E.A.W. The Babylonian Story of the Deluge as told by Assyrian Tablets from Nineveh, London: British Museum, 1920

Burrows D.P. *Jonah, The Reluctant Missionary*, Leominster: Gracewing, 2008

Buttrick, G. A. (ed.) *The Interpreter's Dictionary of the Bible*, New York: Abingdon Press, 1962

Caiger S.L. *Lives of the Prophets*, London : SPCK, 1936

Calmet Dom *La Sainte Bible avec Commentaire*, Tome XI, Arras : Sueur Charrey, 1896

Campolo T. How To Rescue The Earth Without Worshipping Nature, Nashville: Thomas Nelson, 1992

Cary P. Jonah – SCM Theological Commentary on the Bible, London: SCM Press, 2008

Catron J.L.R. *The Minor Prophets*, Dubuque : Emmaus Bible College, 1991

Charlesworth J.H. *The Old Testament Pseudepigraphe – Volume 2*, Massachusetts : Hendrickson, 1983

Chrysostom J. (tr. Christo G.G.) *On Repentance and Almsgiving* (The Fathers of the Church, Vol. 96), Washington: CUA Press, 1997

Cory I.P. *Ancient Fragments*, Charleston : Bibliobazaar, 2008, (1832)

Danby H. (ed.) *Journal of the Palestine Oriental Society Vol. II*, Jerusalem :

Palestine Oriental Society, 1922

de Monléon Dom J. *Commentaire sur le Prophète Jonas*, Clermont Ferrand : Editions de la Source, 1970

Douglas J. D. (ed.) *The Illustrated Bible Dictionary*, Leicester: IVP, 1980

Dray S. Facing the Powers – A Biblical Framework for those Facing Political Oppression, Carn Brae Media, 2013

Edwards R.A. The Sign of Jonah in the Theology of the Evangelists and Q, London: SCM Press, 1971

Ellul J. (tr. Bromily G.W.) *The Judgement of Jonah*, Grand Rapids: W.B. Eerdmans, 1971

Enns P. *Inspiration and Incarnation*, Grand Rapids : Baker Academic, 2005

Erickson M. J. *Christian Theology*, Michigan: Baker Books, 1994 (1983)

Feldman L.H. *Studies in Josephus' Rewritten Bible*, Leiden: Koninklÿke Brill NV, 1998

Ferguson P. *Who was the King of Nineveh ?* Tyndale Bulletin, vol.47 no.2, Nov. 1996

Fretheim T. E. *The Message of Jonah*, Oregon: Wipf and Stock Publishers, 1977

Friedlander G. *Pirke de-Rabbi Eliezer*, London: Kegan Paul, Trench, Trubner & Co Ltd, 1916

Ginzberg L. *The Legends of the Jews*, Vol. IV, Philadelphia : The Jewish Publication Society of America, 1913

Glardon T. *Ces Crises Qui Nous Font Naître*, Génève : Labor et Fides, 2009

Goodwin T. *The Works of Thomas Goodwin, Vol. III*, Edinburgh : James Nichol, 1890

Graystone P. *The J Team – Holiday Club Programme*, Milton Keynes : Scripture Union, 1990

Houtsma M. (ed.) E.J. Brill's First Encyclopaedia of Islam 1913-1936 Supplement Vol. 9, Leiden : Brill, 1987

Jastrow M. Aspects of Religious Belief and Practice in Bablylonia and Assyria, New York : G.P. Putnam, 1911

Jeremais J. Iwnas in *Theological Dictionary of the New Testament – vol. 3*, Grand Rapids : W.B. Eerdmans, 1964

Josephus F. (tr. Whiston W.) *The Works of Josephus*, Peabody: Hendrickson Publishers, 1987

Kendal R.T. *'Jonah'*, London: Hodder & Stoughton, 1978

Kennedy J. *On the Book of Jonah*, London: Alexander and Shepheard, 1895

Khusrau N-I. (tr. Le Strange G.) 'Diary of a Journey Through Syria and Palestine' in Anonymous *The Palestine Pilgrims' Text Society Vol. IV*, London : Palestine Pilgrims ' Text Society, 1888

Kohlenberger III J.R. *The Interlinear NIV Hebrew-English Old Testament*, Grand Rapids : Zondervan, 1987

Lawrence P.J.N. *Assyrian Nobles and the Book of Jonah*, Tyndale Bulletin, No.37, 1986, pp121-132

Layard A.H. Discoveries Among the Ruins of Nineveh and Babylon, New York: G.P. Putnam, 1855

Layard A.H. *Nineveh and its Remains Vol. 1*, London: John Murray, 1849

Layard A.H. *Nineveh and its Remains Vol. 2*, London: John Murray, 1849

Le Strange G. *Palestine Under the Moslems*, London : Alexander P. Watt, 1890

Lewis C.S. (Hooper W. ed.) *The Business of Heaven*, Glasgow : Collins, 1984

Lewis C.S. *Reflections on the Psalms*, Glasgow: Fontana Books, 1958

Limburg J. *Jonah*, Louisville: Westminster: John Knox Press, 1993

Magonet J. *The Book of Jonah and the Day of Atonement*, Service International de Documentation Judeo-Chrétienne (SIDIC), XVIII 1985/1

Martin A.D. *The Prophet Jonah – The Book and the Sign*, London : Longmans, Green & Co., 1926

Maspero G. (tr. McLure M.L.) History of Egypt Chaldea, Syria, Babylonia and Assyria – Volume III, London: Grolier Society, 1903-1906

McBirnie W.S. *Seven Sins of Jonah*, Wheaton: Tyndale House, 1981

Melville H. *Moby Dick*, Evanston: Northwestern University Press, 1991

(1851)

Mermer A. & Yazicioglu U. *An insight into the prayer of Jonah (p) in the Qur'an*, The Journal of Scriptural Reasoning, No. 3.1, June 2003, accessed at http://etext.lib.virginia.edu/journals/ssr/issues/volume3/number1/ssr03-01-e02.html on 07/12/12

Merrill E.H. *The Sign of Jonah,* Journal of the Evangelical Theological Society, vol. 23, no. 1, March 1980

Michel T. *The Prophet Jonah in the Qur'an*, Service International de Documentation Judeo-Chrétienne (SIDIC), XVIII, 1985/1 accessed online at http://www.notredamedesion.org/fr/dialogue_docs.php?a=3b&id=865 on 30/01/13

Miller D.B. & Shipp R.M. *An Akkadian Handbook*, Winona Lake: Eisenbrauns, 1996

Morris L. *I Believe in Revelation*, London: Hodder and Stoughton, 1976

Murray P. A Journey with Jonah – The Spirituality of Bewilderment, Dublin: The Columba Press, 2002

Perrotta K. *Jonah/Ruth – Love Crosses Boundaries*, Chicago: Loyola Press, 2000

Piper J. 'Let The Nations Be Glad!' in Winter R.D. & Hawthorne S.C. (eds.) *Perspectives on the World Christian Movement*, Pasadena: William Carey Library, 1999 3rd ed. (1981)

Piper J. *Jonah – Parts 1,2,3* accessed online at http://www.desiringgod.org/resource-library/poems/jonah-part-1 on 01/02/13

Richardson D. *Eternity in Their Hearts*, California: Regal Books 1984 (1981).

Rodkinson M.L. (ed. and tr.) *The Babylonian Talmud Vol. 1-10*, Second Ed., Boston: Boston New Talmud Publishing Company 1918 [1903]

Rogers R.W. A History of Babylonia and Assyria – Volume II, New York: Eaton and Mains, 1900

Sasson J. M. *Jonah – The Anchor Bible Vol. 24b*, New York: Doubleday, 1990

Sawyer, J.F.A Prophecy and the Prophets of the Old Testament, Oxford: OUP, 1987

Sayce A. Hibbert Lectures 1887 : Lectures on the Origin and Growth of Religion, London : Williams and Norgate, 1898

Schwarz J. *Yunus the Prophet - The Qur'anic Story of Jonah*, Muslim-Jewish Journal, 2008 accessed online at http://www.themuslimjewishjournal.com/articles/yunus-the-prophet-the-quranic-story-of-jonah.shtml on 15/01/13

Shakespeare W. 'Hamlet, Prince of Denmark' (Act III, Scene III), in *The Illustrated Stratford Shakespeare*, London : Chancellor Press, 1993

Shemesh Y. *And Many Beasts (Jonah 4 :11) : The Function and Status of Animals in the Book of Jonah*, The Journal of Hebrew Scriptures, Vol. 10, Art. 6, 2010, accessed online at http://www.jhsonline.org/Articles/article_134.pdf on 21/01/13

Shirsha A. *Jonah, the Whale, the Assyrians, Christianity and Islam – Guest Editorial*, Assyrian International News Agency 11-29-2010, accessed online at http://www.aina.org/guesteds/20101128232122.pdf on 21/01/13

Simpson W. *The Jonah Legend*, London : Grant Richards, 1899

Spence L. *Myths of Babylonia and Assyria*, New York : Frederick A. Stokes Co., 1916

Speiser E. A., 'Nineveh' in Buttrick G. A. (ed.) *The Interpreter's Dictionary of the Bible – Vol. 3*, New York: Abingdon Press, 1962

Stuart D. Hosea – Jonah – Word Biblical Commentary – Vol. 31, Nashville : Thomas Nelson, 1987

Tchividjian T. *Surprised by Grace*, Wheaton: Crossway, 2010

Thompson J.G.S.S 'Sea' in *The Illustrated Bible Dictionary – Volume 3*, Leicester: IVP, 1980

Thomson W.M. *The Land and the Book – Volume 1*, New York : Harper and Brothers, 1880

Tiessen T. *Who Then can be Saved?* Illinois: IVP, 2004

Timmer D. The Intertextual Israelite Jonah Face à l'Empire: The Post-Colonial Significance of the Book's Context and Purported Neo-Assyrian Context, Journal of Hebrew Scriptures, Vol. 9, Art. 9, 2009, accessed online at http://www.jhsonline.org/Articles/article_111.pdf on 22/01/13

Tolstoy N. *The Quest for Merlin*, London : Hamish Hamilton, 1985

Traylor E.G. *Jonah*, Polson: Port Hole Publications, 2001 (1987)

Tudela B. (tr. Asher A .) *The Itinerary of Benjamin of Tudela Vol . 1*, New York : Hakesheth Publishing Co., 1841

Tudela B. (tr. Asher A .) *The Itinerary of Benjamin of Tudela Vol . 2*, New York : Hakesheth Publishing Co., 1841

Von Orelli C. *On the minor prophets*, Edinburgh : T & T Clark, 1893

Wesley K.D. Moving in the Wrong Direction – A study in the book of Jonah, Enumclaw: Winepress Publishing, 2001

Wiseman D. J., 'Nineveh' in Douglas J. D. (ed.) *The Illustrated Bible Dictionary - Part 2*, Leicester: IVP, 1980

Wiseman D.J. *Jonah's Nineveh – The Tyndale Biblical Archaeology Lecture, 1977*, Tyndale Bulletin 30 (1979) 29-52 accessed online at http://www.tyndalehouse.com/TynBul/Library/00_TyndaleBulletin_ByDate. htm#TynBul_30_1_1979 on 31/12/12

Woodward B.L. *Death in Life: The Book of Jonah and Biblical Tragedy*, Grace Theological Journal, 11.1, 1991, pp3-16

Wörhle J. *A Prophetic Reflection on Divine Forgiveness: The Integration of the Book of Jonah into the Book of the Twelve*, Journal of Hebrew Scriptures, Vol. 9, Art. 7, 2009, accessed online at http://www.jhsonline.org/Articles/article_109.pdf on 21/01/13

Yancey P. & Brand P. *Fearfully and Wonderfully Made*, Michigan: Zondervan, 1987 (1984)

Zodhiates S. *The Complete Word Study Old Testament*, Chattanooga : AMG Publishers, 1994

Lightning Source UK Ltd.
Milton Keynes UK
UKHW010807010319
338261UK00001B/70/P

9 781291 945966